MALRAUX

MALRAUX

❈

by Pierre Galante

Translated by Haakon Chevalier

Cowles Book Company, Inc.
New York

To L. de V.
In Memoriam

ACKNOWLEDGMENTS

I am most grateful and profoundly indebted to André Malraux for his warm and friendly encouragement, and for his help, which has been immeasurable. Without his assistance this book could never have been produced.

I wish to express my special thanks to Malraux's two oldest and most faithful friends, Marcel Brandin and Louis Chevasson, and to André de Vilmorin, brother of Louise de Vilmorin who, before her death, shared with me her private insights and reminiscences of André Malraux. Gaston Bonheur, managing editor of *Paris-Match,* gave me steady encouragement and much helpful advice. The letters of Professor André Vandegans, and his able study of Malraux's literary youth, helped to fill many voids for me. Madame Clara Malraux gave me invaluable insights and assistance. I am also indebted to Jean Prinet, curator in chief of the periodicals section of the Bibliothèque Nationale; to Walter G. Langlois; to Harold J. Isaacs; to Jacques Guillermaz; to Charles Grosbois and Robert Jobez, experts on China; to Commandant Jean Esparre and Lieutenant Paul Gambert de Loche; to Professor Max Aub and Jean Sirole; to Louis Page and Boris Pesquine; to Emanuel d'Astier de La Vigerie; and to General Pierre Jacquot and his veterans of the Alsace-Lorraine Brigade.

I especially appreciated the assistance of my friend Yves Salgues. I also wish to thank for their cooperation my confreres Simon Alsot, Louis Cazals, Fernand Gigon, Roger Koeffler, Louis Sapin, Edith Tissier, and the editorial library and photo laboratories of *Paris-Match.*

P. G.

CONTENTS

INTRODUCTION

"Sangre de Jesus! What kind of a frame can I fit this into? It has grown even bigger. It's bursting all its seams!" So Picasso often fumes, half-exasperated, half-amused, as though scolding himself, when his brushes have covered his entire canvas with paint, overflowing the limits he has set himself.

André Malraux's life reminds one of these "disobedient" paintings by his friend Picasso. It too could cover a gigantic canvas, or millions of blank pages, bursting asunder any frame in which one attempted to contain its action, its forms, and its vivid colors.

For Malraux is, first and foremost, a man of action, and at one time or another he has worn just about every uniform, every garb. Multicolored, varied, they relate the epic of our times: from the pith helmet worn by the explorer of Cambodian temples and by the revolutionary in Indochina, from the oil-stained coveralls of the airman in Spain during the Civil War, from the sheepskin jacket of the underground fighter during the German occupation of France, from the uniform of the colonel in Alsace—to the formal frock coat of the minister under two Gaullist regimes. There is no question that, of all Malraux's work, the most vivid, the most tragic, the richest adventure has been the story of his own life.

Even writing is for him a form of action. Malraux's concern has always been with man's relationship with death and his reaction in the face of destiny. His writings reflect this preoccupation. *"Le destin, c'est la politique,"* said Napoleon. The work of Malraux as novelist is political in the same high sense in which Napoleon considered destiny to be political. Because Malraux is a twentieth-century man, he could only paint his contemporaries as engaged in extreme situations, those situations in which destiny plays the major role: revolution or war. All Malraux's heroes—Chinese, Spaniards, Germans, French—are, like himself, men of principle at odds with their society. They are prepared for war—and hence for the idea of death—without accepting it. The idea of death, in fact, is a concept to which they accustom themselves without submitting to it. To borrow an expression from Lenin, Malraux's heroes are "dead men on parole," closely modeled on historical reality. Malraux himself has been for most of his life a dead man on parole—surrounded by the dead, marked, menaced without respite. A fact that caused one of his intimates, Pierre Drieu La Rochelle, whose name will often recur in these pages—and who himself finally committed suicide for political reasons—to say, "How could death surprise Malraux? He has made love to it hundreds of times in his thoughts." Curiously, as though courting risks and danger were a paying proposition, Malraux has proved hard to kill.

He is the only contemporary writer, with the exception of Ernest Hemingway, who has a genuine legend. It is a powerful legend, etched by contradictory and blinding fires, illuminated by fierce passions, warmed by splendid loves tinged with a romanticism that neither Byron nor Chateaubriand would have disavowed. But in this legend, the moment the heart is not involved, adventure comes galloping back. In Malraux's life, it has been a major constant, pointing the way at each crossroads of decision.

Malraux and Hemingway, those two legendary figures, have much in common. They discovered similar centers of interest; they met in various parts of Europe where the cannon thundered, the earth trembled, and men fell. Their great meeting point was Spain during the Civil War; it was a stage on the scale required for two such prodigious actors. Each, in his Spanish testament, was bound to depict the other. Shade, in *L'Espoir,* is Hemingway as seen by Malraux through the magnifying glass of anecdote: life lived with the five senses, a thick-skinned truculence, a Rabelaisian presence—and charming manias, such as the love of cats. In *For Whom the Bell Tolls,* the central character, Robert Jordan—the American intellectual, solidly equipped technically, who fraternizes with the *dinamiteros* and the horse-stealing men of the guerrilla bands—has traits that are characteristically Malrauvian.

When Hemingway formulates the key maxim of his work, "Man is not made for defeat; a man may be vanquished, but not destroyed," one cannot help thinking that he must have written this with the living example of Malraux in mind—Malraux who was defeated, bitterly defeated, in Spain, on the smashed-in Republican fronts, but who, on French ground, never accepted, even for a day, either defeat or his own destruction. And finally, when Hemingway, after having meditated on the writer's calling, reached the conclusion that "all life is a novel," one cannot, once again, rule out the idea that he was thinking of Malraux as much as of himself.

"A life is worth nothing, but nothing is worth a life," Malraux said in the thirties. What an extraordinary living novel Malraux's own life has been! If we believe Flaubert's confession, "I am Madame Bovary," Malraux likewise has already nourished with his own substance a galaxy of creatures whose real or imaginary destiny he assumes. But they all pale before their creator.

His life has been a perpetual journey; from the Indian Ocean, from Aberdeen Bay, to the White House, we are carried round the world at speeds that would leave Jules Verne panting. The deluge of events overcomes us with a kind of dizziness, that of superabundance. You may suggest that this makes easier the task of the biographer; all he needs to do is make a methodical selection. Certain trees bear too many fruits and their flavor suffers in consequence. But this is not the case with Malraux. For him there are no small or great adventures. Each one has its own special savor; each adds its unique quality to his life.

His detractors (there is no lack of them!) have accused Malraux of mythomania, treating him as a fabulator who freely confuses a dreamed event that he would have *liked* to have happen with one that actually did. "He poaches on the event," André Gide used to say, fond of Malraux though he was and holding him, as he did, above all suspicion.

In the couple of hundred books and theses already devoted to the subject of Malraux by writers of the five continents, a good deal of space is given to his role in history. But what of his private life? We know almost nothing about it. Almost deliberately, perhaps, he has kept it a mystery, even to his closest friends. Fascinated by the man behind the legend, I began to ponder the idea of writing a book about the private Malraux, the man nobody knew. But how could I, who did not know him intimately, contrive to penetrate a reserve that seemed so forbidding?

Then an unrivaled opportunity was offered to me, that of receiving

INTRODUCTION

the confidences of that great writer and enchanting personality, Louise de Vilmorin, just as she was on the point of becoming his wife. I had known Louise for many years, and greatly admired both her wit and her writing. Now, thanks to her insight, I came to know a Malraux with whom few people are acquainted—his habits, his tastes, his idiosyncrasies, his foibles. She illuminated the man for me as nobody else could have done. I went innumerable times to the Château de Verrières, Louise's family home, where she and Malraux were living as blissfully happy lovers. We spoke together with complete freedom and frankness, and Malraux agreed to put at my disposal a veritable mountain of documents.

All through the writing of this book, I have had the benefit of his complete cooperation. Our talks lasted for hours at a stretch. They were difficult, exhausting hours, because Malraux would not permit me to use a tape recorder. "I cannot be myself when I have that instrument in front of me," he said to me during our first encounter. So I had to write out hundreds of pages of notes by hand. I used up several ball-point pens. Every evening I had cramps in my right hand. In addition to the notes on our lengthy conversations, there were answers to the questions that I kept sending him from the small village in the French Alps where I had retreated to write the book—more than three hundred of them, which I and my editors felt needed elucidation.

In some cases, however, the answers themselves posed fresh problems. Malraux always thinks that the person with whom he is talking is as familiar as he is himself with the subjects under discussion. This could be embarrassing with someone who has a less omnivorous appetite for information than Malraux, whose fund of knowledge is almost encyclopedic. Once you have "played the first ball" in a conversation, he leaps fully into the subject and catches the ball instantly. Thereafter one only has to listen, and throw it again from time to time. It is a fascinating, but friendly, monologue. The phrases flow easily and genuinely. He is continually digging into the vast resources of his culture, constantly referring to history. But there is no sign of a desire to dazzle his interlocutor. Indeed, to put one at ease, he often charmingly, courteously, interrupts his monologue with, "As you well know yourself . . ."

I remember a luncheon with Malraux, in November, 1969, at his favorite restaurant, Chez Lasserre, on the avenue Franklin Roosevelt.

He arrived, walking fast, his head slightly bent, as if expecting to encounter some obstacle which he could not quite see but which was always present somewhere. He was an elegant figure in a charcoal gray single-breasted suit, immaculate white linen shirt, black knitted silk tie. His pale complexion, his well-groomed black hair, his frail and refined hands, their long, thin fingers yellowed by constant cigarette smoking, seemed the attributes of the man of letters, the intellectual, rather than the man of action, the crusader, the fighter, whose image has played such a major part in Malraux's life.

He sat down quickly, ordered his meal without looking at the menu, and we began to talk—I questioning, he answering, freely, brilliantly, without any apparent oratorical care or preparation.

Then, suddenly, his voice became hoarser, deeper, his head seemed to recede into his shoulders, his gestures grew ampler, faster. Malraux had reached his favorite subject—death. "There is," I remember his saying, "a profound feeling toward death that has not been expressed since the Renaissance—it is curiosity."

Barely a month later, Louise de Vilmorin, his last love—with whom he had planned to spend the remainder of his life—died with tragic suddenness just as she and André Malraux were about to fly to Marrakesh for a joyous vacation in the sun. I remembered the conversation at Lasserre, and the mental picture I had drawn of him then—open as ever for experience, for adventure. To be curious is to be vulnerable. The man whom death had marked so often was alone once more.

1.

Growing Up in Paris

"We shall undoubtedly see other wars and win them too. But never again will our country live through what is in store for it tomorrow."

So spoke Georges Clemenceau—*le Père la Victoire*—on November 10, 1918.

That evening the Paris police reported, "We have reason to fear that Paris will explode. We must be prepared." The following day Paris did indeed explode, but this time there were no casualties. On November 11 World War I ended in a delirious outpouring of joy and relief.

Delirium swept over the city. Exultation. People embraced, hailed, hugged one another. A young man paced the gray, autumnal streets of the Tuileries district without an overcoat despite the November cold. He shared the overwhelming enthusiasm of his fellow Parisians as they crowded the thoroughfares, blocking the traffic, dancing and singing. But deep within him was a profound regret: he had missed the war.

André Malraux was seventeen years old, tall and slender, with unruly dark brown hair and arresting eyes. "Strange eyes, that burn, even at a distance," a police commissioner was to note, ten years later. The eager glance had a restless intensity, which contrasted with the careless elegance that he affected in his dress and manners. "Elegance," Malraux would say, "is not a necessity; it is a luxury."

He was exceptionally precocious and seemed to know everything— far more than one has any right to know at his age. His was a superior intelligence, open to all the rumors as well as the values of the world, obsessed by all the forces that weigh upon this planet, already haunted by man's destiny. Very early, he seems to have impressed those who knew him by his remarkable maturity, both of character and of mind.

"One can think of Malraux as having had a youth," his friend, the

1

writer Pierre Drieu La Rochelle, was to say of him, "but there is no way of telling how old he is."

The war was to give rise to an extraordinarily large and lively body of literature. Drieu La Rochelle, Henry de Montherlant, Jean Giraudoux, Jean Cocteau—all first came to the public's attention with works produced as a result of their war service. A generation separates them from Malraux, however, one artificially imposed by the accident of age. The seventeen-year-old had desperately wanted to be older by just a few months—old enough to take part in the struggle that changed the world.

"I was a pacifist," he explains, across the distance of half a century, "yet I wanted to enlist. But the officer to whom I announced my firm intention of going into battle replied that they were not recruiting soldiers who had not yet been weaned. Since the beginning of that summer of 1918, in fact, the army had been discharging men right and left, whereas before that the soldiers had been packed off to the front after two months' training. When I say 'before,' I am speaking of a period of extravagant propaganda. Ballyhoo has always got on my nerves. Don't forget that Henri Barbusse's *Le Feu*[1] and Ernst Glaeser's *Jahrgang 1902*[2] are pacifist works, and Dorgelès's *Les Croix de bois*[3] is a glorious and solemn requiem for those who did not come back."

The young adolescent was not trying to make excuses for himself. He did not have a guilty conscience, and he was answerable only to himself. He simply felt that he had missed the train. Like his illustrious senior, Captain Charles de Gaulle, who had been a prisoner in Germany since 1916.

The century was a year old when André Malraux was born, and Charles de Gaulle was eleven.

There is a mysterious link between these two men from the north of France, both so taken with eloquence, with the persona, with the theatrical, with the role of aristocracy. Both have their roots in Flanders,

---

[1] Henri Barbusse, director of the Socialist-Communist paper *L'Humanité*, served as a war correspondent until he was seriously wounded in the Battle of the Marne. Discharged because of his wounds, Barbusse wrote *Le Feu*, which was strongly pacifist in tone and became the first literary success to take World War I as its subject.

[2] Ernst Glaeser served with great courage in the German army during the war. A confirmed pacifist, he published *Jahrgang 1902* in 1928. Later, in 1936, he severely criticized the Hitler regime in *Le Dernier Civil*, which was published in France, where he had taken refuge.

[3] Roland Dorgelès enlisted in the French army and became famous in 1919 when he published *Les Croix de bois*. He was subsequently elected to the prestigious Académie Goncourt and is currently its oldest member and dean.

a region where grotesquerie and grandeur go hand in hand. For both men their natural horizon is the sea, for both death is a familiar acquaintance, and both, in their larger-than-life dimensions, are "giants," like those carried through the streets of Flemish towns at carnival time.

Like the de Gaulles, young André was brought up to be very much aware that he belonged to a family and inherited its traditions. The Malraux family was large and its members were fond of each other. Even though they did not see one another often, all sensed a strong bond of unity. Much later, when he became minister of culture in de Gaulle's government, Malraux told his uncle and godfather, Lucien Malraux, then deputy mayor of the city of Dunkerque, "You are my official representative on this soil of Flanders, the cradle of our whole family."

André's grandfather, Alphonse, was a shipowner and cooper in Dunkerque. In his time the shipowners themselves manufactured the barrels that were used to pack the cod their fishermen brought back from the Icelandic banks. Alphonse Malraux was an energetic little man, a tireless worker, who wore a goatee, and a top hat more often than not. He was very proud of his title of "master," a survival from medieval guild traditions; it implied a nobility that placed him above the level of a tradesman.

One night a gigantic storm destroyed almost his entire fleet, including his best vessel, *La Zaca*. Thereafter Alphonse Malraux was ruined, for he considered insurance immoral and had always disdained its protection. He never completely recovered from this tragedy. Though fiercely determined to carry on, he became secretive, uncommunicative, and shut himself off from his children—Georgina and Marie, the daughters, and his sons Georges, Maurice, Fernand, and Lucien, the youngest.

Fernand, the third son, married Berthe Lamy, an attractive young woman of modest family, and went to live in Paris, where he became director of the agency of an American bank. It was in Paris, on the rue Damrémont in Montmartre, that their only child, André, was born, on November 3, 1901. Fernand Malraux, a handsome man who dressed with meticulous care, was something of an eccentric. "One must always mistrust oneself," was one of his favorite maxims.

The household soon broke up. "Marriage kills love," he said to his young wife, and before long the marriage ended in divorce. The Malraux family considered it "a comic-opera divorce." "They no longer live together," went the whispers, "but they see each other all the time."

Fernand and his wife, in fact, were trying to keep in close touch so that their child would not suffer too greatly from the separation.

André made frequent visits to Dunkerque. He appears in the family photograph album, aged three, aged four, dressed in a sailor suit. He was particularly attached to his grandfather, whose physical strength and energy he greatly admired.

"Four sons," was the old man's constant refrain, "and not a single writer. If one of them should turn out to be one, I should be the happiest of men." But Alphonse Malraux was to die without knowing this fulfillment. In 1909 he was hacking out a ship's figurehead representing the lion of Judah with great blows of a double-bitted ax and somehow split his own skull open. He was in his eighties, and his grandson André had just turned eight.

André's aunt, Madame Lucien Malraux, who used to live in a suburb of Dunkerque, Malo-les-Bains, remembered André well at this age:

> He was always a great patriot. He liked to recite *Le Clairon* ["The Bugler"], by Paul Déroulède, which his grandfather had taught him. Very early he had a marked personality, but we were never able to get him to talk about his future. "You'll see," was all he would answer.
>
> When he was ten he surprised us one day. He had hurt one knee very badly, and for a while we were afraid that the leg might have to be amputated. Doctors and surgeons, surrounded by the family, held a consultation at the child's bedside. When they were about to leave the room, little André, from his bed, said to them, "I shall not see you out, *messieurs*."

When he had recovered, he often used to idle around the port, in the old quarter of Dunkerque. Perhaps he was looking for something or someone to remind him of the old man who had made such an impression on his early years.

At carnival time he loved to watch the parades of maskers in which angels and saints, fools and devils intermingled in tableaux that combined the grotesque with the sacred, mythology with religion. This world of dolls and masks, puppet shows and village carnivals—all images that play such an important part in Flemish folklore—excited his imagination; their mystery appealed to him. The impression was to be a lasting one.

"I don't like my youth," Malraux says now. "Youth is a sentiment

4

that pulls you backward. I had no childhood. This has to do with the way my memory works, and I cannot generalize from my experience. The mechanism of memory separates men even beyond what separates them most deeply—their character. For each person, the mechanism by which memory works is absolutely fundamental. Sometimes it involves the idea of fame, as in the case of Chateaubriand, sometimes grief, as in the case of Rousseau. For Proust, memory brings back moments of being present. I personally look to the past above all to bring back the acutest moments of extreme lucidity. For me, childhood is a blank. Yet I have a good memory.

"I can place the turning point, however. There came a time when I left childhood, Alexandre Dumas and *Les Trois Mousquetaires,* behind, in favor of Balzac. It was well before I was sixteen and I wanted to become a great writer. But my schoolmates and I were convinced that a great writer, like a great painter, must be under a curse."

His first friend was Louis Chevasson, a neighbor in Bondy, a rather depressing small town in the northern suburbs of Paris, where André and his mother had gone to live with Madame Malraux's mother after the breakup of the marriage. André's grandmother ran a small grocery store at 15, rue de la Gare, and Louis Chevasson lived close by. The boys first met in 1907, when both were about six years old.

"We were classmates," Chevasson recalls, "day students in a lay school in Bondy. Our teacher used to have long chats with us—there were only a dozen of us in the class! At the age of fourteen André and I discovered Tolstoi. The first book that made a deep impression on us was his *Kreutzer Sonata.* We adored the theater and regularly attended the performances at the Comédie-Française; we often went to the Concerts Colonne too."

At fifteen Malraux won a scholarship to the Lycée Turgot in Paris. There he became friendly with Marcel Brandin, who is still his close friend. "The new pupil was immediately nicknamed 'the Spaniard,'" says Brandin. "Probably because of his dark hair, his pale complexion, and dark eyes." Brandin had fantasies about becoming an actor after finishing school. "Great! Then we'll get free tickets to plays!" was Malraux's instant reaction—a happy thought for an impecunious youth who would gladly have spent every possible evening at the theater.

Malraux never sat for his *baccalauréat,* the essential final examination for those leaving school to go on to university. His studies were constantly hindered by headaches and by nasal and pulmonary infections that kept him out of class. Increasingly, the strength and range of his interests meant that he did the bulk of his work out of school, reading voraciously, constantly questioning, refining upon what he read. He had natural intelligence; culture he was acquiring by himself. He did not need formal instruction, because he was his own best teacher.

"I did not rebel against my family—quite the contrary," says Malraux. "The story that my father was an official in Indochina is quite false. He had studied engineering, and that is how he came to invent a skidproof tire, which he presented in the Lépine competition. I greatly admired my father; he was a tank officer during the war, which I considered very romantic."

"Nevertheless," Chevasson remembers, "one remark of his father's deeply shocked him. Speaking of the famous writer Claude Farrère, who had been in his tank crew, his father said, 'That fellow is nothing but an idiot!' 'How could he say that,' Malraux later said to me, 'about a man who is the author of *Les Civilisés* and *La Bataille?'* "

In his late teens he left school for good, and decided that he wanted to live alone. He first put up at the Hôtel Lutetia, on the boulevard Raspail, then found bachelor quarters on the rue Brunel, in the Seventeenth Arrondissement, around the corner from the avenue de la Grande Armée. His rooms were just large enough for him to be able to have friends in to visit. His father and his grandmother gave him a monthly allowance, enough for the basic necessities. The war was ending; he was on his own in Paris, at a time of remarkable ferment, of variety, of freedom of speech and thought.

His formal education was over, but Malraux is a man whose education has been outside formal limits. He is self-taught, in the special sense that he has learned not only through his own studies and experiences but through the words and the art of others. His intellect is remarkable, and he has always had an exceptional appetite for work, and a near foolproof memory that sees events in visual terms—ideal for a novelist. As the child of divorced parents, he had grown up very much by himself, and it seemed natural that he be his own teacher. His favorite authors, apart from Tolstoi, were Hugo, Stendhal, Dostoevski, Nietzsche, Anatole France, Gogol, and Shakespeare. He was particularly fascinated by the art of the Far East, and, as always, interest led him to become an expert on the subject. He was a constant visitor at the Musée Guimet on the place d'Iéna, France's most extensive collection of Oriental art. He also kept up with current writing, notably by the big four who dominated French literature of the period: Marcel Proust, Paul Claudel, Paul Valéry, and André Gide.

In 1919, Malraux, then aged eighteen, made his appearance in the artistic and literary world—as a trafficker in rare books, first editions, objets d'art, a *chineur,* in the language of the trade.[4] To look at, he was something of a dandy, with black hair and intense eyes; there was an indefinable quality about him, an air of being remote from the world of everyday.

Malraux's first contact in the field was with a bookdealer, René-Louis Doyon, who had a small shop, La Connaissance, at 9 *bis* in the rather dark galerie de la Madeleine, between the *place* of the same name and the rue Boissy d'Anglas. Malraux walked into the shop one day, presented himself to Doyon, and made his proposal. The bookdealer listened with interest. The young man was offering to provide him regularly with first editions and incunabula; apparently he had a wide acquaintance among secondhand bookdealers. He knew rare books and seemed to combine remarkable good taste, perspicacity, and a broad cultural background. Impressed by his obvious ability and air of distinction, Doyon agreed to the arrangement.

Thereafter Malraux came to Doyon's every day at eleven bearing the previous day's haul, set his price, asked to be paid in cash, and then disappeared until the following day. For quite a long time the bookdealer had no other relationship with the cool and reserved young man. Then, in 1920, he proposed that Malraux contribute to a review he was about to launch, to be called *La Connaissance.* It was to be an intellectual journal, on the lookout for ideas, that would analyze and digest them, attack some, and defend others if need be.

"What this country needs now is builders," Doyon liked to say, and this idea appealed to a dynamic, strong-willed young man who was keenly aware of the symptoms of disintegration that were beginning to show themselves in this postwar period. Malraux sensed the prevailing uneasiness and shared it. He was skeptical of systems. Like many young intellectuals of the time, he was unhappy about the maintenance in power of an oligarchy that smugly perpetuated prewar patterns; at the same time, however, he mistrusted parties that, despite their innovations, were still subject to rigid doctrines.

At a very early age Malraux was conscious of breaking with out-

[4] From the métier known in France as *la chine,* dealing in secondhand art bargains of all kinds.

worn ideas and conventions. But at this time he could not see the parties of the Left—nor, indeed, any other party—as pointing the way to constructive improvement. He had little respect for status, and no illusions about the value of conventional ideas or the excellence of existing institutions, but he was in no sense a revolutionary. On the contrary, forms of artistic discipline strongly attracted him—which one might not have expected.

He was impelled by opposing passions of nearly equal force: the passion for order and the passion for freedom, the passion for beauty and the passion for intensity. He was mistrustful of men before he had had a chance to test them. His reaction took the form of a surface gaiety, which was at times quite sarcastic. But he was determined to take his place in the world, to be a winner. This desire found expression in manifold investigations into the most varied realms of knowledge, and in his determined, if capricious, pursuit of encounters with countless aspects of art and of life.

"My ties with religion ended very early, at my confirmation, in fact. After that I studied Catholicism, but in its connections with art, and I have always been responsive to what religion contains of grandeur, just as I have to any philosophy of the individual. Admiration without participation, in short," is how Malraux puts it now.

While still working for Doyon as a *chineur,* Malraux became literary editor and layout designer for Simon Kra, who with his son, Lucien, ran a bookshop on the rue Blanche. Simon Kra was persuaded by Malraux to publish illustrated works in limited editions: *Causeries* by Baudelaire, illustrated by Constantin-Guys; *Etoiles peintes* by Pierre Reverdy, with a frontispiece by Derain; two texts taken from books by the Marquis de Sade.

Young Raymond Radiguet, the author of *Le Diable au corps,* wished to have a book of his published by Sagittaire, a publishing house that also belonged to Kra. He made this known to Max Jacob, the poet, who had become quite friendly with Malraux, and asked Jacob to use his influence with the young editor. Jacob's reply to Radiguet is dated October 22, 1920:

> Malraux would like nothing better than to take a manuscript of yours, but he says, and rightly, that you are not an old enough master for him to offer to do so. It is up to you to go and see Monsieur Lucien Kra, the son of Simon, at 6, rue Blanche. You must take advantage of the fact that these gentle-

men are not yet disillusioned by the works of young writers, and of the fact that they have money. A day will come when our friend Malraux will no longer be there and when the Kra gentlemen will be thinking more of Anatole France than of us.

When the time came for Malraux to do his military service, he was called to the army, his hair was cut short, and he was transformed into a cavalryman. But, by taking an overdose of caffeine, he succeeded in simulating a heart condition, and with the help of a friend he obtained a discharge. And yet he expressed rabidly patriotic sentiments. . . . One wonders sometimes whether his zeal in pursuing revolutionary causes did not come from a guilt he still felt obligated to overcome— having been too young for the war.

His love of action was genuine, however. He was looking for spiritual goals, immediate objectives for action, but found none and became worried. He felt himself being pulled in too many directions, which is a premonitory symptom of destruction. He must discipline himself, pull himself together, and choose a path to follow. But a path in the service of self first and foremost, for he must save himself as an individual. He needed to save the individual in himself through contact with other men and with another world, in order to create— still within himself—a human reality that would no longer be the individual. What kind of reality? He did not know. He would have to see, to experiment, to live, would have to do boldly in the field of existence what he had done timidly in the field of art—explore the "possible." Until now his work had been only the dream of action. He was haunted by the sense of being isolated in a universe in which others led a life he could not understand.

He often showed a precocious boredom in the presence of people other than his intimates, which was pointed up by his predilection for cats. He enjoyed their sublime indifference to human beings. In all the numerous places where he lodged he kept cats, which he baptized Touffus, Tout-ras, and the like. For a long time, whenever he autographed one of his books for a friend he would draw a cat's profile below his signature, with a single deft, whirling stroke of the pen and an additional few touches for the eyes, nose, and whiskers. Nor was he indifferent to the nonchalant grace accompanied by a perverse kind of cruelty that is characteristic of the feline breed. Malraux too had a cruel, sensual streak.

It was in this same period that he came in contact with the group

9

that ran *Action,* a small but influential review with an anarchist slant. Max Jacob was one of its distinguished list of contributors, who included such now well known names as Blaise Cendrars, Jean Cocteau, Louis Aragon, Paul Eluard, André Salmon, Jean Cassou, Carl Einstein, Ilya Ehrenburg, and Maxim Gorky. *Action* also gave a good deal of space to the plastic arts and reproduced Derain, Braque, Juan Gris, Picasso, Dufy, Vlaminck, Fernand Léger, and Utrillo, among others.

In *Action*'s offices Malraux met most of the contributors and quite a few painters. He took part in the review's activities and appeared at the dinners it organized. (The poets Max Jacob and André Salmon rarely showed up at the *Action* offices. They were usually to be found in the corner bistro or at home, Jacob in Montmartre, on the rue Gabrielle, and Salmon on the rue Joseph Bara, in Montparnasse.)

Jacob, who was born a Jew and converted to Catholicism in 1909, tried to discipline and organize his life by regularly attending the services at the nearby Sacré Coeur, but one evening a week he and his friends would gather at the café-restaurant La Savoyarde on the rue Lamarck, close to the Sacré Coeur, and on those evenings Jacob really let himself go. He would dance and do imitations—of a Radical deputy on an electioneering tour, of a young Breton girl in Paris who has just strayed from the straight and narrow.

Malraux was surely appreciative of Max Jacob's talents, and still more of the many kindnesses the poet extended him, but Jacob, who was extremely sensitive and loved flattery, was somewhat vexed by the reserve that the younger man rarely threw off.

Malraux saw more of the poet Pierre Reverdy, who lived on the rue Cortot in Montmartre, like the painter Demetrios Galanis, another friend. In the evening they would go strolling in the nearby districts.

"I remember," Malraux writes, "that one evening in 1920, an evening when the wild demons of poetry still haunted the provincial Old Montmartre and a light, willful intoxication liberated in a few men a world of incomparable stories, we dropped in, for want of anything better to do, on a painter who lived across from the Sacré Coeur in an immense wooden structure that was called Le Panorama, because a faded Christ was suffering the Passion in the center of two hundred meters of canvas. Painters lived there. They would paint to the sound of a harmonium tormented by a blind old man."

At about this time Malraux also struck up a friendship with the poet Georges Gabory, author of *Coeurs à prendre,* and with René Latouche. The three of them would frequent certain Montmartre and

Montparnasse night spots. Gabory, Malraux's elder by two years, was also a friend of Jacob and of Derain. He cultivated a refined cynicism. In 1920 he wrote a "eulogy of Landru"[5] that was highly revealing about his philosophy. One of his sentences is suggestive of Malraux's style: "In its very principle art is a revolt. To express submission is a beginning of escape from it. True submission is mute and passive."

René Latouche, an extremely promising young poet, published only one poem. In despair at finding nothing worth living for, he committed suicide when he was barely twenty. Eight years later Malraux was to dedicate his book *Les Conquérants* to him.

His contacts with Latouche and Gabory gave Malraux experience of two extreme reactions to the anguish of the West, both of them reactions of escape—one into death, the other into frivolity.

Another close friend was Marcel Arland, two years Malraux's senior. They spoke of their common literary heroes: Barrès, Gide, Claudel, Dostoevski, Stendhal. But they also talked a lot about painting, and Malraux confided to Arland that someday he would write about art. Both felt a distaste for the shrill manifestations of the contemporary spiritual confusion. Rather, they respected age-old traditions, worshiped pure and perfect forms. They were alike in their keen desire to break with false conventions perpetuated by routine and self-interest and instead to blaze their own trails. "In my hopes," says Malraux, "the feeling of the need for revolt far outweighed any aspiration to notoriety."

By far Malraux's most important encounter of this period came as a result of his work for *Action*. At a lunch given in honor of the magazine he met Clara Goldschmidt. She was an attractive, extremely cultivated young girl of his own age, with a gentle voice that concealed an iron will. Her intelligence and love of independence greatly appealed to him. Clara was very much a child of the twenties—50 percent dream and 50 percent business. And, like most girls of that immediate postwar period, she had liberated herself from her parents' tutelage and lived her own life. Her father had been a wealthy businessman of good Jewish middle-class family of German origin, and Clara's childhood was divided between Magdeburg and Paris, where she lived with her widowed mother and two brothers in a town house in Auteuil, at 10, avenue des Chalets. Jean Jaurès, the great French socialist leader,

[5] Landru was a famous French murderer. He was arrested in 1919 and later charged with killing ten women after having proposed marriage to each in turn. His story inspired Charlie Chaplin's film *Monsieur Verdoux*.

11

had lived on that private street prior to his assassination in 1914, and Clara as a tiny girl had often played with the Jaurès children.

André Malraux soon found Clara to be the only woman with whom he could talk about all the things that interested him. Recalling this period of their acquaintance, which so rapidly deepened into something far more meaningful, Clara confesses that in particular they shared what was almost an obsession with death. As an adolescent, she had been haunted by the subject—she had lost her father before she was fourteen. "And then I am a Jew and it is not easy for Jews to accept the idea of death because there is nothing in the Bible that really says that God has promised man salvation. André too thought constantly about death, rebelling against it. It is something that brought us enormously close to each other. . . . André is someone who has found no consolation for death." He is too lucid an agnostic, in fact, to believe that agnosticism can offer anything in the face of death.

In the summer of 1921 André and Clara traveled to Italy. They wandered through Florence together, dawdling in the streets, visiting museums, peering into shopwindows. André would become irritated when Clara lingered longer in front of a dress shop than in front of a shop that catered to men. He was especially fond of the leatherwork that is one of Florence's supreme crafts, and whose smell one could guess at through the plate glass.

The Italian trip was to be the first of many journeys together. From the main post office in Florence they sent Clara's mother a telegram announcing their engagement. It would be a marriage of youngsters, as was the fashion of the period, for he was nineteen and she twenty. "In six months we shall divorce," Clara proposed, out of bravado, wanting neither to tie herself nor to tie her wonderful companion, having a presentiment that great things lay in store for him.

Without apparent effort, but rather to prove to herself that she was not middle-class, Clara had rejected the tribal law. She conceived love to be the search for a double equilibrium, marriage as a simple experiment, a test. The liberated young girl who had always been made much of, treated as a little prodigy by her family, was hardly prepared to become an unobtrusive, submissive wife. In marrying André, she wanted, in her own words, "to be something for someone who would be something for others."

Both families were opposed to the match. The Goldschmidts had wanted to see Clara make a "good" marriage, in worldly terms, and were worried about André's financial status and prospects. Fernand

Malraux, an ardent patriot who never spoke of his country without calling it *la douce* ("sweet") France, disapproved of Clara's German connections. But André had ceased to have close ties with his father. Fernand had remarried, fathered two more sons a great deal younger than André, and spent most of his time on his small country estate, appropriately named Bois-Dormant,[6] making occasional forays on the stock exchange.

Recently the son, like his father, had begun playing the stock market, which was in a period of violent inflation. The young couple were comfortably off, with André's earnings added to the inheritance Clara had had from her father. They did not plan to live grandly save in the mind. They shared a hunger for reading, for works of art, a passion for ideas and for travel; both of them being inclined to hazardous undertakings, marriage seemed an appropriately exciting adventure.

In the end, of course, both families accepted the inevitable. Clara and André were married, in October, 1921, and went to live in Auteuil, with Clara's family. Sharing a house was not a success, and there were soon many clashes, especially with her two brothers, who did not appreciate their brother-in-law and did not get along with their sister. The newlyweds soon took to traveling, and made trips to Italy, Germany, Greece, Czechoslovakia, and Spain:

> So sometimes we lived here and sometimes there, sometimes in Paris, marvelously free in our movements, seizing upon one facet of this earth every day, delighting in our bodies and our minds, finding out about ourselves through the knowledge that we were acquiring by means of travel, reading, long wanderings in museums and galleries, hours spent in the cinema, nightclubs, at the Russian ballet (the real one), the theater (not often), dawdling about the streets, under arcades, under colonnades, sitting in squares drinking clouded white *anis,* mint tea, and indefinable mixtures, believing ourselves to be wealthy and in fact scarcely being rich at all.[7]

The spring before his marriage, Malraux had been introduced by Max Jacob to Daniel-Henry Kahnweiler, a German by birth, who had

[6] The title of the fairy tale *The Sleeping Beauty* is, in French, *La Belle au bois dormant.*
[7] The above and subsequent quotations from Clara Malraux in this chapter are from the abridged edition of her *Memoirs,* translated by Patrick O'Brian (New York: Farrar, Straus and Giroux, 1967).

an art gallery in the courtyard of 29 *bis,* rue d'Astorg. He was then (and remains today) one of the most respected gallery owners in Paris, handling Derain, Picasso, and Braque. He liked to discover promising young artists and was prepared to publish deluxe editions limited to one hundred copies to bring their work to public notice. In April, 1921, Kahnweiler published *Lunes de papier* ("Paper Moons") by André Malraux, a fantasy about death that André had begun planning as early as 1918. The book was dedicated to Max Jacob and had strikingly fine woodcuts by Fernand Léger. It made only a modest stir, however. In the *Nouvelle Revue Française,* Georges Gabory wrote: "Malraux, the doll ripper, is also a vendor of little red balloons and a puppet master. He shows the seven deadly sins dancing elegantly, Death in a dinner jacket, and other pleasant personages."

It is interesting to note that in his very first published work Malraux was already writing about death. "The world is bearable," says the character of Death in *Lunes de papier,* "thanks only to the habit we have acquired of enduring it. It is imposed upon us when we are too young to defend ourselves."[8]

Malraux became friendly with Kahnweiler, at whose house in the Bois de Boulogne he often went to spend Sundays *en famille.* Max Jacob seemed not to take kindly to this, for in June, 1921, he wrote to Kahnweiler: "Say hello to our friends—to good old [Erik] Satie and to the learned and fickle Malraux. . . ."

But neither literature nor his work with publishers could bring in the sums of money that André and Clara needed for travel. They added Clara's dowry to his own money in order to play the stock market. The economic situation of the twenties favored them. "On working days," Clara records in her memoirs, "by which I mean those when the stock exchange was open, as soon as lunch was over we used to go to the nearest bank and decipher the messages that came over the machines imprisoned in their glass boxes. Everything was going along very well for us: often we saw the little + sign to the right of the name of the stock certificate that we had in pledge with the stockbroker."

Malraux had left Doyon and was now working only for Kra as art editor. Clara describes how he would run up a book "as a dressmaker runs up a frock," working at home in the evenings with trays of type, illustrations, scissors, and paste. He was extremely skilled at layout and art work, with his visual imagination and extensive knowl-

---

[8] *Lunes de papier* was reissued in 1945 by Editions Skira in Geneva.

edge both of typography and illustration, but the post at Kra's demanded that he make fairly regular appearances at the office, which Malraux found conflicted more and more with his liking for travel. So he gave up the job and devoted himself instead to the occasional production of what Clara called "bawdy books, with no less bawdy illustrations"—a task that fitted more easily into their vagrant way of life.

Clara, living with him, entertaining his friends, traveling with him, often wondered exactly how much she knew about the young man whom she characterized as "my companion":

> Yes, what did I know? That he handled ideas remarkably well, that he was well-read in many fields, that he was brave, sometimes full of fun and often touchy, that he had an unusual ease in discussion, and that he was not exempt from a certain degree of snobbery and social awkwardness . . . and I knew the shape of his fear of death. . . . I knew little and everything that mattered.

She would have liked to know more, being a woman. Yet she asked no questions, content to let his mysterious personality emerge by degrees as they read, traveled, looked at things together. They did not know many people, but they did succeed in getting to know each other. André, something of a misogynist, had expected to find foolishness, hypocrisy, and unfairness in Clara, and was delighted at the extent of her virtues. She was surprised at his separate characterization of "woman's painting," "woman's *esprit de corps*," having never been aware of it before. "It did not take me long to discover the masculine *esprit de corps*, and then a little later everything that that same feeling contained in the way of conscious or unconscious contempt for women," she commented wryly. One day, André remarked that since the values of their civilization were masculine, it would be amusing to imagine those that would have been produced by a predominantly feminine civilization, and he and Clara spent some enjoyable hours in the compilation of various hypotheses.

Their life in these years was strangely frivolous, nonchalant, unreal, and change was to come about abruptly. The couple had taken a boat trip down the Rhine, watching the vine-covered hills glide by, day after day, while André talked to Clara about the Rhenish civilization that stretched the length of the river and had brought about the

15

region's specific arts, customs, even landscapes. The trip was a vacation from reality in every sense; all the time they were traveling they did not look at a newspaper. If they had, they would have learned that the Paris stock exchange had collapsed, and with it any claims they had ever had to being well off. Their shares in Mexican mining stock had not merely collapsed, as Clara put it, they had vanished. André had no job. The pair arrived in Paris to find out that they were ruined.

This crisis presented André with the opportunity he had—perhaps unconsciously—been waiting for. He had been seeking a chance for some immediate action that would be linked to his need for independence. The Orient—Asia—fascinated him. It was a subject on which he was remarkably well informed. Oriental art was familiar to him. The next step seemed to him exciting but quite natural. Clara tells how he suggested it to her:

A decision had to be taken. I asked him a few questions; upon this he simply replied, "You don't really suppose that I'm going to work, do you?" . . .

"Certainly I don't," I said, "but then . . .?"

". . . Then," said he, "then . . . do you know the road that the Compostella pilgrims took from Flanders to Spain?"

"No," I said, not seeing much connection between my question and his reply.

"It doesn't matter," he said. "The road was studded with cathedrals, and the greater part of them have come down to us intact. But as well as the great sanctuaries there must certainly have been little chapels, many of which have vanished."

"Oh," I said, "I had never really thought about the subject."

"Well, from Siam to Cambodia, all along the Royal Road that runs from the Dangrek Mountains to Angkor, immense temples were built, the ones that have been located and described in the [Khmer] Inventory, but there were certainly others, little ones that are unknown at present."

"Yes," I said. How could I have known what he was getting at? So "Yes," said I.

"Well, then, we'll go to some little Cambodian temple, we'll take away a few statues, and we'll sell them in America; and that will give us enough to live quietly for two or three years."

Clara was surprised by the plan, yet less surprised than if André had announced his intention of entering some import-export firm. They had often been to the Musée Guimet together and had studied the inventory of Khmer monuments compiled by the Ecole Française d'Extrême-Orient that was kept there. André had made visits on his own to the Bibliothèque Orientale. She questioned neither his judgment nor his decision. It was the temper of the times for young people to travel in far distant countries, to enter and attempt to understand other civilizations, and to report subsequently on their experiences. It seemed to her, as well as to André, a natural extension of their joint adventure for them to travel to Cambodia, halfway round the globe, to wrench from unknown temples in the jungle centuries-old statues for which they would find buyers in the United States, the richest country in the world.

2.

The Adventure of Banteay Srei

In early September of 1923, Clara and André embarked in Marseilles on a steamer sailing for Hanoi. The rainy season was in full force in Cambodia when they had made their decision, so they had had plenty of time to prepare for the journey in their own inimitable fashion.

André set about procuring a ministerial commission, which he hoped would give their expedition official backing from an archaeological point of view. The officials at the Musée Guimet whom he approached on this quest were amazed at the breadth of his knowledge, and the order was duly signed by the minister of colonies, Albert Sarraut. It authorized him to visit Cambodia to study the Khmer temples, at his own expense, and permitted him to recruit farmers and carts to transport his expedition's baggage. His sole obligation was to give an account of his travels on his return.

Clara's task was to equip the expedition as cheaply as possible without letting anyone know of their financial straits. She coped with her own wardrobe by having copies of models from the great dress houses run up by the corner dressmaker. She also, more practically, bought quinine, to guard against malaria, a snakebite serum (which came with a syringe they did not know how to use), and a dozen compass saws. The tropical outfitting—mosquito nets, cooking and camping equipment—they left to be done in Pnompenh.

Malraux knew that the Cambodian jungle, a forest of lianas and banyans—a kind of ficus whose branches send out aerial roots that grow down to the ground—was one of the most arduous to break through. The strength and resistance of the vegetation in those damp, hot regions is unimaginable; the lianas and banyans can wrap themselves around a five- or six-ton rock and lift it out of position. They would need not only skilled guides and porters, but also the help of a male friend who could be trusted implicitly. André asked Louis Chevasson, his old school friend, to come along. Chevasson, small and dark, had remained friendly with Malraux and saw him often enough to have been given a nickname, "Coffee Bean," by Max Jacob. Clara did not particularly like Chevasson, but André trusted him, and he was free to make the journey. They agreed to meet in Saigon.

Clara and André made the voyage to Indochina as first-class passengers on a Messageries Maritimes vessel. The journey was a long one, lasting a couple of months, and made a profound impression on the idealistic young people.

The boat docked at Djibouti, capital of French Somaliland, at the mouth of the Red Sea, where Malraux was appalled at the wretched conditions in the native slums that crowded around the artificially clean and spacious streets of the European part of the city. He had known, had read about the gross inequalities between the lives of the colonial French overseas and those of the natives over whom they ruled, but to see the juxtaposition of comfort and misery at first hand brought it most vividly home.

This impression was reinforced by the conditions on the boat, on which he and Clara were traveling as first-class passengers but with minds free, so to speak, to roam where they would. Their shipmates, by contrast, seemed to have separated into groups that were aligned in a social hierarchy very different from the loose structure with which Malraux was familiar. It was his first contact with the rigid, unsparing outlook of the typical *colon*. These Frenchmen, he realized, thought of Indochina as a vast feudal state of which they were the overlords, and regarded its people as little better than the serfs of medieval times. What of the incredibly rich civilization of the past, which was all he and Clara yet knew of the country they were about to visit? To these bourgeois colonists, it seemed not to exist. They lived in the present, with all its petty considerations of position, wealth, and influence.

"Given his habit of speaking his mind," remarks Walter Langlois in his book on Malraux's Indochinese experiences, "young Malraux, brilliant, liberal, and haughty, must have made quite a few enemies and few friends on the long voyage across the Indian Ocean."[1]

On their arrival in Indochina, André and Clara went first to Hanoi, where they visited the Ecole Française d'Extrême-Orient, the headquarters for archaeological activity in the country. There they

[1] *André Malraux, l'aventure indochinoise*, Mercure de France, Paris, 1967.

19

were warmly received by Professor Henri Parmentier, who arranged for them to visit Angkor Wat, the marvel of the Khmer civilization. As a result of reading the *école's* bulletins, which gave regular accounts of the explorations carried on by the school, André had already settled on the object of his interest, the abandoned temple of Banteay Srei, some forty-five miles northeast of Angkor, in the midst of the jungle. It had been visited by Parmentier himself in 1916, but had never been explored and was not included in the inventory of Khmer temples. Small, hard to reach, almost unknown, it seemed ideal for Malraux's purposes. Parmentier was dazzled by the extent of Malraux's knowledge. "He is so young, and so wealthy," he confided to Clara. "How astonishing to have made such good use of his time! And so disinterested!" Naturally, the loyal wife did not disabuse him.

From Hanoi they went to Saigon, where they were met by Chevasson, who had made his own way to Indochina, and then journeyed on by train into Cambodia.

From Pnompenh, a riverboat, specially chartered from the Messageries Fluviales, took André, Clara, and Chevasson as far as Siemreap, where the curator of the Angkor complex had a car waiting for them. They stayed with him briefly, enlisting his help in procuring buffalo carts, drivers, horses, and a guide—who turned out later to be a spy. Then, mounted on the tiny Cambodian horses, preceded by natives who hacked a path through the brush, and followed by oxcarts to transport the huge camphorwood chests in which they planned to conceal the statues they were hunting for, the three improvised explorers set off into the jungle. Fresh from Europe, conditioned to urban life, they suffered acutely from the tropical heat. In *La Voie royale,* a novel he wrote some seven years later, Malraux included a passage that vividly describes this mad adventure into an unknown world full of repugnant insects and deadly snares:

> . . . Obliterated by centuries, the Way revealed its presence only by those rotted mineral masses, with the two eyes of some toad sitting motionless in an angle of the stones. . . . Would the caravan eventually reach the sculptured temple toward which the boy was guiding them? . . . The forest and the heat were, however, more overwhelming than the anxiety. Claude felt himself succumbing as to a disease, in the fermentation in which forms swelled, stretched, rotted, in a world in which man did not count, which separated him from himself with

the force of the darkness. And insects were everywhere. . . .

They lived on the forest, from the black balls that were crushed by the hooves of the oxen yoked to the carts and the ants that quiveringly climbed the porous trunks to the spiders held by their grasshopperlike feet to the center of webs four meters across whose threads caught the light of day that still lingered near the ground, and appeared from afar, phosphorescent and geometric, against the confusion of forms in a motionlessness of eternity. They alone, on the mollusklike movements of the brush, fixed figures which an obscure analogy linked to the other insects, to the cockroaches, to the flies, to the unnameable little creatures whose heads emerged from their carapace on the surface of the mosses, with the sickening virulence of life seen under a microscope. . . .

The tall and whitish termitaries, on which the termites were never visible, lifted their abandoned planetary peaks in the semidarkness as though they had taken their substance from the corruption of the air, in the odor of mushrooms, in the presence of the minuscular bloodsuckers agglutinated beneath the leaves like flies' eggs. . . .

The horses walked with necks bent, in silence . . . the young guide made his way slowly. . . .

The wall stretched across the vegetation like a road, but covered with a sticky moss. A fall, if Claude were to try to walk on it, was fraught with danger: gangrene was as much a mistress of the forest as were the insects. He got down and crawled on all fours; the rotten-smelling moss, covered with leaves half-viscous, half-reduced to their veins as though they had been partly digested, reached up to his face, enlarged by the proximity, vaguely stirring in the calm air, recalling the presence of insects by the movement of their fibrils. When he had progressed three meters he felt a tickling.

He stopped, rubbing his neck with his hand. The tickling sensation passed over to his hand, and he immediately withdrew it. Two black ants, big as wasps, their antennae sticking out, were trying to slip between his fingers. He shook his hand hard, and they fell. He was on his feet again. No ants on his clothes. At the end of the wall, three hundred feet away, there was a break. The gate, probably, and the sculptures. . . .

21

Guided by an old man who was by no means sure of his and their objective, the three finally reached Banteay Srei. "There was a doorway in the bush, a doorway opening onto a little square courtyard, with its paving all heaved up," goes Clara's account. "At the far end, partly fallen, but with two of its walls still standing firm, a pink, carved, decorated temple upon which the splashes of moss looked like ornaments . . . lovelier than all the temples we had seen hitherto, at all events more moving in its forsaken state than all the naked and swept Angkors."

Banteay Srei—its name meant "the virgin's fortress"—offered everything that Malraux had hoped for: uncommon difficulties, an incomparable artistic and archaeological interest, and the possibility of a profit that would be remarkable. But the luxuriant vegetation made the temple almost invisible. Before they could reach the sculptures they had to hack their way still farther through masses of vines. From a bas-relief Malraux chose seven sculptures of *apsaras*,[2] which they cut out with the saws they had brought with them. Each of the sculptures formed a stone block some twenty inches high and twenty-six to twenty-eight inches wide. They packed the precious figures carefully into the camphorwood chests and heaved them up onto the oxcarts, then headed again in the direction of Angkor Wat and the river. Once arrived they boarded a riverboat for Pnompenh, their chests safely stowed in the hold, addressed to a company in Saigon.

It seemed that everything had gone well for the little expedition, but unbeknown to them their guide had reported their activities to the authorities in Pnompenh, who had sent the curator of the Pnompenh museum to intercept the boat secretly some sixty miles upstream from the city and assure himself that the cargo of stolen sculptures was indeed aboard. When the riverboat stopped in Pnompenh on December 24, the police at once boarded the vessel with a warrant of arrest. The local paper reported the facts as follows:

> On December 24, 1923, at about midnight, at the very time when the church bells of Pnompenh were inviting the faithful to celebrate the anniversary of the birth of Christ, two *Sûreté* inspectors boarded the Messageries Fluviales steamer arriving from Siemreap and after informing two passengers, MM. Malraux and Chevasson, that they were authorized to search their

---

[2] Goddesses of inferior rank in Indian mythology, dancers and musicians.

baggage, had these opened and found fragments of statues which came from the Angkor ruins. When cases addressed to the firm of Berthet & Charrière of Saigon were searched, seven blocks of stone were discovered, one of which represented two divinities and the six others *apsaras*.

These various items were immediately seized and transported to the Musée Albert Sarraut, where M. Groslier [the curator] identified them and established that they belonged to the bas-reliefs of the temple of Banteay Srei.

Malraux was going to pay dearly for his success.

What had happened? Malraux had no sooner arrived in Cambodia, according to the local press, than he had been reported to the local authorities by the Department of Colonies as a suspect to be closely watched. The chief of the Second Bureau, the area in which the expedition had taken place, had had the archaeologists followed and spied upon throughout their expedition. Once it was completed, he had only to alert the Pnompenh police.

Malraux was accused of having intended to engage in "illicit" trade. He had not, however, intended to violate the law. Legally, any object unclassified in the official inventory of monuments is *res nullius,* something to which the law does not apply, and which therefore belongs to its finder. How many of the settlers in Saigon and Pnompenh who displayed antique Khmer statuettes and bas-reliefs in their houses could vouch for their being from equally blameless sources? When these colonists were short of money, the first thing they habitually did was to sell their statuettes, without a word to anyone. At least Malraux had had the courage to attack a monument situated in an almost inaccessible spot, which no one had until then seen fit to classify in the official inventory.

The judicial inquiry into the Malraux case lasted six months, during which time André, Clara, and Chevasson stayed, in increasing discomfort, at the so-called best hotel in Pnompenh, the Manolis. They were not allowed to leave the city, and they could not pay their bill. Meanwhile Henri Parmentier, director of the Ecole d'Extrême-Orient, personally visited Banteay Srei to appraise the depredations on the spot.

On July 16, 1924, at 8:00 A.M., the case came before the Pnompenh court of summary jurisdiction. Half an hour before the deliberations began, the courtroom was filled. Malraux was quite a drawing card. He and Chevasson were accused of "willful damage to monuments and of misappropriation of fragments of bas-reliefs stolen from the temple of Banteay Srei, belonging to the Angkor group." The case lasted for three sittings. Malraux began by undertaking his own defense.

"He is a tall youth," wrote the editor of *L'Impartial*, "thin, pale, with a beardless face illuminated by two extremely intense eyes. He is very eloquent and defends himself with a keenness that reveals in him unquestionable qualities of energy and tenacity. He appears to have a solid cultural background." (In order to show proof of his erudition, Malraux had to recite a passage from Vergil's *Aeneid* in Latin. *L'Echo du Cambodge* reported: "The public had the impression that they were attending a veritable course in archaeology, Malraux was so remarkable.")

After the pleadings, the judgment was postponed until the following Monday, July 21. The court sentenced Malraux to three years' imprisonment and Chevasson to eighteen months.

The colonial administration had taken its revenge. It did not forgive Malraux his arrogance, his intelligence, his culture, and, most of all, his intolerance of the colonial way of life.

The French government had always made a point of singling out able people from the admixture of cultures and countries that comprised French Indochina and sending them to France for professional training as doctors, civil servants, officers. But whether they returned to Cochin China (which was still a colony) or to Cambodia, Annam, Tonkin, or Laos (which were French protectorates), the situation was still the same. Despite their French qualifications, they were invariably placed under the orders of administrators or settlers who were often less educated than they, and sometimes, indeed, grossly ignorant. How could a fiery, intelligent person like Malraux help being severe toward colonial administrators whose spelling mistakes in their reports had to be corrected, surreptitiously, by their Indochinese subordinates? If the long months of awaiting trial in Pnompenh served no other purpose, they made André Malraux supremely aware of the inequities of the colonial system. So did the verdict, which patently ignored the fact that André had carefully chosen Banteay Srei because it was unclassified and hence its contents did not legally belong to anyone.

Malraux and Chevasson did not acknowledge themselves beaten, and immediately filed an appeal. They were scheduled to appear before the court of appeals in Saigon on September 22, 1924. The manner and the tone in which the news of the case had been presented in the French press—there was talk of the "pillage" of the temple—worried some of

Malraux's friends in Paris. On August 9, 1924, René-Louis Doyon, André's old employer, published a lengthy open letter in the Paris newspaper *L'Eclair* in which he deplored the nearly total aggressiveness of the press. He drew a eulogistic portrait of Malraux and expressed his fear that this highly original and distinguished young man had been treated as a commonplace thief.

Max Jacob, whose initial reaction to the news of Malraux's departure for Indochina had been sarcastic, now expressed concern over his misfortunes. "A mission for Malraux!" he had written to Kahnweiler the previous year, when the dealer informed him of André's departure for Indochina bearing the minister of colonies' official sanction. "At last he will find his vocation in the Orient. He will become an Orientalist and will end up at the Collège de France, like Claudel. He was born to occupy a professor's chair." But on learning of the trial in Pnompenh and Doyon's declaration of support for Malraux, he remarked: "I was told about our misfortune too late to have been the first to act; I have been only the second. We owe our gratitude to Doyon for having had the idea and the courage to get the press to act."

Two days before Doyon's letter appeared in print, however, another supporter, the staunchest one of all, had reappeared on French soil—frail, exhausted, but determined to move heaven and earth to save her husband—Clara Malraux.

What had happened to Clara meanwhile? After three months of awaiting trial in Pnompenh, Clara had had the "brilliant idea" of feigning a suicide attempt. She took an overdose of phenobarbitol and succeeded in getting herself out of the Manolis Hotel, but only into the hospital, where she remained for another three months, seriously underweight and weakened by a bad attack of malaria. Finally her case was dismissed (on the grounds that it is a wife's duty to follow her husband, and she was therefore not responsible for her actions at Banteay Srei), and André at once cabled the news to his father. Fernand Malraux responded nobly with a boat ticket home, a check to pay the hospital bill, and a small amount over for pocket money. Clara embarked for France early in July, just before her husband's trial began.

It was a long voyage, and in its course Clara met a fascinating man, the colonial official responsible for French education in China. One night, when the boat was in the Gulf of Aden, the inevitable happened —he became her lover. "There are few men whose image is so sharp in my memory: he was capable of being a lover without ceasing to be a friend," wrote the incurably honest Clara long afterward. "If we were not both married . . ." he said to her once. But if they were not, Clara decided, then things would not be as they were—and maybe that would not have altered anything.

On the ship she also made the acquaintance of a distinguished Saigon lawyer, a Frenchman named Paul Monin, who was known as "the natives' lawyer" because of his sympathy for their cause. He and Clara exchanged addresses before they left the boat at Marseilles, and Clara took the train to Paris, where her mother and brothers were waiting for her. News of Malraux's arrest and trial had preceded her, of course, and she returned home to a barrage of criticism and suggestions that she divorce her "criminal" husband immediately. When she indignantly refused to do so, the family challenged her on another front, André's idleness. He had not worked since they were married. She could not possibly stay with him.

"How could I make them understand that there are enriching forms of activity? To have convinced them of this I should have had to be able to show them the books he wrote later. 'In two years he has advanced to a point that it would have taken him ten years to reach in other circumstances,' I murmured."

Their response was to throw her out, in her words. She went to stay in a hotel, and got in touch instead with André's mother, whom she had never met, suggesting that Madame Malraux might like to have firsthand news of her son. The two women met in the lobby of Clara's hotel and fell into each other's arms. Madame Malraux was tall, slim, pretty, and looked much younger than she was, with a voice to match. She and Clara at once set off to look for a furnished apartment, for the little house and grocery at Bondy had just been sold, and Madame Malraux was planning to have Clara come and live with her and her mother until André's return. Clara's first meeting with André's grandmother impressed her greatly. "She was tall and as straight-backed as one of Franz Hals's female regents, but with her own family she displayed none of their severity or harshness. . . . She was a great lady, and she ruled her world firmly," Clara reported, adding how impressed she was when the old lady said to her that she considered society to be out of order these days. "When I was young people came out to fight in the streets," she complained, and Clara had a vision of her bending in her dignified way to pick up a stone that she would then carefully add to the nearest barricade.

Strengthened by the support of André's family, Clara Malraux undertook to circulate a petition on her husband's behalf. She wrote it herself for the most part, with the help of Paul Monin, who gave her advice and friendship. The day arrived, all too soon, when he had to return to Saigon. As they parted Clara said, "Go to see André. He's an extraordinary person. Everything takes on meaning when he talks. I'm sure you and he will like each other."

Was she trying to make amends for her infidelity on the boat? It does not seem so. The pair were a most unusual couple, who considered themselves above prejudices and who tried by means of an absolute sincerity to disarm jealousy as a manifestation of the instinct of property.

No, the explanation is rather the one she gave long afterward, to an American reporter: "It was a very tempestuous marriage. We seemed to live from one quarrel to another. But I was never bored and it was the great adventure of my life."

Clara's petition was signed by just about every member of the literary vanguard, from André Breton to Jean Paulhan.

In an article in *Les Nouvelles Littéraires,* the influential French literary weekly, André Breton invoked ". . . the well-known dilemma of the desire for possession that will impel a young man of twenty-three, endowed with a fiery temperament and rather heroic, to seize what he loves, even money or what may represent money, in one of those impulses of absolute innocence which it is customary to overlook in poets after they are dead and which are then regarded as only adding to their glory. . . . Everything that matters to us is involved in this, for—beyond Malraux himself—what is at stake is the safeguarding of a certain quality of spirit. All of us, I hope, will stand by Malraux, and we shall not abandon him to what he has called the brother of change, the wind."

The Malraux-Chevasson case came up before the Saigon court of appeals on September 23 and was held over to October 8 at the request of Chevasson's attorney. On that date the deputy public prosecutor presented a charge establishing Malraux's premeditation, making him the principal defendant. "This man," he said, "a fop and a liar, has succeeded in taking advantage of the minister of colonies by claiming a university degree which he does not have, by passing his father off as being something he is not, by promising, finally, to hand over to the Ecole Française d'Extrême-Orient the fruit of his searches."

The third audience, that of October 9, was devoted to the pleadings. Malraux was represented by one Maître Béziat. "The case, reduced to its real proportions, does not justify all the stir that has been made over it," the lawyer concluded, and asked for an acquittal. "For, after all, those stones are nothing but pebbles," said Maître Béziat to Chevasson as he was leaving the courtroom.

On October 28, 1924, the court of appeals rendered its decision. It reduced Malraux's three-year sentence to a suspended sentence of one year of imprisonment and that of Chevasson from eighteen months to an eight-month suspended sentence.

Still dissatisfied with a verdict that made them into criminals, Malraux and Chevasson determined to appeal their case to the Supreme Court of Appeals in Paris. On November 1, at six o'clock in the morning, the two friends boarded the liner *Chantilly* for Marseilles and their return to France.

Many people in Saigon were beginning to say that instead of having Malraux and his companion followed as though they were spies, the government should rather have warned them of the risks they were running by disturbing the statues of the Cambodian temples. What proof was there that Malraux had intended to carry out an illicit operation in Cambodia? He might well have believed that operating at his own expense placed him under no obligation to the government, such as a civil servant, who was appointed by the state, might have had. The legislation concerning the conservation of monuments in Indochina was based on grounds that were certainly open to challenge. And had not much more serious cases recently been settled amicably?

The Indochinese adventure had confronted Malraux with the bourgeois spirit in its most unattractive forms: indiscriminate veneration of authority for its own sake, approval of police intrigues and their techniques, pleasure derived from the crushing of the weak. This avid, jealous, and timorous society seemed to him concerned only with the values of conformity and convention, and it could not but arouse his contempt. He was determined not to let himself be bullied by it, and his recent trial only strengthened him in his determination. During the judicial inquiry into his case, he had had plenty of time to observe many aspects of colonial society and its relation to the native population, whose hatred for the settler he now so well understood.

He had become aware of the stupefying quality of French imperialism as it manifested itself in operation in a colony. He had become aware also of oppressed peoples, with a centuries-old civilization, who were slowly and powerfully rising—the spirit of revolution. He would be on that side:

THE ADVENTURE OF BANTEAY SREI

The origin of my whole revolutionary commitment is colonialism, and not the proletariat. Indochina was the touchstone. I became involved in the revolutionary movement when I found that it alone was ready to come to the aid of the Indochinese, to grant them a liberal status. My Marxist, self-taught education, too, is linked to Indochina.

3.

Return to Indochina

In late November of 1924, Malraux arrived in Marseilles. He was wearing a white tropical suit. It was snowing. He announced to Clara, who had come to meet him, nearly beside herself with joy and emotion, "We are leaving, both of us, in a month or six weeks, for Saigon. Or as soon as we can get enough money together. The Annamites need a free newspaper. Monin and I will publish it."

Paul Monin had indeed gotten in touch with Malraux, as Clara had suggested, and the two had quickly become friends. Monin, a youthful hero of the war, had emigrated soon afterward to Indochina under the impression that it was a happy country where he and his wife and child could make a new life for themselves. Instead he found disorder and injustice under the shadow of the French flag he loved. Monin was thirty when he arrived in Indochina. His battle experiences were behind him; he was acquainted with death; revolted by the falsehoods invented by his French countrymen to justify the slavery they imposed upon *les jaunes* ("the yellow race"), he set himself, through the practice of law in Saigon, to combat the monstrous reality.

It was natural that his name had become anathema to the Saigon colonial bourgeoisie; equally natural that he and André should immediately have struck up a friendship that was to color both their lives. Monin had already had the idea of publishing a newspaper that would plead the cause of Indochinese nationalism. He and Malraux met regularly for long planning sessions, on their own or with politically minded Indochinese, mostly members of the Young Annam movement,[1] which was closely allied with the Kuomintang, the revolutionary movement that was growing in China, and attracting increas-

[1] This left-wing youth movement was widespread in Annam, the most urbanized area of Indochina, hence the name Young Annam. Annamite was also widely used to mean Indochinese generally.

ing interest and concern in other countries. Monin had already attracted notice and outrage by organizing a waterfront strike and by waving a red flag in the streets of Saigon; he would later be accused of being an active agent of the Kuomintang in Indochina.

Malraux's short stay in Paris was spent in getting in touch with lawyers to arrange for a motion to appeal the decision in the Malraux-Chevasson case to the Supreme Court of Appeals in Paris, and in trying to raise the money needed for the new project. Malraux went to see André Breton, Max Jacob, and others who had combined their efforts in the petition to save him. But he found them not too eager to become involved in a political commitment.

He kept Monin informed of the various steps he was taking toward the publication of their projected paper. In the course of several interviews with editors at the publishing firms of Fayard and Hachette, he was successful in getting them to agree to pay in advance for reprint rights to a stated number of articles that would be excerpted from various issues of the as yet nonexistent paper, which was to be called *L'Indochine.*

André also introduced Clara to the pleasures of using hashish—he had brought her a parcel of it as a present.[2] "You chew it until nothing is left but the woody part," he told her, "and that you spit out. Then a wonderful music starts to play and words give rise to colored images. . . . You can guide the show that goes on inside your head— I'll help by reading poetry aloud. . . . And the splendid thing is that you don't get hooked on this stuff."

While she was on the hashish trip, Clara told her husband about the affair she had had on the boat, and became dreamily aware, suddenly, that André was sitting at the foot of the bed, in tears. "Why did you do that?" he demanded. Then, after a pause, he murmured, "If you had not saved my life, I should leave you."

He did not, however, and somehow the two reconciled their problems in the light of the more pressing urgency of planning their return to Indochina and the difficulty of finding the money to do so.

"We sold everything we could still sell," Clara writes, "what we had left in the way of books, paintings, jewels, the sale of which brought us in enough money to buy two third-class tickets to Singapore."

---

[2] Like everyone who has lived for any time in the Far East, André and Clara Malraux had also smoked opium. Later on, it is said, Malraux experimented with other and more dangerous drugs, but definitely cured himself of the habit.

Before they left, two miracles occurred that put an end to at least some of their difficulties. André Malraux's father, convinced by his son of the importance of the task he was undertaking, gave him a present of fifty thousand francs (the stock exchange was having a small boom), which he was to collect in Singapore and which would pay for them to complete the journey to Saigon. Fernand Malraux made it plain, however, that there was no more to be had once that sum was exhausted. "Anyone can make a mess of things once, but if you do it twice you no longer deserve to be helped," he said. Then, three days before they were to board ship, Bernard Grasset asked Malraux to come and see him, and had him sign a contract for three books, on the recommendation of François Mauriac. On the same day he handed Malraux an advance of three thousand francs.

A sea voyage of nearly a month in third class was by no means agreeable. The passengers were segregated by sex in cabins of six, which meant that the two were separated just when they were so full of exciting plans! In Saigon, Monin was busy collecting the funds needed for the launching of their paper.

"What we were planning was nothing less than a daily," Clara writes. "He [Monin] was sure he would obtain the major part of the needed financial support from the leaders of the Chinese community of Cholon, and the rest from the Young Annam groups which were beginning to organize in the country, not yet in order to achieve autonomy, but simply to live on a footing of relative equality with the French."

Out of a native population of twenty-five million, only a thousand could hope to have a higher education. The French functionaries had more power over the natives than the Mandarin conquerors of earlier centuries had ever had.

When the harvest was poor—a harvest on which high taxes were levied, leaving only 25 percent for the peasants—the natives were imprisoned for debts! They were also constrained to buy a product taxed by the state; the Annamite villagers must at least buy, if not drink, so many liters of alcohol distilled by the French under the excise administration. The tax on salt was even more distressing, since it applied to a population whose basic foods were rice, tasteless without salt, and dried fish, which demands the use of salt as a preservative.

The Indochinese did not have the right to vote, so they were not even citizens in their own country.

In a situation of such obvious inequity, it seemed to liberal intellectuals such as Monin and Malraux quite natural that the elements eager for change in Indochina should look, not to France, but to nearby China for encouragement and example.

The situation in China deserves a word of explanation. Not only was it by far the largest country in the Orient, but its far-flung overseas population, those merchant Chinese who dominated all the major trading areas of the Far East, gave events in China enormous importance. The Kuomintang, the Chinese nationalist and republican party, which was headed by intellectuals who had studied abroad, had warm advocates in Europe as well as in Indochina. Among them was Bertrand Russell, who wrote: "The Chinese military chiefs who fight among themselves are ambitious brigands, serving the interests of rival foreign powers. One man alone, Sun Yat-sen, is disinterested and works for his country."

This man, who held the destiny of China in his frail hands, was then an aging and ailing visionary. He had been born into a very poor family and spent many years in exile before returning to China to participate in the revolution that overthrew the Manchu dynasty in 1911. He led the country briefly and later set up a separatist republican government in Canton. In 1922 he deliberately allied his Kuomintang party with the Communists, in order to get Russian backing and sympathy for its cause. The Communists for their part realized that an alliance with the Kuomintang was the only way possible for them to get control of China, a vast land of 400 million inhabitants, with an urban proletariat of barely 5 million, few of whom had any conception of trade union action, let alone the principles of Marxism. In 1922 China was still semifeudal; rival warlords with their private armies controlled small areas and fought each other with a barbarity little changed since the Middle Ages. Even with external aid from the Russian Comintern, the Chinese Communist party could not hope to wage a successful struggle against the established social order without a powerful ally within China itself.

On October 10, 1924, there was a bloody uprising in Canton in which a volunteer corps sponsored by the Cantonese merchants turned a peaceful workers' demonstration into a massacre, and then was itself routed by a "workers' army" organized by Sun Yat-sen. The Communists seized on the occasion to extend their hold over the Canton region, and two opposing factions became evident in the Kuomintang, one, led by Sun Yat-sen's able lieutenant, Chiang Kai-shek, of right-wing tendencies, the other, led by Wang Ching-wei, readily available to underground pressure from the Russian Communist party. As long as the ailing Sun Yat-sen lived, they were somewhat under control, but after his death in March, 1925, the division would speedily deepen into outright schism and war.

When Clara and André arrived in Saigon from Singapore early in 1925, Monin was waiting for them on the docks—tall, slender, deeply tanned under his pith helmet. He was full of enthusiasm, and they at once plunged into planning sessions, but three months would pass before they could actually bring out the new periodical. Monin was full of ideas but had no practical experience in publishing; Malraux was an expert at book layout but had not worked with newspaper composition before; most of all, they lacked money. In the evenings at their hotel André would make mock-ups of *L'Indochine* with Clara's interested help. "Number zero of our periodical was composed, decomposed, recomposed. Number one suffered the same fate," she wrote. The composing room where the paper was eventually set in type was lit only by a skylight and had no ventilating fans; since they had no other help, they corrected their own proofs as they came from the printing press, smudging the paper with sweat as they did so.

For relaxation, Monin and Malraux often indulged themselves with a little sword practice on the roof terrace. They were both quite expert and enjoyed the sport—which may be the only one that Malraux has bothered to become expert in.

The men never lost confidence that the money would come in, collected from distant provinces and even from Canton, whence the successes and defeats of the Kuomintang were regularly reported to Monin and Malraux by the Chinese settlers living in Cholon, the Chinese section of Saigon. Clara's comments on the Chinese situation offer a vivid insight into how they felt during this time:

> At a distance of a few days from this Indochina that Europeans presume to insert in their universe, some yellow men, Chinese, are trying to become once more masters of what belongs to them. I do not quite understand all these comings and goings of generals, these towns taken and soon abandoned, these relationships with Occidental thought—that Occident from which they want to free themselves—by means of the thought of the Russians, part-European, part-Asiatic, a thought revised and corrected, no doubt an indispensable stage of a reconquest of themselves. Thus I am learning certain names:

34

Sun Yat-sen, and the names of some warlords, Chiang Kai-shek, for one; and I now know that the Kuomintang exists. . . . And thus we come into contact with problems ignored by most Europeans. We run into these problems, we see them, feel them, touch them, almost. Isolated in Cambodia, we had barely suspected them. . . . Now they are becoming our most disturbing subjects of reflection, we have cast behind us what were, until now, our usual themes: the arts, metaphysics, psychology. . . .

Some large sums are being given by men who are almost poor, and small sums by little functionaries and little land-owners, but also by some moneybags who want their names to be kept secret. The Chinese, for their part, are active. . . . We are going to have a fine periodical, combative, generous, at the service of this admirable people. . . . Westerners consider the natives to be cowardly. They have not read what Le Lo'i, the Liberator, wrote about them when the country was occupied by the Chinese: "Sometimes we have been weak, sometimes we have been powerful, but never have we lacked heroes". . . .

From our first contacts with the Chinese of Cholon, I had faith in them. . . .

The day came when the Chinese of Cholon celebrated our new membership in the Kuomintang. Suddenly, without invitation, without instruction, we had entered a community! As for Monin, he had certainly given more proofs of his convictions, which was to our benefit.

At the end of a lavish banquet, Monin stood up and spoke, declaring his attachment to the Chinese cause, and at the end of his speech he exclaimed, "Long live the French Republic! Long live the Chinese Republic!"

Then it was André Malraux's turn. Tossing back the lock of hair from his forehead, he declared: "We are going to make a periodical together. . . . We are going to fight together. It would be wrong to think that our aims are absolutely the same. . . . The thing that unites us is the fact that we have the same enemies."

The first issue of *L'Indochine* came out on June 17, 1925.

"*L'Indochine* is an independent journal, open to all, having no ties with banks and business groups. It makes a principle of respecting the right of its contributors to express themselves, whether their contributions are regular or occasional." This statement of principle was in the first editorial Malraux and Monin wrote. The first and second numbers of the newspaper were distributed free of charge in Saigon streets. The editors had printed five thousand copies of each. By the time the fourth edition of the eight-page daily paper came out, people were sufficiently interested to buy it. The editorial slant was instantly evident; the paper plunged straightaway into controversy. To take a case in point:

In the spring of 1925, the governor of Cochin China, Maurice Cognacq, had made a tour of inspection in the newly cultivated sectors of Camau, the richest agricultural region of Cochin China. The government press celebrated the event lyrically and declared that the governor had "seen everything and heard all the pleas and satisfied all the claimants." He had made it a point of honor, the papers added, to see to it that the illiterate peasants should not be exploited by "certain sharks and politicians out to feather their own nests."

Shortly afterward, a brief notice in the *Bulletin de Commerce* announced that an auction of lands situated in the region of Camau would take place on July 27.

On July 23, four days before the date set for the Camau auction, the governor-general of Indochina came to Saigon on a tour of inspection.

The evening before his arrival, Malraux ran a page one editorial in *L'Indochine* that could not escape the governor-general's attention. In it he denounced three big scandals in which Governor Cognacq had been involved along with Henri Chavigny de Lachevrotière, managing editor of *L'Impartial* (the right-wing Saigon daily)—arranging a monopoly of the port in 1924, a real estate swindle in Khanhhoa, and now Camau. In each of these frauds, the colonial administration had allowed a financial consortium to profit from the affair, to the detriment of the unfortunate Indochinese. The press had played the role of accomplice in almost every case by remaining silent and allowing the exploiters to get away with it.

In the present case, wrote Malraux, apart from *L'Indochine* "not one French paper in Saigon printed the letter of the dispossessed Camau proprietors, which we have printed. . . . It is a moving document and is based on a certain law. No one has published it."

Chavigny could move fast, he went on, when it was a question of accusing others, notably the editors of *L'Indochine,* of stirring up the ill will of the Annamites against France. Yet Chavigny and Cognacq refused to listen to the unhappy peasants who were demanding justice.

In the final paragraph of his editorial, Malraux addressed himself directly to Chavigny:

These proprietors . . . came to settle in Camau a long time ago. They were poor folk. Little by little they have turned the bush into fertile land. I need not tell you about the torrid heat or the fever they endured. They are exceptional people. . . . But they have been known here for such a long time that they have been forgotten. I am merely asking you to look at their faces and see how all the suffering of the Annamite farmer is imprinted there; the long travail of their forefathers has left deep marks on them, which inspire pity.

You and your good friends who covet their lands, make no mistake. All their toil, all their trouble may be seen, you think, in the magnificent rice grown on their lands. Well, you know, under each field you will find the corpse of the man who cleared it. You imagine him, at night, counting the piasters he has earned—the value of his land. You count with him. . . .

And you will tell him: "The French law has foreseen and provided for everything. This dispossession, if it does take place, will not cause you to suffer. Your work on the land will be evaluated by an expert, and you will be paid the value!"

Yes, but before they are paid that money they will have to sue for it and carry the suit to the State Council. By the time the lawsuit is ended they will be dead. And France, alas, too far away, will cast on their grave a great melancholy shadow.

True, you will also tell them that their death shows to what point they have comprehended their duty. More than ever before their lands are rich and the rice will grow ever more densely over their graves. The most beautiful rice fields of Cochin China, those over which the wind blows with the rustle of shifting coins, are those where lie countless sufferings, countless numbers of the desperate dead. . . . Especially, *monsieur*, if they were living skeletons.

L'Indochine and its two editors won their case. The unjust clauses were suppressed and the auction of the Camau lands took place without incident. The twenty-one thousand acres that remained after the withdrawal of the cultivated fields were sold in fourteen parcels. The public treasury received close to 280,000 piasters, which surpassed by a great deal the 100,000 piasters that the Cognacq consortium would have paid for the same lands had the sale at auction remained unchanged.

The Camau affair made the Annamites clearly understand that the new periodical was resolved to defend their interests and put an end to government corruption in Cochin China.

In March of 1925, Sun Yat-sen had died and the situation in China began changing rapidly.

L'Indochine started publishing a new feature on its front page: "From our private wire service." The news printed in that column came from independent sources to which the other newspapers had no access. Cognacq made repeated but unsuccessful efforts to suppress these reports about the nationalist agitation that was triumphing in a country so close to Indochina.

In telegrams from Shanghai and Canton, notices of uprisings came in day after day. *L'Indochine* followed the situation very closely. Later these reports were to provide Malraux with material for his first long novel, *Les Conquérants*. Some of these news items about the bloody Cantonese revolt of June 25–29 were even inserted word for word in his book.

The editors of *L'Indochine* were in close touch with sources of information situated in China; probably these were Chinese journalists. There may even have been someone in the general headquarters of the Kuomintang to wire the news. From time to time this connection was interrupted, however, and some of the telegrams indicated that a struggle was going on between the several Chinese factions for control of the liberation forces.

One such message, published in *L'Indochine* on July 31, 1925, announced that an army supporting the Kuomintang (which governed Canton) had defeated another and rival Chinese army recently arrived from Yunnan. This telegram made it crystal clear that the Kuomintang troops were commanded by "Chinese cadets and Russian officers."

Another telegram, published three days later, gave another glimpse of what was happening behind the official scenes: "CANTON: The struggle between the Communist party and the first section of the Kuomintang has begun. From now on the Kuomintang will be affiliated with the pan-Asiatic federation being formed in Japan."

Relations between the Chinese nationalists and the Communist party were of capital importance for the future of the revolution. Malraux could not take up this problem in *L'Indochine,* though he later expounded it fully in *Les Conquérants.* Naturally the colonials in Saigon were convinced that the Kuomintang had stirred up the troubles in Canton with the sole aim of promoting the international Communist revolution. Malraux and Monin refuted this idea both in articles and in editorials. They published a long interview with one of the chiefs of the Kuomintang, Sun Fo, son of Sun Yat-sen. Sun Fo declared that the Kuomintang was a republican party and not a Communist organization. Its only program was "Chinese liberty." *L'Indochine* warmly supported the ideals of the Chinese nationalist movement as represented by the Kuomintang, and this attitude was made clear by Monin in an editorial that appeared in one of the paper's earliest issues.

Conservatives in the colony were indignant. Not only did *L'Indochine* heckle the French colonial administration and uncover the corruption prevailing among its top functionaries, while at the same time inciting the Annamites to demand reforms, but it went so far as to espouse the revolutionary cause of the Chinese republicans! This was enough for Cognacq and his clique to consider Malraux and Monin as agents of "the Communist Kuomintang." And at the beginning of July, the governor decided to start a vigorous offensive in the press he controlled.

L'Indochine's ultraconservative rival, *L'Impartial,* accused Monin of being in the pay of the Chinese Bolsheviks and the newspaper of being financed by the Chinese revolution's secret funds. The other publications in the colony of Cochin China quickly followed *L'Impartial*'s lead. Those that, like *Le Courrier,* had welcomed their new fellow journal quickly recanted, probably after being subjected to strong pressures.

Malraux carried on a violent exchange of polemics with Henri Chavigny de Lachevrotière, managing editor of the misnamed *L'Impartial,* which culminated in Malraux's challenging Chavigny to a duel, a challenge that the latter failed to take up, perhaps because of the younger man's reputation as a swordsman.

Then Malraux, in the pages of *L'Indochine,* attacked in a new direction—the *Saïgon Républicain* and its director, Camille Delong. This quarrel was even more virulent. Delong had literary pretensions, which Malraux dismissed with the passing remark that Delong's writings were "like a bouquet of poppies or of onions: they made the readers either weep or go to sleep."

Delong had told some Saigonese friends that he was preparing "something along the line of Nietzsche, Epicurus, and Spinoza, but with, in addition, what they all lacked."

He had warned Malraux that he would no longer tolerate any unpleasant comment.

Malraux retorted, "Let me tell you right away what I think of you: you are not an upgraded version of Nietzsche, Spinoza, and Epicurus. You are a downgraded version of Prudhomme, Homais, and Pécuchet.[3] And if this should strike you as an impoliteness, I should be delighted."

Delong then launched a volley of low insults at Malraux's head: "Having escaped from the lap of André Gide, hesitating between literature, business, thievery, and prostitution . . . a young ninny . . . spreading in his journal the filth that is in his heart . . . a plagiarizer of Anatole France and of Voltaire."

Malraux simply replied, "Monsieur Delong holds my youth against me. Forty years of stupidity have never added up to intelligence."

Hippolyte Ardin, coeditor with Delong of the *Saïgon Républicain,* attacked Malraux in turn and called him Isaac. Malraux retorted, "Everyone can't be called Judas."

But a few days later Malraux reverted to Ardin's anti-Semitic insinuation: "I am not a Jew. If I were, I should not care. But in any case I am not. And as the name 'Isaac' may insultingly be aimed at a woman who is close to me . . . I should be obliged to you if you would explain yourself. Otherwise I should be very sorry to have to repeat to you that in my opinion a man who tries to insult a woman because he is incapable of getting at a man is called a cad; and I mean this, not in the journalistic sense, which is necessarily attenuated, but in the fullest sense of the word."

The polemic finally concluded with a quip of Malraux's: "We repeat that we have not replied, that we do not reply, that we shall not reply to the *Saïgon Républicain* so long as that paper has only thirty-three readers."

Malraux had flung himself into the fray with vigor and passion, writing editorials, composing open letters, replying to attacks, attacking in turn, denouncing the abuses to which the naïve Indochinese peasants were subjected, protesting against the maneuvers that were

---

[3] Joseph Prudhomme is a *petit bourgeois* character created by the caricaturist Henry Monnier in the late nineteenth century. Homais and Pécuchet are characters, one stupid, the other vain, in Gustave Flaubert's *Madame Bovary*. Malraux's satire is evident.

preventing the Annamites, in violation of existing legislation, from traveling to France if they had not proved their unconditional fidelity to the colonial administration.

He had no reason to humor an administration that had no compunction about thwarting him at every turn. It added its formalistic vexations to the calumnies of the Chavigny de Lachevrotières. Indochinese citizens who read *L'Indochine* were summoned to appear before the Labor Administration and threatened. From his editorial office on rue Tabard, Malraux retaliated by threatening to call for an investigation of the facts by the parliament in Paris.

The police, in turn, intervened and found a variety of good and bad reasons for preventing the distribution of the paper. But postal employees sympathetic to the Young Annam movement nevertheless continued to insure its dissemination.

In the midst of the struggles and the annoyances to which the administration was subjecting *L'Indochine* there was one cheering event. Malraux received news that, by a judgment pronounced on June 15, 1925, the *Cour de Cassation* (the Supreme Court of Appeals) in Paris had annulled the judgment of the Saigon court of appeal on the grounds of *vice de forme*.[4]

Finally, on August 14, 1925, the blow fell. The printer told Malraux and Monin that he had been so constantly threatened by the government that he was no longer prepared to print *L'Indochine;* there was no other printer they could turn to. It had been an unequal struggle, for the administration was bound to triumph. The paper ceased publication—it had been in existence for exactly two months.

"The fundamental datum of the relations between Indochina and China," Malraux says, looking back, "was a democratic one and carried with it the recognition of independence. The alliance between Chinese and Indochinese was a substantiation of the reality of the principles of Sun Yat-sen. We were allies, for their struggle was similar to ours.

"When I met Ho Chi Minh for the first time, he did not tell me, 'After Community[5] we shall do something different,' and for good

[4] This French legal term means a flaw in the drafting of a juridical document that renders it null and void. In Malraux's case the flaw was the noncommunication by the defense of an important item of evidence—a telegram that had been delayed in reaching the defense lawyers.

[5] The ironic fact is that the original aims and demands of the Indochinese people were for "community" with France—a kind of loose association similar to that of the British Commonwealth. It was repression that drove Ho Chi Minh and his followers into the Marxist camp, as Malraux makes clear.

reason. The seizure of power by the Indochinese trade unions was ruled out—there weren't any. Ho Chi Minh, initially, was not a Marxist. There was no vehemence in his attitude. We were asking for community in the name of an old romantic kind of liberalism going back to the French Revolution.

"In 1925 there would have been no Indochinese problem if the people had only been given the right to vote. We wanted to create a kind of Senegalese Indochina in which Ho Chi Minh would have had the place occupied by Léopold Senghor. Yes, it would have been enough for France to make shift with an Indochinese nationalism, as de Gaulle worked it out with Senegal. . . . It does no good to *pretend* political liberalism. The right policy would have been to accept community twenty years earlier. That was already the last chance.

"When Ho Chi Minh returned from Europe, he had become a Communist and he tried to create a Marxist party. But the slogans remained the same: community—becoming a dominion. For a long time there was no real communism in Indochina. It grew out of a certain romanticism, which was enhanced by the reputation of the convict prison of Poulo Condore to which Ho Chi Minh had been committed.[6] But there was neither a trade union base for communism, nor an ideological base, to begin with."

What became of Malraux after the disappearance of his newspaper? The facts are not absolutely certain, and Malraux makes a habit of never refuting books written about him. Still better, he says he doesn't read them. He has allowed it to be believed that he journeyed to Canton in 1925 or 1926, without confirming or denying it. Malraux is an exceptionally polite man, who never utters a vulgar word. One might almost call him too refined.

According to Clara Malraux, what happened was as follows:

In order to bring out *L'Indochine* once more, new type was needed. Malraux and Monin had a printing press set up with the aid of old pieces of type, but this was not enough. They tried to buy type in Saigon, but in vain. No one would have anything to do with them. When they realized it would be impossible to get anywhere in Saigon, Malraux resolved to seek aid in Hong Kong. As a leader of the Young Annam movement and friend of the Chinese nationalists in Cochin

---

[6] Poulo Condore, today known as Con Dao, is an island in South Vietnam where there was an Alcatraz-like penitentiary noted for its rough treatment of prisoners. It received chiefly common criminals, but some important political prisoners were sent there also, which gave them a kind of inverse prestige.

China, he was welcomed and aided by the agents of the Kuomintang in Hong Kong, and found the typefaces he needed. They were English, and lacked French accent marks, but he hoped to remedy that without too much trouble.

Did he at this time briefly visit Canton? If so, did he meet Borodin, the Russian agent of the Comintern, who had acted as Sun Yat-sen's right hand and whom he describes so vividly in *Les Conquérants?* Clara categorically says no. Monin knew Borodin and could have described him to Malraux, in sufficient detail for him to assemble the rich portrait in the novel. It is possible . . .

At any rate, Malraux will settle this question once for all in the second volume of his *Antimémoires,* on which he is now working and which he promises will deal with his China experiences.

By the time Malraux returned to Saigon, he was tired, ill, and disappointed, too. "I saw him enter the hospital where I myself was under treatment," says Paul Morand, the writer-diplomat, who was on his way to take up a diplomatic post in Bangkok and had had to visit Saigon en route to be treated for fever. "He was pale, emaciated, looking much more ill than the patients."

His state of health did not prevent Malraux from resuming the struggle, however. The type was scheduled to arrive in Saigon in two installments. The first shipment was instantly confiscated, on the express orders of Governor Cognacq, but the customs officers refused to obey the governor's orders the second time around, and Malraux and Monin were able to take possession of their precious packing cases.

L'Indochine, rebaptized *L'Indochine Enchaînée,* could thus reappear in November, 1925, about two and a half months after Cognacq had obliged the office to close. Most of the issues of this new series bear no dates, for the editors were never sure of being able to bring out their paper regularly; there is also a scarcity of accent marks, for Malraux could not buy any and had to rely on the kindness of his printers, who used to "abstract" some from the type trays in other printing houses where they worked.

The paper appeared until the beginning of 1926, at which time Malraux, completely exhausted, decided to return to France. For a year he had had to fight a venomous press, to appear twice in court. His experience had been in many ways a disappointment. To fight for man is also to meet other men on one's way, usually mediocre ones. It means coming up against sordid interests. But unquestionably he now bore within him the experience and the material that were going to bear fruit and find expression in *La Voie royale* and *Les Conquérants*.

Toward the end of December, 1925, André Malraux wrote in *L'Indochine Enchaînée*: "We must appeal to the workers by every means: speeches, meetings, periodicals, tracts. We must persuade the workers to sign petitions in favor of the Annamites. It is necessary that our writers—and they are numerous—who still have some generosity, address themselves to those who love them. The loud voice of the people must be raised to demand of their masters an account of all this heavy burden, this anguish which weighs on the plains of Indochina. It is to this end that I am undertaking a journey to France. . . ."

The Chinese of Cholon gave Malraux the money that permitted his return to France with Clara.

"We voyaged second class," wrote Clara Malraux. "It comprised a mediocrity worse than poverty. The curtain fell . . . hiding the scene where the Asiatic drama was taking place, a drama that daily became less our own. Their hopes deceived, the wrath of the Annamites became rebellion, alienating all idea of collaboration with France. . . . In China, the Asians were discovering simultaneously nationalism and social revolution. . . . The man to whom I had given myself at last tried, with his own weapons, to dominate the world which until then had resisted and on which, by his writings, he was to impose his vision. Our Indochinese adventures were to culminate in some big books. . . . The literary talent of André was to reach an ever greater maturity: it was ripe for the novel. Later on he told me that his journalistic experience had greatly helped him in his literary writings."[7]

In March, 1926, *L'Echo Annamite* announced the departure of Monin for Canton. He returned two years later to Saigon, where he died. The Annamites asked his widow for the right—which was granted—to inter his body in the soil of Annam.

In 1942, Nguyen Ai Quac—whose patronym was Nguyen Van Coong—became known as Ho Chi Minh ("he who enlightens"). In September, 1945, he proclaimed the independent Republic of Vietnam.

Henri Chavigny de Lachevrotière, the editor of *L'Impartial*, was killed early in 1950 by a hand grenade that some Vietcong tossed into his car. He was on his way to the tennis courts, where he went every afternoon.

---

[7] Like the rest of the quotations from Clara Malraux in this chapter, this extract is taken from Vol. III of *Le Bruit de nos pas*, her memoirs, which were published by Grasset in 1969.

4.

The Road to the Prix Goncourt

André Malraux returned home in the spring of 1926 to find France greatly changed. The country was coming out of an economic crisis and recovery had become the order of the day. Ended were the postwar period and its extravagances. "Seriousness" had become fashionable. In this atmosphere Malraux could feel more at home, and his two great dimensions, art and adventure, could express themselves majestically. The activity of the *Nouvelle Revue Française*,[1] to which he was an important contributor, and of *Action Française,* mouthpiece of the Catholic revival, were manifestations of the same longing for order. The yearning for escape, to be sure, had never been so strong, and escape that found expression in dreams and in the magic realms of the imagination had kept its fascination. But the landscape of reality, preferably exotic, was even more appealing. Malraux, ripened by his Oriental experiences, found himself in harmony with the new French mood.

He was, however, without illusions about finding any speedy solution to the problems that he had encountered. His recent adventures had brought no triumphs and left him seared and nervous. The writer and critic Jean Prévost observed him in those early months of 1926:

> He could not look you in the eye, as if he were following the circling flight of an invisible bee. His shoulders contracted as though someone had stuck a dagger in his back. His fingers

---

[1] The monthly *Nouvelle Revue Française* has always been published by Gallimard, which was originally founded in 1911 as Editions de la Nouvelle Revue Française. In 1919 the firm became the Librairie Gallimard, and under the direction of Gaston Gallimard has published many great names in literature. Frequently a work would first be serialized in the *NRF*, then published as an *NRF* special edition by Gallimard. This gave a book added prestige.

burned, trembled, tried to free themselves. The moment a man approached, the haggard face seemed to grow more anxious. A punished child, a youthful rebel, who as yet has embraced only death: such was Malraux on his return from Asia. He tried to take refuge from others and from things with politenesses, doctrines, farfetched reveries. Pen in hand, he stripped life bare. His work took on the character of a revenge, marked by sadism and an elaborate, unshakable obsession with death. He was able to find solace in his genius. Action, rather than age, had matured him. Danger had muscled his heart. He even seemed capable of repose.

The Indochina experience had caused a break with certain friends, but it also brought about the tightening of a few bonds. Malraux continued to have a good relationship with his father, whom he went to see at his country home or his Paris apartment on the rue de Lübeck at least once a week. Fernand Malraux had stood by him at the time of his Cambodian expedition, and André was grateful to him for his support.

Malraux struck up a friendship with the writer Edgar Du Perron, just a little older than himself, who was from Java in the Dutch East Indies. Du Perron had broken not only with the bourgeoisie, but with idealism, even with the modern world. Obsessed by boredom and images of eroticism and death, he sought escape from these phantoms by recourse to a breezy irony borrowed from Voltaire, Stendhal, Gide, and Paul Morand.

Malraux too had brought back phantoms from the Orient, and his way of exorcising them was to write his experiences into his books. It is interesting to note that he did not directly plead the Indochinese cause as he had promised his Young Annam associates he would do. Maybe he assumed that the cause to which he had given so much energy and enthusiasm was a hopeless one. Maybe he was, quite simply, drained by the ordeal he had been through.

He was feverishly busy; he owed Grasset three books, under the terms of the contract signed before he left for Indochina, but he also wrote articles and reviews to help pay the rent. He and Clara had taken an apartment at 122, boulevard Murat, near the Porte d'Auteuil, where they lived in dire poverty. Clara too was hard at work, translating an Austrian book by an anonymous author, *The Diary of a Young Girl*. It was published by Grasset in 1926, but made no particular stir. Nor did it bring the impoverished pair any money to speak of. Almost as soon as he returned from Saigon, Malraux had delivered the first of his books for Bernard Grasset, *La Tentation de l'Occident,* which he had dedicated to his wife. It was published in July, 1926. Throughout 1927 he labored on the second, *Les Conquérants,* his first full-length novel, which would be published the following year.

But the *NRF* was to be the crucible in which, over the months, the slow fusion of the art enthusiast and the committed writer would manifest itself. A few months before his *Tentation de l'Occident* appeared, Malraux published in the *NRF "Les Lettres d'un Chinois,"* a short article embodying many of the ideas in the book. It was extraordinarily densely written, and revealed a synthesis of the Chinese mind when confronted with Western reality. This Chinese, who in a sense represents Malraux, manages in a few lines to speak of everything that matters in our consciousness—time, life, death. "Each one of us," he writes, "venerates his dead, as being the symbols of a force which envelops us and which is one of the modes of life, although all he knows of it is its existence. But this existence is something that we *experience;* it dominates us and shapes us and we cannot grasp it. Rather, we are penetrated by it. . . ."

The Chinese visits Greece in order to try to discover in its ruins the sources of our disconcerting civilization: "The West has its birth there, with the hard face of Pallas Athena, with its weapons and also the stigmata of its future dementia. The ardor that wells up in us is about to be lost and, you may be sure, to bring about our own loss. The ardor that burns you creates. But it is wise to let the dragons that sleep in the earth rest in peace."

The line of Malraux's work, the ideas that are embodied in action in *Les Conquérants, La Condition humaine,* and later *L'Espoir,* is sketched in the scattered writings that he published in these years in the form of letters, reviews, and critical articles. His journey to the Orient, the experience that he gained from it, put him in a special category. Others before him had traveled, and had seen different worlds. But Malraux found man, everywhere, at a moment in the evolution of humanity in which he was the sole parameter. The struggles that he undertook were no longer a sport, or a clash of interests. They were struggles for the right of every individual to freedom and to dignity. Though in varied aspects, the entire species seemed to be animated by one impulse. Malraux, with his intelligence, his cosmic vision of life, seemed to have been chosen to make this synthesis, to explain this *élan*. His reasoned exaltation made him the ideal instrument and interpreter of mankind to man.

In the *Nouvelles Littéraires* of July 31, 1926, he wrote: "The essential character of our civilization is the fact that it is a closed civilization. It is devoid of spiritual aim; it constrains us to action. Its values are founded on the world that depends on facts—the world of gestures, analogy, control. . . . The concept of man that we have inherited from Christianity was built upon the exalted consciousness of our fundamental disorder; such a disorder does not exist for the Oriental, for whom man is a place rather than a means of action."

In this same article we find hints of an essay that he was to publish the following year on the qualities of European youth. The arguments that he makes for this youth make it clear why today, despite all the upheavals we have witnessed, Malraux's ideas still exert a strange fascination on students:

The outstanding fact in the West is in my opinion the need that nearly all European youth feel to break with the past effort of a whole century, even though their sensibility has not ceased to respond to it. The whole passion of the nineteenth century for man asserts itself in the vehement affirmation of the eminence of the ego. Well! this man and this ego, who are built on so many ruins and still dominate us whether we wish it or not, no longer interest us. Moreover, we are determined not to listen to the appeal of our weakness, whether it offers us a doctrine or a faith. It is said that no one can act without faith. I believe the absence of all conviction, like conviction itself, incites certain men to passivity, and others to extreme action. . . .

What Western youth is looking for is a new concept of man. Can Asia bring us any enlightenment? I do not believe so. Rather, a special discovery of what we are. One of the most compelling laws of our spirit is that temptations overcome are transformed into consciousness.

Despite his disappointments in Asia, Malraux remained mentally in contact with the Chinese adventure, but he would no longer attempt to be a participant in it. "The events in Shanghai in 1927 were for me nothing more than an *imagerie d'Epinal*,"[2] Malraux has told me. "I was not present. When I went to Shanghai [in 1929] it was to be not as a warrior but as a 'stroller.' "

Nevertheless, this picture show in Malraux's visually active mind was to produce, a few years later, what is probably his most stirring and most powerful novel, *La Condition humaine*. It was dedicated to his friend Eddy Du Perron, and its principal character, Kyo Gisors, was partly modeled upon another friend, the Japanese Komatsu—who later translated the novel into Japanese.

Shanghai in 1927 was a great industrial metropolis with a large working population. As one of the few heavily industrial areas of China, it was natural that it should be the center for modern Chinese capitalism and that its powerful labor unions should be controlled by Communists. But as well as being the commercial hub of the Yangtse Valley and the heart of the wealth of China, Shanghai was also a center of intrigue—for bankers and merchants, for politicians of the right wing of the Kuomintang, led by Chiang Kai-shek, for professional plotters, and for the underworld of the Green Gang.

The Green Gang was a secret society that had come into being along the banks of the Grand Canal at the time when this important artery handled the flow of China's inland traffic from Peking to Canton. The canal boatmen, who were mostly from the north, had felt the need to meet when they were in the southern provinces, and a kind of guild had developed. Over the years, it had turned into a kind of Mafia.

The Kuomintang had grafted itself onto the Green Gang, and, while still a young officer in the Shanghai garrison, Chiang Kai-shek had met the gang's leaders. The opium traffickers, too, were under the gang's protection. In Shanghai, in fact, the Green Gang was all-powerful. It had numerous cells, ranging from ricksha coolies and police officers to peddlers and gangsters. Some of these cells had hierarchies composed of people of a far higher social standing than the ricksha coolies and the water carriers. The cells also admitted Europeans, who thus became the "pupils" of a given "master" of the Green Gang and who took their share of the advantages that went with such affiliation.

The chief of the gang in 1927 was Du Yueh-sheng. His influence was enormous. He could initiate a strike or bring it to an end. At his

[2] Crude colored pictures that were printed at Epinal in the Vosges and chiefly sold to schoolchildren.

order, the members of the merchant sailors' association would have brought their bags ashore, streetcar service would have been paralyzed, there would have been no more water in the city. In Yunnan Province, the market price of opium would have dropped, had he so wished, and the provincial government would have been on the brink of ruin. In Shanghai itself, it was he who controlled the price of cotton and of gold, the stocks of rice, the distribution of newspapers, and the "orchestration" of press campaigns.

Du Yueh-sheng was a frail man, with a shaved head, an intermittent cough, apparently ageless. Was he forty, fifty, or even older, in 1927? It was impossible to tell. He dragged his feet as he walked; his hands, already shriveled, were nervous. He did not impress one at first, but in his eyes and in his expression there were signs that betrayed energy, cunning, and also great cruelty. He was a native of Ningpo, like a great majority of Shanghai's underworld. In his youth, having quarreled with one of his compatriots from Ningpo who had made off with one of his concubines, he had one of the offender's feet amputated. Just by way of warning.

Du had some ten thousand men under his orders, all members of the Green Gang, utterly devoted to him. Reactionary unions of pseudo workers, supported financially by the major banks and the Chamber of Commerce, were organized to act against the authentic trade unions, nearly all of which were controlled by Communists. Chinese capitalism —which had been built up with the aid of the foreigners in the Shanghai concessions—had once been all-powerful. But the power of the Communists was increasing; not only were many of their workers armed, and organized into military cadres, but their agitators were arousing a large part of the population. Force, armed force, was necessary.

It was at this point that Du played his part. He "discovered" in the French concession huge stores of weapons, which had been taken by the French from the troops of two Chinese warlords who had been fighting each other. When the Chinese government now demanded that these weapons—five to six thousand guns—be handed over, the French representatives could not refuse to surrender them. To whom? To the master of Shanghai, General Chiang Kai-shek, who promptly turned them over to the Green Gang. Du was now able to arm his men and undertake the "cleanup" of Shanghai.

For several months there had been numerous, serious incidents of schism between Chiang Kai-shek and the Communists. Chiang was gradually losing almost all his special powers as generalissimo and saw his personal position within the Kuomintang seriously threatened. He was not going to consent to having his powers whittled away without a struggle. He saw all too clearly the disastrous consequences this could have for his personal future. He determined to act.

At dawn on April 12, 1927, General Chiang Kai-shek disarmed the pro-Communist trade unions of Shanghai by force, thus finally breaking both with the Communist party and with the government in Wuhan (the left wing of the Kuomintang, which was still cooperating with the Communists). Neither the Russian Comintern advisers nor the Chinese Communist leaders dared to take action, to throw Chiang in prison and indict him for counterrevolutionary plotting. So the workers were once again told that everything was being done in their best interests....

That dawn those workers got up to discover that the unthinkable, the impossible, was happening. Machine guns were crackling all over the city.

"There were some Communists," Malraux says, "who wanted to organize resistance." Kyo, his leading character in *La Condition humaine,* wanted to fight. "But the official speeches of the Chinese Communist party, the entire propaganda of union with the Kuomintang, paralyzed him." "How are we to fight," Kyo asks in the book, "being one against ten, nearly unarmed, in violation of the instructions of the Chinese Communist party, against an army which would bring up its corps of bourgeois volunteers armed to the teeth and having the advantage of the attack?"

The Green Gang had worked feverishly organizing its forces to have that advantage in the dawn attack. The men had been supplied with white armbands bearing the character *gong* ("work"). At the given signal they attacked the workers' positions, which were scattered throughout the city. All those who resisted were shot down on the spot. It was a massacre. By four o'clock in the afternoon the Green Gang and Chiang Kai-shek's soldiers announced that they had the situation "well in hand."

The following July, the left-wing faction of the Kuomintang, led by Wang Ching-wei, the head of the Wuhan government, in its turn separated itself from the Communists, and the Soviet political and military advisers were given orders by the Comintern to return to the USSR.

The Communist party was now forced underground and henceforth had to conduct its struggle against Chiang and the Nationalist government as an illegal party. It was this "People's Army of Liberation"—which came into being as a result of the violence in 1927 —that would triumph in the end, bearing out the words of Mao Tsetung: "War is the highest form of the class struggle."

In December, 1927, Chiang Kai-shek and the American-educated sister of the financier T. V. Soong were married in Shanghai by a representative of the YMCA. The couple thereby paid a debt of gratitude to the American Methodists who had hurriedly baptized the future husband so as to give this marriage a religious consecration. Chiang now definitely entered the political alliance of the Cantonese and international financiers. His involvement with liberal causes was over.

"In 1927," André Malraux told me, "all China still believed in Hankow, the political capital of the rebellion, controlled by the Russians. But in Hankow there was no Red Army. The Japanese and the American secret services knew this, and they immediately put their resources at Chiang Kai-shek's disposal. The latter, deciding to steal a march on the Communists, applied the principle of Asiatic heads of state: 'You want to kill me, so I murder you.' This is the Chinese way of retaliation, the Ping-Pong technique. Hence the Shanghai massacres. The key to these massacres was the opposition between the non-Marxist revolutionary urge and Marxism. It was like the events of May, 1968, here in Paris, but in Shanghai it was serious. If there had been tanks firing on the Sorbonne, here in France, there would have been thousands killed. De Gaulle said to himself, 'Those Sorbonne kids are a pain in the neck, but they don't want to kill me.' And besides—he was de Gaulle!"

After this parenthesis Malraux came back to the Chinese question.

"Chiang became nothing when he allied himself with the Right. His army deteriorated. The volunteers left him. All he had left was mercenaries, paid with American money. After having been the master of five hundred and sixty million Chinese,[3] Chiang Kai-shek ended up in Formosa, not very proud, with fifteen million inhabitants. So be it. But it's not too bad for a colonel. . . ."

Malraux turned to his hero in *Les Conquérants,* the Jewish Comintern leader, Borodin, who had organized the 1925 riots in Canton.

"As for Borodin, Stalin had it in for him. He wanted his hide. Stalin's anti-Semitism became even more a factor in turning him

[3] By 1970 the count was 800 million.

against Borodin when the latter, in 1927, seemed to him to be following a Trotskyist line. Then Stalin put the blame for the Shanghai disaster on poor Borodin's shoulders and used him to wash his hands of the Russian defeat there.

"Trotsky, on the other hand, never had a bad word to say about Borodin, nor did he speak of him as a renegade. And yet God knows he had a way of tossing people into the wastebasket!"

Malraux had met the exiled Trotsky in 1933 when he was living at Royan, not far from Bordeaux, and had some interesting conversations with him. Asked why he had failed in his bid for power in Russia, Trotsky told Malraux, "Because I was expecting too much." When he spoke of Stalin, who had exiled him in 1929, Trotsky always referred to him as "the other one." But whenever he spoke of Russia, Malraux noticed, his national loyalty came to the fore.

"When I asked him how the Russians would manage, with their single-track railroads, should the capitalist states, led by America or Germany, attack the Soviet Union, Trotsky replied, 'We would fight on Lake Baikal.'"

Malraux told me one other story about Trotsky. They were speaking of Chiang Kai-shek's oldest son who, as a student at Moscow University in 1927, had publicly repudiated his father, accusing him of going back on all of Sun Yat-sen's principles and saying he was ashamed to be his son and to bear his name. Trotsky's comment was brief and to the point. "People," he said, "have the children they deserve."

Although the events that took place in Shanghai in 1927 and that marked—provisionally, as Malraux himself says—the end of the Soviet experiment masterminded by Borodin in China were not "physically" witnessed by the author of *La Condition humaine,* his feeling and understanding of them were surely more intense than the reactions of many others who both participated in and described them.

A six-year gestation period would be needed for that book to be written. But while the combats continued in the streets of Shanghai, their logic and the motivations of the protagonists were sensed and understood by Malraux. In 1927 he was at work on *Les Conquérants,* but he was also writing articles, and it is fascinating to see how they reflect his essential ideas.

At the time of Chiang's triumph, Malraux wrote for the *Nouvelle Revue Française* an important review of *Défense de l'Occident* by

Henri Massis. According to Massis, it was necessary to fight those who were working to organize against the West that great amorphous Asia constituted by the Soviets. "In reality," wrote Malraux, "this is aimed at the Third International. The danger does not seem very pressing. That the Third International is anxious to unite Asiatics against the capitalist governments of Europe and of America there can be no doubt; but we see it everywhere in retreat. . . . Chiang Kai-shek's opposition to the Communists is certainly the most serious defeat the movement has suffered. For along with force our civilization brings its individualism; it organizes Asia, yes, but into factions opposed to one another, which is very evident in Far Eastern revolutionary circles."

It is through these scattered texts that we can really measure the impact of his Indochinese experience and the opportunity it had offered to observe the Chinese conflict with an insider's understanding. Malraux could have come back from his great adventure with travel accounts and news reports, and surrounded himself with a comfortable notoriety. His experience, on the contrary, provided him with substance for profound thought, and through discreet and prophetic phrases culled here and there we can trace the evolution of a work in embryo.

"Before its dead gods the entire West, having exhausted the joy of its triumph, is preparing to vanquish its own enigmas. One is reminded of those ancient tragedies, inhuman and at the same time poignant, in which the night resounds with the lamentations of the earth. What notion of man will the civilization of solitude—the civilization that the possession of human gestures has separated from all others—be able to derive from its anguish?"

These lines appeared in the 1927 article *"D'une jeunesse européenne,"* published in *Les Cahiers Verts.* In the *NRF* we can read: "The fact that certain peoples of Asia have inherited nationalism from Europe at the same time as the means of using it is not surprising, but the consequences of such a heritage are unavoidable and it is we who have determined them." Or, "The substitution of the values of persevering energy for those of the spirit is the very mark of modern times. By destroying those spiritual values we have prepared the way, both at home and abroad, for the reign of force, and especially of the greatest force, that which endures."

Despite these signs, which are obvious in retrospect, those who realized at the time that they were the testing ground for a writer whose works would mark his period were not numerous: the *NRF* authors, a few friends, such as Maurice Sachs, who seems to have been one of the first to have a premonition of what Malraux might become. As early as 1926 he had written:

"There are writers about whom knowledgeable people are beginning to talk: Julien Green, Georges Bernanos, André Malraux. I have met Malraux. He makes the most vivid impression. There is something about his eyes that irresistibly evokes adventure, melancholy, and decision; a fine Italian Renaissance profile, yet at the same time his looks are very French. He has about him something of the young officer, of the *dilettante,* of the romantic poet, he speaks very fast, and well, seems to know everything, never fails to dazzle, and leaves you with the impression that you have met the century's most intelligent man."

Les Conquérants, Malraux's novel about the Canton uprisings of 1925, appeared in five consecutive issues of the *NRF* from March to July, 1928. Interest was aroused, and the work's publication by Grasset that September confirmed its success.[4] "It is the book of the year and the success of the season," Du Perron noted. It was mentioned for the Prix Femina,[5] but failed to win, perhaps because its brilliantly drawn scenes of horror and murder somewhat frightened the jury.

Almost simultaneously, as if to disconcert the critics who were busy analyzing his *oeuvre* and pronouncing final judgments upon it, Malraux published *Royaume farfelu,* a short poetic meditation that could not have been further removed from a novel of action. It was a limited edition, brought out by Gallimard, whose staff Malraux had joined, and the author-editor acted as his own layout man, designing a handsome format that did justice to the fantastic and haunting tale. It was dedicated to his old friend Louis Chevasson. The whole thing recalled Malraux the aesthete of the "mad years" when Jean Cocteau's Boeuf sur le Toit was all the rage.[6]

After *Les Conquérants* appeared, Du Perron recalls that Malraux dreamed successively of Dahomey, of Persia, and of Afghanistan—a further proof that such a man could hardly feel satisfied with only

[4] Malraux has always said that in literature he owes everything to two men, Jean Paulhan and Daniel Halévy. It was Paulhan, editor of the *NRF,* who first liked *Les Conquérants* and arranged to publish it; Halévy, Grasset's literary director, brought the work out in book form in the *Cahiers Verts* collection, Grasset's series of deluxe editions.
[5] The second most prestigious literary prize in France, ranking after the Prix Goncourt. It is called the Prix Femina because the literary selection board is entirely composed of women.
[6] Le Boeuf sur le Toit ("the ox on the roof") was a cabaret named by Darius Milhaud and launched by Jean Cocteau, who was the leading promoter of jazz in France in the early 1920s. The Boeuf owed its success chiefly to two pianists, Wiener and Doucet (their first names were never used), and smart young Parisians went to the Boeuf to listen to them, drink cocktails, meet friends—and even, sometimes, pick up drugs.

one mode of activity. Some of the dreams, at least, were shortly to come true.

That summer Clara and André made a visit to Persia, a land that so enchanted them that they returned annually for the following four years. In the course of these lengthy visits, they also managed to include side trips to Afghanistan, the Soviet Union, India, China, and the United States, which Malraux saw for the first time in 1929. Fortunately, Gaston Gallimard was generous with vacation time, and it paid off—because after Malraux published *La Voie royale* in 1930, his contract with Grasset was fulfilled and he transferred to Gallimard, who would publish all his subsequent books.

Malraux now found himself recognized as an important writer, and as one difficult to define or to catalog—a fact that he could hardly take exception to. All those who then counted in the world of letters showered praise on him. The royalist writer Léon Daudet was one of the first to recognize his "daring and dangerous talent," and compared his writing to the somber and luminous chiaroscuro of Rembrandt. "In these dishonoring times of spiritual do-nothingness," Daudet went on, "in which hundreds of idlers amuse themselves by blackening paper, Malraux paints with his pen. . . . Yes, this young man who is said to come from a ruined middle-class family[7] is a painter who writes fast and who thinks hard. He thinks with a knife; this accounts for those teeming colors which, as the chapters run on, make a noise as of gunfire or like a regiment of insurgents assaulting a fort."

The literary bourgeoisie, infatuated with the psychological novels of Jacques de Lacretelle, was furious. Malraux horrified them, yet there was no keeping him out.

Drieu La Rochelle, Malraux's friend, wrote perceptively in the *NRF* summing up the three works that stemmed from his Indochinese experiences:

> I don't know what Malraux did in Asia. I don't know what his role there was, but I do know that he sampled a variety of things. Whatever it was, he derived from it a palpitating kind of meditation—these three books in which, from one to the next, the intellectual divests himself, strips himself, and becomes, little by little, a naked man, a flesh-and-blood man.

[7] Daudet refers to the fact that Fernand Malraux had had heavy financial losses, which would eventually bring him to the verge of bankruptcy.

The first, *Tentation de l'Occident,* was an essay, a youthful essay, revealing a brilliant and highly endowed young man. But an excess of complacency deprived it of decisiveness. One sensed influences wrapped in a labored style, which was too cautious to be effective. (There is in Malraux a twenty-year-old aesthete who has not yet wholly died; witness *Royaume farfelu,* a collection of prose poems that reek of literary opium.)

Next came *Les Conquérants,* the first product of the union of thought and action. *Les Conquérants* revealed Malraux overnight as a writer of stature.

La Voie royale has a theme and a manner no different from those of *Les Conquérants.* But a hand that had shown itself to be firm at the outset shows itself to be even firmer.... The specific nature of his genius is to make felt first of all the power of absorption of a solitary ego—he always has an overwhelming protagonist—and afterward the duration, the lasting quality, of this ego in action....

Malraux appeared two years ago on the European horizon. The fact that he was known or esteemed, from the first, in Germany and in Russia as well as in France is an additional example of the broadening of all audiences. It is especially evidence of the fact that what is human reaches beyond national borders....

In December, 1930, Malraux's father committed suicide. He had had a severe stroke, and, fearing that he might be permanently paralyzed, preferred to take his own way out. Two years later, his first wife, André's mother, was to die of an embolism, which would leave Malraux without any immediate family, his grandmother—the old lady whom Clara had admired for her character—having died before her daughter. He remained in quite close touch, however, with his father's second wife and his two much younger half brothers, Roland and Claude, whom he saw fairly often and who idolized their famous older sibling.

Fernand Malraux's death hit hard, and not only because, as a result of his depression losses, he could leave no money to his sons. Malraux was deeply, permanently shocked by the suddenness and the manner of his father's passing, although he has always admired those who commit suicide purposefully. It would be a theme he would use much

later, in *Les Noyers d'Altenburg,* in which the death of the grandfather is patterned on that of Fernand Malraux.

While Malraux, in order to fulfill himself, needed to live dangerously, he also needed to create.

As we know, he had a thorough knowledge of publishing techniques. He also had many friends who were writers, painters, and
engravers. Soon after his return from the Orient, at a time when he
had absolutely no money—"unlike Claudel," he says, "I have never
been interested in money, either for or against"—he had begun publishing deluxe editions, under the imprint of Les Aldes.[8]

Clara remembers what it was like:

"We sold our books at a high price, when we sold them! And we
had a simple system. We made a hole in our budget that we plugged
with the sale of a book. Then we made another, and so on. This game
could have lasted indefinitely. It was a little tiring and did not earn us
a living, but then *Les Conquérants* became a success. And Gaston Gallimard took André on as editor of the *NRF*'s deluxe books. . . .

"Then we began to travel for our pleasure and we went to Persia.
Persia was more wonderful than we had dreamed; it was extraordinary.
I believe, as a matter of fact, that André had dreamed about Persia
since he was an adolescent.

"We left with the two volumes of the *Thousand and One Nights*
in the Mardrus translation as our most precious baggage. I can still
see us reading it!"

A dreamy look came over Clara's face, as she went on, "We left on
a cargo boat, via the south of Russia, crossed the Black Sea to Batum,
in Georgia, took the train to Baku, and from there a boat again to cross
the Caspian Sea to Persia. It was even more enchanting than everything we had imagined.

"The following year we returned to Persia, and then the year after
that. . . . We stayed for several months each time, and we made friends,
who got into the habit of saying, 'Look, the swallows have come back.
The Malrauxes can't be far away.' For we always went there in the
spring. . . .

"I loved Persia passionately. André had already written things on
Persia, the Persia he dreamed about, in *Royaume farfelu*. He never
wrote the novel on Persia that I thought he might write—I have often

[8] After Teobaldo Manuzio, known as Aldo, the sixteenth-century Venetian master
printer who designed the classic italic type font that still bears his name—Aldine.

wondered whether reality, repeated several times, did not disturb him."

The "two swallows" were soon to separate.

In his passions Malraux has always committed himself wholly, as in a war, wanting children every time even if he did not always get them. "Maternity is women's war," he writes. By the early thirties he no longer felt for Clara more than affection and tenderness. They had one daughter, named Florence, who was born in March of 1933. (An elder child, a boy, had died as an infant.) They had waited a long time to have a child—perhaps too long.

"When one has loved a woman passionately," says Malraux, "and then one comes to love her in a different way, there is no longer any point in living together. The appeal of another woman is often irresistible. Love is too important a thing. Man has no right to deny himself love, to refuse passion."

Today Clara lives with her memories and perhaps her bitterness, though this was not obvious when I went to see her, in October, 1970, at her modest two-room apartment not far from the famous La Santé prison. She lives simply, writes quite a lot, and has become intensely involved with Israeli affairs. Her short hair is gray these days, but she is still a vivid, attractive woman, especially when a subject really excites her. Her manner is authoritative, expressive of a lively intelligence, though her voice is soft and gentle.

I asked her about her feelings for André.

"Admiration and disappointment," she replied. "It's always been one way with him, his way—never mine, and that was impossible. He used to ask me to be a clever woman in public and a completely effaced one in private. But he was twenty then, and one is awkward at that age. I take pleasure in the fact that he did dedicate his first real literary work to me—*La Tentation de l'Occident*, you know."

She went on to tell me that her daughter, Florence, who is close to her father and sees him quite often,[9] had told her that Malraux had changed for the better, was no longer so intransigent. But I had the feeling that Clara Malraux was just as stubborn in her view of him as he had ever been about her. She is currently at work on the fourth volume of her memoirs, which will cover the years from 1926 to 1934,

---

[9] Florence is a screenwriter who has lived for long periods in the United States; in June, 1970, she married the film director Alain Resnais, in San Francisco. They now live in Paris.

when they became estranged. It was the hardest of all her books to write, she told me—"those were the gray, gray years!"

It was in 1933 that Malraux met one of the most charming women in Paris, Louise de Vilmorin.

She bore a name that sounded like a pseudonym, like the name of a character in a play, "a name to go streetwalking with to capture hearts," Malraux once told her. Yet this romantic-sounding name is an authentic one. It belongs to the Vilmorin-Andrieux family, seedsmen and landscape gardeners to the kings of France, who, in the gardens of the Tuileries and Versailles, grew the "dear roses" Marie Antoinette loved so well. "I was born among baccarat roses, next to an enormous poppy flower that frightened me," Louise used to say.

On June 24, 1933, at the annual end-of-the-season reception given by the *Nouvelle Revue Française* in the garden of the town house on the rue Sebastien Bottin that houses the Gallimard offices, Gaston Gallimard, the head of the firm, took two hands in the crowd that surrounded him and united them. This was the first contact between André Malraux and Louise de Vilmorin.

"You are made not only to understand each other, but to like each other," said Gallimard.

Only a few days before, Malraux had delivered to Gaston Gallimard the manuscript of *La Condition humaine*. The publisher found the title very striking[10]—believing, as he did, in titles—and he was deeply impressed by his reading of the novel. The book, he felt, had a very good chance of winning the Prix Goncourt. His only fear was that the powerful action, the exotic psychology of the locale, and the sometimes disconcerting lyricism of the style might go over the heads and try the patience of certain members of the jury.

In Gallimard's judgment, which was uncannily accurate, *La Condition humaine* would not be an essentially popular Prix Goncourt, but it would have a strange and savage impact upon the literature of its century. Long after the award it would continue to sell, regularly and progressively. Gallimard felt that the book had already taken its place as a classic of its time, even before it was displayed for sale in the bookstores.

But on that June day in the Gallimard garden Malraux was not thinking of sales of hundreds of thousands of copies, nor of the numer-

[10] It was inspired by a phrase of the philosopher Montaigne.

ous translations that his book would go through, a bare five months later.

He had before him a dream creature. Louise de Vilmorin, two years younger than he (he was thirty-two), seemed a *jeune fille en fleur,* straight out of a chapter of Proust's *A la recherche du temps perdu.* She exhibited a *snobisme* that was utterly genuine, without a false note, and expressed herself—this was what struck Malraux most—with an innate sense of the French language.

"She speaks with perfect naturalness, without preparation or precaution, with a kind of chastened delirium, radiant and colorful, which makes one think of the great lady companions of queens. One does not weary of listening to her, one's ear remains glued to her voice. This young society woman was unquestionably born to tell love stories, adventures of stolen jewels, treasures rifled from stagecoaches. . . . And here you have an example of the incoherence that Chamfort[11] had noted in women: this she-devil, who has the subtlety and wit of Madame de La Fayette, toys with painting and daubs no matter what. . . . In a sidewalk exhibit I should be ashamed for her, but she won't commit the madness of exhibiting."

This was the first "intellectual" portrait of Louise de Vilmorin by Malraux.

As for the physical portrait—Louise was already the figure she would continue to be through the years, as though age had no hold on her: an eternal fiancée on the eve of her marriage. A slight, almost invisible limp, which vanished before the grace of her speech and the beauty of her face, affected her walk. With her fair skin, prominent cheekbones, regular features, and pale, gray-tinted blue eyes, Louise really made one think of no one—save of Louise de Vilmorin.

"If I had had a previous existence, I should have liked to be Mary Magdalene! She is my Bible heroine. Or Mary Stuart, Queen of Scots! What a well-filled destiny! I have a horror of courtesans. . . ."

In 1933 Malraux nicknamed her "the intimidating lady." This was just a quip, but Louise, slim and willowy, was five feet, eight inches tall, and he only an inch or so taller. "Chanel, for one of her great prewar collections, wanted to have me present her wedding dress," Louise said once. "She changed her mind. 'My customers, both men and women, would have been floored,' said Coco. 'Brides are so much smaller!'"

The gossip columnists immediately put the relationship between

---

[11] Sébastien Nicolas, known as Nicolas de Chamfort, was an able satirist who used to improvise witty sayings in the salons of pre-Revolutionary Paris.

Louise and Malraux, so innocent in appearance, into the category of society liaisons that have no chance of survival.

In 1933 Louise painted. She made abstract cubes that piled one atop another like the buildings in Manhattan. She drew oval, multi-colored lines in gouache. But Louise also went in for figurative painting. This was her calvary as a creative artist; she would have liked to be the Berthe Morisot of her period, the impressionistic lens always ready to register the constant whirl of impressions in the midst of which she was living.

"Do put this into your head—your painting is bad, dear Louise," Malraux told her. "And in my opinion there is no chance that it will improve, either from the point of view of form or of color. I can think of no worse thing to say about a work, but your painting lacks soul. One seeks in vain for any passion motivating it."

Georges Braque, who in Malraux's opinion was the greatest painter then living, called Malraux the only really constructive French critic, and said that "he smells good painting with both his nostrils."

There was therefore nothing for "dear Louise" to do but to rip up her canvases and put away her brushes.

But Malraux was not a sadist. He was frankly expressing his opinion to a woman who was dear to him and whom he saw blindly losing her way. It was not as though there were no recourse. Louise with her brilliant, unexpected conversation studded with surprises had too many verbal gifts not to have a writing gift as well.

"Write," Malraux advised her. "Write as it comes to you, but at the same time watch that intoxicated butterfly exuberance that comes over you whenever you're in company. Writing, literary creation, is a solitary and controlled art. You have to mistrust words. I remember how I began, with a dictionary within reach. . . ."

To this appeal of André's, Louise responded in a vexed tone, "In other words, you're telling me to stop talking!"

Malraux, exasperated, shrugged his shoulders.

"That was the only tiff we ever had," Louise later remembered. She knew perfectly well what Malraux expected of her, above all that she not be deaf and dumb and that she get to work like a studious school-girl. And that was how she began to write her first novel, *Grâce de Sainte-Unefois.*

She would submit pieces of chapters to Malraux.

"This is impossible. Bad!" he would say.

"Then I'll tear it up!"

"For heaven's sake, no!"

"It breaks my heart, but I'm going to tear it up!"

"Mothers always prefer their most ill favored children. . . . Everyone writes, dear Louise, but there are fewer and fewer writers. You are a writer. . . ."

When she left for the United States to return for a brief time to her husband, Henry Leigh Hunt,[12] Louise continued to send pieces of chapters to Malraux.

Unanimously accepted by the Gallimard reading committee, Louise de Vilmorin's first novel was published in May of 1934.[13]

"This is my bouquet of lilies of the valley," Louise wrote in her dedication to Malraux. "I have picked all these sprigs for you in my Verrières meadow, for you who are responsible for them, *vilain monsieur,* and who will see me weep all the tears of my body if the fate of this thing is a catastrophe. If it is otherwise, *gentil monseigneur,* all the stars of heaven will follow you in procession; and I myself shall lead the dance of love while reciting to God every evening the prayers that shall protect you. Your very affectionate Louise."

Criticism was divided. "Let us hope this first time will be the last," some said. But Jean Cocteau, that discoverer of new and able young writers, devoted a dithyrambic article to the book in the *NRF.* "There is no limit to what we are entitled to hope for from Louise de Vilmorin," he concluded. "Henceforth every word of hers will count. She is not a *précieuse ridicule;* she is a clever scholar who knows nothing, except how to write."

Much later, referring to his discovery of *Sainte-Unefois,* Cocteau wrote, "This book revealed the person who had written it, that is to say a young woman in whom the singular despises the plural and flames with that exquisite fever that childhood feels in disobeying grown-ups. It can be imagined that I longed to meet the original of that mysterious self-portrait. That is how, dear Louise, to the utter dismay of your entourage, who took me for the devil, you came to pay me a visit in my humble hotel room and we discovered, at first glance,

---

[12] Her marriage to Hunt, a Wall Street broker, was a series of separations followed by temporary reconciliations, but it was going downhill; in 1935 Louise would divorce him and return to France to live at her family château of Verrières in the Essonne department.

[13] It is a story about an amorous emancipation within a family framework that is solid only in appearance.

that we both belonged to the family of itinerants and that we lived in the same caravan."[14]

And so there was *la petite* Vilmorin settled, as it were, on an insolent throne. Cocteau's admiration alone was almost sufficient for overnight celebrity in those days—at least for a while.

Malraux warned her, "Beware of that beautiful blue Danube whose waltz often is heard only once. Literature is a vanity fair in which one must defend one's display foot by foot. Believe me, nothing is more uncomfortable than this celebrity, sometimes so artificial, which brings you more false courtiers than real readers."

Malraux spoke feelingly, and he knew what he was talking about. On December 1, 1933, six months before Louise's literary debut, he himself had been awarded the Prix Goncourt, on the first ballot and unanimously, for *La Condition humaine*. After the announcement of the result at the Drouant restaurant, in accordance with the established ritual, he could think of only one thing—how to get away, leave the members of the Académie Goncourt who had selected him, leave the celebrity hunters, avoid the reporters, and go to join Louise. He had a date with her for lunch at Marius's, a restaurant on the rue de Bourgogne, within easy walking distance of the Chamber of Deputies, many of whose members dined there regularly.

Malraux sat across the table from Louise. Over dessert—an *omelette flambée au rhum*—he said to her:

"It is with you that I shall end my life."

"Is it a probability, or a certainty?"

"More than that," Malraux replied, "a deep conviction."

Less than a year later the Atlantic Ocean would separate Louise and André, and after that all manner of events would come between them. Yet they would always remain in each other's memory, part of its essential mythology. And more than thirty years after their first meeting Louise would say, "That man whom I met in 1933, who does not like to remember and who every morning tears the page of the day before from his calendar, has decided to end his life with me."

It was 1934. Neither Malraux's literary success, his important friendships, nor the advantages of his position at Gallimard's could dispel his somber mood. Hitler had become chancellor of the Third Reich in 1933, and the news from Germany grew ever more alarming.

---

[14] It was, of course, simply a meeting of minds, because Cocteau loved everything but women.

5.

Saba: The Secret City

"How did it come into my head, thirty years ago, to go and look for the capital of the Queen of Sheba?" Malraux was to ask himself when he came to write his *Antimémoires* in 1967.

To a historically minded adventurer, the search for the legendary palace of the Queen of Sheba represented a challenge too romantic to resist.

The land of the Queen of Sheba (known as Saba) has historically been identified with the area of Yemen in southwest Arabia at the mouth of the Red Sea. Its history has always been linked with a legend that tradition has perpetuated for nearly three millennia. It marks the beginning of the Ethiopian dynasty, the oldest in the world, which has been Christian since the fourth century.

About the year 1000 or 950 B.C., Queen Makeda (known in the Koran as Balkis), who reigned over the kingdom of Saba, was attracted by the reputation for wisdom of Solomon, son of David, king of the Jews—so attracted, in fact, that she journeyed from her capital of Marib to the kingdom of Israel. Solomon welcomed her to his palace and initiated her to his religion. But when, after six months, the queen wished to return to her own country, he could not conceal his despair that he had not been able to initiate her also to his bed.

To honor her departure he offered a sumptuous dinner, at which he saw to it that she was served only highly spiced dishes. Before retiring to her bedroom the queen, guessing Solomon's intentions, made him promise not to make any attempt upon her virtue.

"I so promise," said Solomon, "on condition that you take nothing that is in my dwelling."

The queen accepted the condition and went to bed. During the night, however, she was so tortured by thirst that she got up to take a cup of water. Solomon, of course, was waiting for that moment.

"You are freed of your promise," said the queen, "but let me at least drink this water."

After which she gave herself to him.

The return journey lasted nine months, and just before reaching her kingdom she brought into the world a child whom she called Ibn El Hakim ("the son of the sage").

At the age of twenty-two, Ibn El Hakim went to Israel to visit his father, Solomon, who proposed to him that he become his successor. The young man was anointed and crowned in the temple at Jerusalem and, in memory of his grandfather, took the name of David. But he could not forget the land of his childhood. He fled, taking the Ark of the Covenant with him, and mounted the throne of Saba, adopting the name of Menelik I.

Thus, according to tradition, was founded the Solomonic dynasty, which later linked the land of Saba with Ethiopia, on the far side of the Red Sea, and which still reigns over Ethiopia in the person of Emperor Haile Selassie. His land's history is a succession of epic struggles, of desperate resistance, fierce combat against enemies from without who have unremittingly challenged its beliefs, coveted its riches, and attempted to subdue its people.

Ethiopia is a country upon which nature has set its seal of grandeur, and this dry, desert land across the Red Sea, with its jagged ranges of mountains, almost unexplored by westerners, is no less a setting for an epic.

The Queen of Sheba has taken her place in history with a romantic grandeur due not only to Ethiopian tradition but to references to her in the Koran and in the Bible. The air of mystery about her and her kingdom has always fascinated historians and writers. Gustave Flaubert found her particularly intriguing and devoted more than ten pages to describing her in *La Tentation de saint Antoine,* which of all his books most completely reflects the profundity of his nature. Malraux had read with intense pleasure Flaubert's account of her arrival, on the back of a white elephant caparisoned in gold, to tempt the virtuous St. Anthony in the desert.

The queen, seated upon cushions of blue wool, cross-legged, her eyes half-closed, is so splendidly dressed that she "emits rays" all around her. The attendants prostrate themselves, the elephant kneels, and the Queen of Sheba, gliding down by its shoulder, steps lightly on the carpet and advances toward the saint. She tries to seduce the hermit, who draws back from her lavish gifts and sensual blandishments, his teeth chattering, pale as death. She draws nearer, tries to caress him:

> "If you placed your finger on my shoulder, it would be like a stream of fire in your veins. The possession of the least part of my body will fill you with a joy more vehement than the conquest of an empire. Bring your lips near! My kisses have the taste of fruit which would melt in your heart. Ah! how you will lose yourself in my tresses, caress my breasts, marvel at my limbs, and be scorched by my eyes, between my arms, in a whirlwind. . . ."

Antony makes the sign of the Cross.

"So then, you disdain me! Farewell!"

She turns away weeping.[1]

Haunted by the image of the queen, Malraux grew increasingly interested in putting together information about her and in locating the lost city that had been her capital. Was it mythical? Malraux believed not. Few lands are more fertile in legends and in mysteries than Arabia, that vast, mostly deserted country of which westerners know so little. According to legend, the Sabaeans, the subjects of the Queen of Sheba, had occupied the southwestern section of Arabia. But their territory had for centuries been in the hands of dissident, bloodthirsty tribesmen, which had led to its remaining the most mysterious area of all that mysterious, unexplored land. The Sabaeans had traditionally maintained close relations with Egypt, and with the ancient kingdom of Punt, whence came the cedars of Lebanon. The Greeks and Romans, familiar with Lebanese cedarwood, which they used in building their ships, knew about the kingdom of Saba but did not know the exact location of its capital. Diodorus of Sicily, the Greek historian, situated it on a wooded mountain of Arabia Felix. Pliny the Elder identified it with a stronghold in the center of Yemen. Other historians placed it close to the Bab el Mandeb pass, in a region fertile in spices and in perfume.

Malraux probably first heard about Saba and Marib at Djibouti, in French Somaliland, where the ships on the France-Indochina route regularly docked to take on water, provisions, and passengers. Later, on visits to Persia, he listened to professional storytellers' accounts of

[1] Gustave Flaubert, *The Temptation of St. Antony, or, A Revelation of the Soul* (printed for subscribers by M. Walter Dunne, New York and London, 1904).

how a Roman army, defeated by Sabaean troops, had been placed under a curse by the enemy stargazers and, after wandering the desert blindly for months in search of the sea, had finally perished to a man in the inland wastes. In the museum of the Société de Géographie in Paris, he studied whatever documents he could find on the subject of Saba and its lost capital city.

Most important of these was a report in the *Journal Asiatique,* brought to his notice by the scholar-explorer Jean Charcot, which described the adventures of a mid-nineteenth-century pharmacist named Arnaud—the first European to reach Marib. Arnaud, living in Jidda in the 1840s, became fascinated by accounts of the mysterious city and managed to find his way there, enter the town in disguise, and take rubbings of several inscriptions he found among the ruins. After a lengthy return trip filled with vicissitudes, he finally reached France and published a report on his adventures, with copies of the inscriptions.

"Why should there not be another city, still inviolate, intact, with its ramparts, its palaces, its towers, unknown even to the Arabs themselves, concealed in these unexplored territories?" Malraux asked himself. For a man with an insatiable thirst for adventure, who could combine the imaginary and the real with supreme felicity, such uncertainty made the idea of an expedition to find either Marib or some other city, still lost in the wastes of Saba, all the more attractive.

One evening, among friends, he broached the subject to Captain Edouard Corniglion-Molinier, a young officer in the French air force reserve, who had made his name as a brilliant pilot in the closing stages of World War I.

"He told me," Corniglion later related, "that he was planning to explore Yemen and try to find the city of the Queen of Sheba, disguised as a Persian.

"I was able later, and on many occasions, to verify the exaggerated idea Malraux has of his knowledge of the Persian language and history. Every time he tried to use the language, the Arab porter or the erudite old man to whom he was speaking would register utter surprise and show that he understood nothing of what he was saying.

"I said to Malraux, 'Why add to the list of scholars or romantic adventurers killed in such expeditions without reaching their objective, when there is a much greater likelihood of finding the city, if it exists, by flying over it?'

"That evening Malraux hardly said another word and only pretended to listen. . . ."

Corniglion's suggestion had made an instant appeal to him, and his thoughts at once turned to Jean Mermoz and Antoine de Saint-Exupéry, France's two most famous pilots, who were employed by the Aéropostale, the French airmail service, and constantly making the perilous and lengthy crossing of the South Atlantic. The very next day he asked Jean Mermoz to go with him, but the airmail service refused to liberate its best pilot. He then made the proposal to Saint-Exupéry, who accepted enthusiastically. But Consuelo, his young wife, thought differently. "Antoine," she told him, "if you go, I'll go to bed with every man in Paris!" Faced with this threat, Saint-Ex gave up the idea.

Malraux then telephoned Corniglion-Molinier.

"I think your idea is an excellent one. Can you give me some technical information about the preparation for such a flight?"

"It's a distance of twelve hundred miles without a stop," Corniglion replied, at once accepting the idea that he act as pilot on the flight. "If we try to land, it's certain death. If the city is on a hillside it will be hard for us to make a pass very low, because it's easy to shoot down a plane if you can fire down on it from above. . . ."

"Then it looks as if there's less than a fifty-fifty chance of coming back alive from such an adventure. But the danger makes it all the more attractive," was Malraux's conclusion.

"My own love of adventure matched André Malraux's," Corniglion said later, "but I did not dare to assume the sole responsibility of piloting one of the few remarkable men of my generation, especially on such a special venture.

"I telephoned to one of my fellow aviators, whom I considered one of the best, Captain Maurice Challe.[2] He was willing to accompany me and we decided to make preparations for the flight."

As the two pilots studied the few maps of Arabia available, they were filled at first with amusement, and then with perplexity. None of the maps showed the important landmarks in the same place. It became quite clear that the exploration would involve a nonstop flight of fifteen hundred to eighteen hundred miles, at an altitude of ten thousand feet. There were very few French planes with such a range, and Challe and Corniglion thought enviously about all the foreign planes that would

---

[2] Later General Challe, who played a prominent part in the Algiers putsch in 1961.

have suited them, which included two English models and one American. The money for the venture was limited, however; Malraux planned to finance it in part by writing articles about the expedition for *L'Intransigeant*.[3] Since they had to make do with a French plane, they decided—not wanting to be too demanding and dream about certain three-engine planes—that the Farman 190 would suit their needs, despite its having only one engine, provided that this was sufficiently powerful and thoroughly reliable. The three-hundred-horsepower Gnôme and Rhône K 7 engine seemed to meet this condition.

Corniglion then had the idea of approaching an old comrade, Paul-Louis Weiller, who was the president of the Gnôme firm. His wartime reputation for dash and bold resourcefulness made Corniglion confident that he would view their somewhat risky project with sympathy and interest. Corniglion visited his ex-commander, with results that were favorable indeed:

> Weiller was willing to lend us his own private plane, even allowing us to have it undergo all the needed changes. In a very few days his handsome touring plane with its streamlined wheels, its comfortable seats, with electrical starter, central heating, and soft carpets, became a machine bristling with extra tanks and radiators, a maze of ugly pipes, big wheels, innumerable tachometers, thermometers, and outlandishly large compasses. After a few consumption and altitude tests we were ready.

At the last moment, Challe could not join them, so they took one of Weiller's mechanics instead, a cheerful, competent man named Maillard. Daily stages of twelve hundred to fifteen hundred miles brought them rapidly to Djibouti under skies that were almost uniformly favorable.

One afternoon in March, 1934, Captain Jean Esparre, commander of the French Somali Coast Squadron, was out on the Djibouti airfield (an unimpressive 650 yards long by 225 yards wide) when without any announcement or signal a Farman suddenly came in low and landed. Three passengers stepped out.

"They introduced themselves to me," Captain Esparre remembers. "They were French. It was the first private plane coming from France

---

[3] Paris' most popular evening newspaper in the thirties.

ever to land on this field. They were Corniglion-Molinier, the pilot, a mechanic from the Farman plant, and a distinguished-looking, slender, rather nervous young man. This was André Malraux, the author of *La Condition humaine,* which had just been awarded the Prix Goncourt.

"The Farman had come from Cairo, after a stop in Port Sudan. Corniglion informed me of the objective of the flight—Arabia, where they hoped to find some vestiges of Marib, the capital of the Queen of Sheba. Djibouti was therefore the best possible base of departure, and the best place to make their final technical preparations. I placed my local facilities at their disposal—first off, a roof."

Captain Esparre and Lieutenant Paul Gambert, his adjutant, had set up their command post in a vast dwelling surrounded by a garden with trees, known as the Nocetto house. It had been built by an Italian tradesman who had made his fortune in Djibouti and wanted his home to look like a colonial palace. Indeed, Haile Selassie regularly stayed there when he stopped over in Djibouti. The squadron had taken over the ground floor for its offices, and the single floor above provided living quarters and a mess for the men. The house was not only impressive to look at but was well adapted to the demanding local living conditions; Djibouti is said to be one of the hottest spots in the world, a real furnace, where the *khamsin,* the wind from the desert, covers everything over with a coating of sand.[4]

For centuries the people who have landed on this savage coast have baptized it with the most discouraging names—the Land of Thirst, the Bay of Desolation, the Valley of Death. Since France created the port of Djibouti in 1888, to serve as a port of call for the shipping lines running through the Suez Canal to the Far East and to Madagascar, the local life has had a north-south orientation, or vice versa.

When Malraux and Corniglion landed there, the famous zinc palm tree put up as a bitter joke by an early settler was still the showpiece of the bistro in front of which it stood, but many palm trees, real ones, had been planted and had grown. Those of the Ambouli oasis sheltered numerous fertile gardens, where water, brought from wells in leather bags, trickled between lettuce and radish patches.

Famished-looking goats grazed in the streets of Djibouti. But what could they find to eat? For, apart from sand and old tin cans, what was there in those streets? To prevent the starving goats from suckling

---

[4] *Khamsin,* or *chamsin,* is Arabic for "fifty," and hence is the name given to the simoom, a wind that blows for fifty days.

one another, their teats were encased in small sacks. The streets had no names. Some had numbers, like the avenue 15. The black women came every day, carrying huge pitchers on their muscular shoulders, to fill them with water at the fountains of avenue 15.

At noon, when the sun was at its zenith in the heavy sky, a leaden pall would fall on the city. The streets became deserted. There was no longer a hint of sea breeze—only the despairing and nerve-racking cry of the rooks in the thorny shrubs bordering the gardens of the city.

The traditional tourist attraction was a trip, in the cooler evening hours, to the native quarters of the town to see the "sewn-up women." It had long been local custom to sew up young girls to preserve their chastity; a solemn unstitching took place just before the marriage ceremony. Some of the fishermen of Djibouti, anticipating lengthy voyages at sea, have been known to sew up their wives to prevent them from being unfaithful. But most of the wives, when they got tired of waiting, cut the stitches with the slivers of broken glass that the local people use instead of knives.

Djibouti fishermen have always been fortunate, for immense colonies of dolphins, rays, tuna, mullet, and porpoises are to be found in nearby waters. The sea is full of coral reefs infested with sharks, but the boats venture out fearlessly. Slender sailboats known as *boutres,* and the native *zarougs,* which require the skill of an acrobat to maneuver, streak across the water.

Djibouti in 1934 had a polyglot population of local Somalis, Isas, Afar, and Arabs from the Yemen; in addition, there were Greeks, Turks, Armenians, a few Italians, and many Hindus. The French population, whether military or civilian—aviators, officers of the colonial army, tradesmen, civil servants, employees of the Franco-Ethiopian railroad, navigation line agents—was naturally involved in all questions relating to the Orient and to India. The arrival of André Malraux, who had already produced impressive work despite his youth—he was thirty-two—undoubtedly caused a considerable stir.

Although their guests were totally unexpected, Captain Esparre and Lieutenant Gambert planned to make them as comfortable as possible while they were preparing for their expedition. Corniglion and Malraux were allotted vast rooms in the Nocetto house, separated by a common bathroom. André Malraux was barely installed in his when he went into Lieutenant Gambert's room, which was next door, and sat down on the *angareb,* the local bed, under the ceiling ventilator. In front of him was a wall shelf with some books, including *La Condition humaine,* which by mere chance stood next to T. E. Lawrence's *Seven Pillars of Wisdom.*

"I took *La condition humaine* and handed it to him," Paul Gambert relates. "He let the pages flutter between his thumb and forefinger. I asked him, 'Do you enjoy rereading what you have written?' 'One should never reread what one has written,' he replied. His tone was so natural, so devoid of intellectual pride, that it impressed me, coming as it did from a writer who had just become famous and was in the limelight."

The atmosphere was relaxed and open from the start.

"We deserved no credit for this," Paul Gambert explains, "since we were at home here, nor did our senior, Corniglion-Molinier, since he naturally felt at home in air force surroundings. The ease we felt was due essentially to Malraux, who immediately adapted himself to our ways when it would have been easy for him to impose his personality on us."

In the mess kitchen Ali, the *bep* (chef), cooked his roasts and browned his *cassoulets* in an oven he had contrived from an old gasoline can. He even managed to make delicious sherbets, with the temperature at 104 degrees Fahrenheit in the shade, in an equally makeshift freezer.

"Our guests," Esparre recalls, "enjoyed the highly spiced local dishes, which seemed to be no novelty to Malraux. He loved the shrimps and the enormous crabs prepared with curry and strongly peppered. With this we drank an Algerian wine, which could stand the Somali climate."

India inevitably had influenced the style of living in the small French colony. The soldiers' uniforms were made and sold by Hindu merchants, modeled on those worn by the Indian army. The food, with rice and spices as major ingredients, was markedly Indian; so was the pattern of domestic service by "boys" wearing long white coats and red turbans. Even the fuel for the planes came over in drums from Aden, the British colony on the opposite shore of the Red Sea. Much of the everyday ritual, in fact, had an Indian flavor.

"We would talk late into the night before going to sleep," Paul Gambert recalls. "Without pressing me, but coming back to the subject now and then, so that it struck me, André Malraux would talk to me about the search for absolute truth and would question me. His questions gave me the strange feeling that it was himself he was questioning, as though the fact of speaking to someone enabled him to go further along this path.

"More precisely, because we were living in a country that was somewhat influenced by India—we felt its closeness and a sense of its 'pressure'—Malraux asked me what I thought of the possibility of pursuing the search for absolute truth by the methods of the Hindu sages. The fact that this man of action in the full vigor of youth was pursuing problems that challenge the highest level of intelligence dumbfounded me."

One of Malraux's favorite subjects, too, was madness and the insane, who he claimed became normal under the influence of opium.

He would question Esparre about the country, about aviation, about the customs of the inhabitants, even though he never manifested any desire to go and see the sewn-up women.

"He would particularly question me," says Esparre, "about our relations with the RAF, based at Aden. Our British comrades, under the orders of Group Captain Boyd, and later of Group Captain Portal, would set out on mysterious bombing missions, but we were never able to determine what their object was, despite our discreet surveillance. We had good reasons for believing that the British bombers were sent out to lambaste some dissident tribes on the fringe of the Hadhramaut."

Meanwhile Corniglion-Molinier spent his days preparing for the coming expedition in search of Marib. Malraux would have liked to take off from Aden, which was a good thirty miles closer to the spot they would be looking for. He would have had more time to explore a territory designated as *terra incognita* on the maps of Arabia. But the British would not allow anyone to fly over Aden without authorization, nor over Perim, a small island in the southern Red Sea that was an oil center. The Farman's flight consequently presented a delicate problem, because, lacking authorization from the British Foreign Office, it would have to cross the Gulf of Tadjoura, passing south of Perim, and skirt the Hadhramaut, in order to avoid the British sector.

Great Britain's attitude of intense suspicion even applied to the French, who were presumed to be her allies. Only the tiny Shell Oil planes were authorized to take aerial photographs. If a foreign plane equipped for photography were to make a landing on soil that was British or British controlled, such as Egypt, its trap door for taking pictures had to be tightly locked shut. Any film already exposed was automatically developed by the British photography services, and then either seized or returned intentionally "fogged" to its owners.

Esparre told his guests about the French emergency landing fields at Labbé and at Obock, which were closer to their destination than Djibouti itself. If they ran short of fuel, it was vital that they be able to land without too much risk after a flight navigated solely by a clock and a compass. (A map of the area is included in the first of the two illustration sections.)

"We'll leave tomorrow morning at dawn," Corniglion-Molinier told Maillard, the navigator-mechanic, one night. "I hope you've checked everything."

"Everything is ready," Maillard replied. "I have my Colt. Your Arab disguises are on board. . . . For myself, I haven't even been able to find a tarboosh to fit me. I'll try to borrow the Somali sergeant's."

"My dear Maillard," said Corniglion, "it's very decent of you to want to come with us, but I don't want to expose you. It's a nine- or ten-hour flight over unknown country inhabited by dissidents and the capital of the Queen of Sheba, after all, doesn't specially interest you."

Maillard flushed with indignation. "You're not leaving me behind!" he exploded.

In the early dawn on the tiny airfield Esparre and Gambert were on hand, with last-minute advice and reminders.

"Have you checked the oil pressure? Have you tightened the controls, which were a little loose yesterday? Are you sure all your compasses have been well compensated? Are you sure the drain cock on the right-hand tank no longer leaks?"

Maillard, in a white flying suit, looking very trim, was waiting beside the white plane.

"Maillard is the Roman soldier," said Malraux.

Soon they would be passing through the gate to the unknown. . . . They would be heading for the desert in search of the buried city of the Queen of Sheba, the famous Shulamite. Of this voyage above the desert of dunes where only plunderers, vicious as famished wolves, now roam, André Malraux brought back the following account:[5]

The plane waits in the predawn. How many such planes I have seen, sitting squat on a long field that stretches out to

---

[5] This material, based on the notes Malraux took on his trip for the articles he subsequently wrote for *L'Intransigeant*, has never before been translated or published in book form.

the edge of the dawn, in a Muslim odor of burned grass, pepper, and camels! Fields of southern Persia, steppes of central Asia—with their Russian pilots who spend the night naked on swings to escape the frightful heat—at the foot of the Himalayas in the scorched gardens, beneath the wild and torrid fragrance of the dried lavender of the mountains. . . . Islam surrounds us on all sides, to the very heart of Africa.

Yonder is the dawn. Light slowly asserts its ascendancy over the night, slowly releases from the darkness the motionless details of the landscape.

We have of course no information as to the weather on the Arab coast. All we know is that at this season the coast is almost always obliterated by clouds, the mountain region almost always clear, but the geographers mention a short rainy season in March. Today is the seventh of March. Every day lost would increase the chance of running into bad weather. What shall we find 150 miles away, beyond the Asiatic banners of those scattered clouds? Blue sky, or other clouds? In other words, the impossibility of distinguishing the mountains in an almost unknown region.

We are here, shadowless in the predawn, beside this engine, in this plane, which bears the seal of the West, inspecting the clouds and the sky with the seriousness of peasants and the wariness of the shepherds of old.

We cast a last glance at the contradictory maps that we carry with us for conscience' sake, like torn parachutes.

The night falls back slowly, slips behind the mountains of Ethiopia. The plane has become white. The imperious light of the tropics begins to make the mist and the clouds tremble. It seems to want to join us, to tear away the hostile multitude of those clouds, to join the low, swift wind that flattens the grasses in the field and sweeps away the last shreds of shadow.

Yonder, the wind, the mountains, the desert—the Plutonian forces, the monsters with the muzzles of demigods, which rediscover the old lurking-places where they have lain in wait for man since the beginning of time. How many pilots have undertaken this departure for the unknown!

Djibouti is behind us. We reach the clouds. Above, the sky is blue. No birds. The solitude of Genesis. Thus we advance for half an hour in the absolute, while below the African territories of the earth prowl. But this landscape of cosmogony, without limits, is also without dimensions: to the right the light vanishes in a russet blur that might be either mist or the heaviness of the air. The mountains of Arabia are surely not far off, and yet we do not see them.

Luckily the air is clear. We descend. Through holes in the clouds the coast appears, and then the strait. In the middle, a glimpse of Perim; beyond, the Arab coast. Is it really the Arab coast? Yes, obscured by a reddish mist. We make a wide detour round Perim, flying over it being prohibited. Besides, it it Tuesday, and the English airmail is due here. We don't want to meet it.

So this coast to which we keep our eyes glued is Arabia. All those coves that we pass one after another with an insect's patience, and the softness of whose dunes seems to dissolve in time, were once the small forgotten ports of pre-Islamic civilizations. This coast is connected to San'a[6] by radio; we fly in the clouds in order not to be spotted, and it is through long rifts that we perceive, down there in the mist, an inexhaustible solitude, surrounded by the surf line. Will the mountains and the north be more favorable to us?

Beneath the clouds the same mist prevails and when we again descend we see Mokha at the far end of its sandy gulf, a white mosque and ruins of palaces scattered in the emptiness of the sand.

How many dreams have these remains nourished? In the russet and greenish light of the sand and the sea, do we see just enough to continue to dream, or is it the obscure working of Saba in me that makes me think of the city of the devil worshipers, near Mosul? There, the main parts of those mud houses had almost everywhere returned to the earth; only the stone facades remained standing, cut through by immense windows in which prostitutes were sitting, a last flash of the setting sun resting on their enormous earrings and their thick necklaces; a cat passed on a cornice with the sacred pace of an Egyptian cat. As far as the eye can reach, it seems indeed that here too the facades are inhabited only by their shadows and that, from the fraternal depth of death, the kingdom of Saba ironi-

6 The capital of Yemen.

cally holds open to travelers, like a vast gate, the sumptuous skeleton of a Muslim city.

What is sung here, in the mist?

The sand, the sand, the sand.

The map becomes more real than the soil, and we climb northward, like a beetle up a ladder.

I calculate our speed: 160 per hour. A head wind. If the wind does not die down we shall not reach Saba; or, if we reach it, we shall not have enough gas to fly back.[7] And the mist, below the clouds as above, remains just as dense. Let us wait. Perhaps the mist does not extend as far as San'a. Perhaps it does not fall on the desert, on the other side of the mountains. What is the great inland desert like, toward which we are heading? Probably very much like this abandoned coast, covered with brush quickly conquered by the sand.

With its short brush from which the shadows of the morning spread despite the mist, the coast is still full of antique presences and of demons. As in Tibet, as in Mongolia, as in Persia, something supernatural can be sensed. Not for nothing have the world's last great legends taken refuge on the snows of Central Asia and in the desert that those pointing mountains still conceal from us.

We are now approximately at the latitude of the Sabaean centers that await us on the other side. Of the unknown city, what do we know that is not legendary? The Persians claim that in the desert, close to Yemen, there is a vast abandoned city that was the capital of the Queen of Sheba. This is confirmed by the Bedouins. A German adventurer whom I met in Bushire, where he had come from Mecca, dressed as an Arab, told me he had glimpsed it and then been chased away by nomads. He spoke of seventy temples. . . . That is a lot. Joseph Kessel had heard tell of it in San'a. Helgritz had nearly reached it. It is said that at the moment in Hodeida, which we shall soon reach, an English expedition is in preparation. The mystery has been rather well preserved: Langer, Seetzen, Durchart—all killed. And how many others. . . . It would probably take only a very small European column to reduce those nomads; but there is nothing to justify sending one. For a cen-

[7] Additional cans of gasoline had, however, been loaded on the plane to fill the tanks in the air in order to increase its range for the flight.

tury people have wondered if the legendary Saba, the city of the desert, was not Marib. Archaeologists have visited Marib. All confirm that it has been destroyed. Yet Marib was the capital of the Sabaean confederation. Were there two Sabas, successively? Such a thing would not be without example in Arabia, for in Marib there is no trace of the queen. If the city that we are looking for does not exist, all this is absurd. But what if it *does* exist?

Hodeida grows bigger; here are the mandibles of its jetties. We again climb into the clouds. According to all the maps, two peaks over thirteen thousand feet overlook San'a. They therefore are conspicuously higher than the mountain chain and we can get our bearings by them. Let us go find them. . . .

These mountains, and those of Tibet, are said to be the world's most startling; indeed, they awaken and stir in us the souls of primitive sorcerers. Above a mist as thick as that found in Japanese prints, but reddish and menacing, a colossal set of sharks' teeth now appears, detached against the sky; and as we advance, the disappearance of the ground gives a more and more unreal character to those forms, as though their vertical slopes met nowhere, as though those fangs were sunk into the depths of the earth. They nevertheless advance toward us in a gigantic prehistoric troop, as though still lifted by the cry addressed to them by Allah speaking of the prophet: "And you, mountains, join him in singing my glory!" They rise in tiers, higher and higher, as for a song of triumph round the one and only God. The plane rears and climbs with the movement of a horse that hesitates before an obstacle he is about to jump over; the second barrier appears to us less sharp, more massive, very blurred—we can see hardly more than five or six miles. Much less dense than on the ground, the sand mist, as it lightens, reaches a considerable height. Everything that could help us disappears at once; it is useless now to look for the road, which is in fact no more than a trail, or telegraph posts, or the mountains that could guide us. . . .

The compass and that is all.

Three hours ago we looked at the sky with the anxiety of the ancient shepherds; now it will be necessary to live the life of primitive navigators. Few people, other than those who have had something to do with aviation, know that a plane is a big blind beetle once it has taken off from the earth. The safety that the European lines provide is due to the transmission stations that send and receive radio messages, but there are no transmission stations in these regions. Besides, we have no radio receiver; we had to reduce our weight to the minimum. Which leaves us only the compass and our speed to establish our bearings.

The compass? But in this fog that surrounds us, the cross-wind can blow us fifty or more miles off our course without its showing on the compass card. Whether we are now moving crabwise or straight ahead, the compass still shows the direction of the axis of the plane and not the direction in which we are moving. There is a device for measuring the drift, but it refers to the ground. And our previous observations are of no use—it was in order to cross the mountains that we changed our direction, and the same cause makes the wind carry us off our course and brings us into the fog.

The speed? Apart from the extreme caution that must be used in relying on the instruments aboard a plane, our speedometers give us no sound indication. In a car, the instrument indicates the speed in relation to the ground; in a plane it indicates speed in relation to the wind. Ours, at the moment, marks 190, I think. What is our actual speed in relation to earth in this crosswind? 160, as it was earlier? 210?

This would all be unimportant if we had more than ten hours' worth of gas.

At moments the mist is less dense, the ground appears. Aided only by his experience with planes, Corniglion corrects our direction as best he can. It has been right up to now, for here is the region of Manakha, halfway to San'a.

The villages are now perched high. We can make out fairly well their romantic towers atop the peaks. We have not given up hope of finding at least the general direction of the large rivers. Here is a caravan led by its small guide donkey. I can imagine it advancing like those I have come upon in Persia, in Afghanistan, in a sustained noise of cattle bells, each of its travelers protected by the most effective charm—a foxtail or the shoe of an infidel child. . . . As we descend to see it at closer range, in the narrow strip of shadow cast by the mountain, brief flames appear. We are being fired on. With old-fashioned guns, because we can see the flash; perhaps also with modern guns that we do not see. But it is nearly impossible to hit a plane in flight from below.

We are some sixty miles from San'a. We know that the city, despite its size, is hard to see, buried as it is in a deep valley. And this is our only landmark on our route, before we venture over the desert.

No more villages, a geological solitude. The mineral kingdom returns to life, the mountains emerge from the mist as if at God's call. The duel will resume between the mountain chain, the fog, and the inventions of men. As far as the eye can see—and it is not very far—there is no place where a landing could be attempted.

At times the mist is lighter, and, while we continue to have poor visibility ahead, we at least can see down below. Even the English-Turkish map indicates to us rivers that are nowhere to be found; everywhere, in this season, in the inextricable network of valleys, rivers and tributaries merge. . . .

The mountains, huddled together like sheep, are separated by deep, narrow valleys. The villages on the heights can be made out; but those in the valleys appear suddenly, as if behind a wall we had just jumped over.

We race above innumerable hiding places, looking for villages burrowed into their holes like crabs; in this atmosphere San'a, like the mountains, becomes animate, becomes a hidden creature. It is already late. If we bypass San'a, if we circle round for more than an hour without finding it—and just now it seems impossible to find anything whatsoever in this geological forest—we shall have to go back and start over again tomorrow. But will we find tomorrow? And the bad March weather will start any day now. . . . Our eyes keep jumping from one to another of those ever more rugged, ever more secret mountains. In the photographs, San'a is surrounded by three peaks that are closer together and less high than those I spoke of earlier; they are jagged in a quite peculiar way. We look for them even more intently than for the city hidden in its valley, of which Anis Pasha told us: "You see it only when you are on top of it."[8]

---

[8] Hassan Anis Pasha, an Egyptian pilot, the first man to fly over San'a, had lent them his map.

Still the solitude. And suddenly—where does it come from?—there is the road.

Five minutes later it has disappeared in the gorges. Over yonder it ramifies, curiously, in three directions. But it is the road to the sea; San'a therefore is east, and we are heading in the right direction. In fact, here are the three peaks from the photographs.

Here are the three peaks. But no city. We have made a mistake. Ah! Beyond, enveloped in mist behind an enormous flat mountain mass, a kind of sacrificial table, there are the right peaks, in the right direction.

No. Again, nothing. For how long are we going to pounce on those peaks as on empty treasure chests? I remember a saying that is traditional in the Far East: "If you want to keep a man from leaving a place, you must have him look for a treasure." We shall see San'a everywhere. I have some experience with this particular illusion, which is more tantalizing than a mirage, having come upon it on the dirt roads of Persia. The forms of those ranges are all alike, and one is sure of finding them wherever one looks for them. We shall continue in this way until we reach the desert. Much too far south. And the gas we have allowed for the outward flight is running low.

We suddenly realize what has happened. The roads shown on the maps mean nothing, because they are constantly changing, a trail becoming a roadway, then dwindling again into a trail. The broad road we saw is not the highway, but the small road running south. The wind must have blown us off our course, and we must have come upon it south of San'a. We should have headed north then, and instead we continued eastward. We shall have to change our course completely and find the road again.

Having noted the time we crossed it, we find it easily. Now we head north. We lose it again, but instead of trails that vanish like the tributaries of a river we fly over roads or tracks that vanish and reappear, all converging northward. For the first time since Hodeida—since we have seen a town—man reasserts himself on the scale of the earth, of the mountains, of the clouds. Like a bird's talon encrusted in this gigantic rubble, the tireless convergence of the trails stamps the imprint of a human force. Geology is ended, the fantastic exhausted; henceforth the mountain is something that can be vanquished. . . .

We begin again to look for our three peaks. Before us is a plateau with a north-south orientation; it must be the valley of the Kharid. Here and there, ridges of lower mountains. But still no San'a.

And all at once, at the top of a peak that is like all the others, a geometric form appears. We look at it as though it were a lighthouse; is it another illusion? No, it is a modern fort. No three peaks, no city, and yet, in the whole of Yemen, San'a alone is dominated by a fort. We head toward it. And when we are less than a mile away, through a break in the mountain wall the San'a valley suddenly appears, cultivated to its last hollows, with the city in the middle inside its sloping walls, and dismantled Rauda right by, like a snake's sloughed-off skin—San'a, round, all stone, an arid and magnificent basket of white and garnet corals, at the foot of those vertical mountains.

The unknown begins.

We head due north. We must now find Shira, and from there go up the valley of the Kharid as far as the Valley of the Tombs. As far as the desert, between Ma'in and Marib. That is where the city should be. Exactly where? Neither my German, nor the Persian, nor the Arab historians and geographers say where exactly (and what does even the word "exact" mean, when the most recent maps can show a discrepancy of as much as forty miles for a given spot?). But their indications will have to do for us, if the altitude allows us to see; all we can do is explore while circling patiently. . . .

The mist to the east seems to light up from within, to become marbled with great streaks and bluish phosphorescences. Shall we get past it soon? Halévy, who explored this whole region as far as the desert toward which we are heading, who visited Marib and discovered Ma'in, mentions a grandiose ruin beyond Shira that he was unable to reach. Shira, toward which we are flying, is in the valley of the Kharid.

The mist, surely, does not extend eastward; it becomes more and more diluted. Numerous villages appear. I look at

them with passion and with anguish, calculating, accumulating
multiplications that are unreliable since we do not know our
speed, afraid of finding that something far away, as at San'a,
is very close.

Now we can distinctly make out the ground. We are north
of San'a. Shira, a dot on the map, is in fact a cluster of villages,
according to the texts. The landmark is the Kharid, the largest river in the region. We must be sixty-five hundred feet
above it.

The river is underground. . . . There is no Kharid.

We continue ahead at our fullest speed, which we shall
have to reduce, no longer having a single landmark. Only the
Kharid appeared on all the maps. Eastward, nothing. Nor is
there any trace of the Adana River. The towns are villages that
we shall be unable to make out at twenty miles, which is the
smallest error on the maps.

We fall back on the compass, take our chances. The edge
of the desert may perhaps enable us to get our bearings. As I
look at the speedometer I see the clock: we have a little more
than five hours of gas left. We are still scrutinizing the pattern
of the villages and valleys below us. We cannot possibly be anywhere but over the Kharid.

And almost abruptly the mist, from which we have been
gradually emerging in our flight, is behind us. We are over the
Kharid! Yes, the river is underground, but in this relatively
sterile region the dark green line of the vegetation—we can
make it out now—follows that of the water. The invisible river
is painted on the ground by trees. We are now hot on the
scent.

Mountains and mists disappear behind us. The steppes
begin. At last, the desert!

The visibility is twenty miles. We have reached the desert
south of Ma'in. For ten minutes we need not strain our eyes.
And yet . . .

It is not a desert with long soft dunes, like the northern
Sahara; it is rocky or flat, but always bare, the yellow and
white skeleton of the earth, full of shadows, teeming with
mirages. Chalky ochers, jagged or flattened out beneath those
trembling mirages, the landscape, intensely *mat,* rejects any

precise form as though it were already fighting the human eye
intruding upon its planetary solitude. It seems as though innumerable rivers, dried up geological epochs ago, can be traced
in the sand. . . .

It is a fantastic new world, altogether inhuman, in which a
tree twisted in the ground has the form of the first Semitic
dragon, of the dragon of Babylon bristling with claws. . . .

Mind and eye, however, gradually become habituated. The
fantastic subsides, we get used to the trembling shadows. At
last, to our right, ahead of us, we begin to make out a vast,
almost white spot, a stretch of colossal cobbles in the middle
of the sand. Is it a geological accident? An error? We tell ourselves that we must wait, get closer; but already, deep within
us, we have recognized towers, and we know that it is the City.

We get closer and closer; we watch it grow as eagerly as
a starving man eats.

The shaken mind must choose in a jumble of dreams. If
we follow both the Bible and the legend, if this city was the
queen's, it is contemporaneous with Solomon. Was that enormous monument, which looks like a tower of Notre Dame,
below which a whole series of terraces tumbles down to the
petrified skeleton of a river, the palace about which the Envoy
says in the Koran, "I saw there a woman governing men on
a magnificent throne; she and her people worship the sun," the
queen to whom Solomon sent the one among his seals that can
be deciphered only by the dead? . . .

We make out more and more details as we descend and,
like frantic café waiters juggling with their trays, we struggle
with the cameras in the plane banking at 45 degrees above the
wreckage of that fleet of dreams. It is no longer the desert, but
an abandoned oasis, with the traces of its gardens and cultivated fields; the ruins touch upon the desert only to the right.
Those oval, massive surrounding walls, with their broken
columns and their debris on the ground, are the temples. In
their sand will undoubtedly be found, as in Marib, a whole
miniature bronze fauna: fish, children, camels, seals, rings,
intaglios, bulls, rams with enormous curved horns. We see today that the mother religion from which those of Mesopotamia

and Judaea sprang was destroyed with these elliptical crum-
blings; in the earliest primitive thinking, even before the soul
was born, it was from these Arab sands that the triad of God
the Father, God the Mother, and God the Son first came into
being. Here the Trinity was all but conceived. And the bronze
figure with arms open in a gesture of welcome that the Bedouins bring from the desert might perhaps also have come
from here. . . .

Abstract divinities vanish beneath the inscriptions like
shadows, but if they have their incarnation in the constella-
tions, their very names invoke the presence of the stargazer on
these crumbling terraces. The moon god, Sin, who is masculine
—he is feminine in all the other mythologies—Dat-Badan, the
sun goddess, and the strange Ouzza, called the mascot Venus,
who is named by so many inscriptions and yet wholly unknown, were worshiped here. On this site of mystery, one is
puzzled by the sexuality of the strange people who, alone
among all peoples, conceived Venus as a man, saw in the sun
the feminine sign of fertility, and in the moon, not the mistress of anguish, the closed fist of the Semitic fatalities, but a
clement and pacifying Father. Is it in the desert that gratitude
to night was born? But the other peoples of the desert, in the
same period, make of the moon a cruel god. What disturbed
or pure sexuality gave this vanished race a conception contrary
to that of all others, and, according to its legend, as yet confirmed by no historic fact, made it want to be governed by
queens?

It is not the charming woman with a limp, her hands full
of flowers tossed at Solomon's beard, who passes here from
terrace to terrace; it is the enchantress, the sister of Semiramis,
who soars with the hawks in the vertical light of noonday
above the mysterious gods returned to the sand. At this very
moment the shadow of a bird of prey glides slowly from
temple to temple, wings outstretched like a silent and distant
protection.

The shadow reaches the surrounding wall and slips on to
the desert. Partly standing, partly broken, the wall stretches its
dazzling stones far into the distance with its tall windowless
towers. As we continue to drop, I see that the monuments are
outside the wall, on the tower side, and not within. There

must undoubtedly have been two surrounding walls, and this center still standing above its ravine was an acropolis. The city was probably built of hollow bricks, like Nineveh and Babylon, and, like them, has returned to the desert; the vast horseshoe walls open only on the void. How can we land? On one side are soft dunes where the plane would be sure to capsize, on the other side a volcanic soil where rocks break through the sand. Near the ruins, fallen stones are everywhere.

In another mass of stones stands a temple of almost Egyptian appearance: trapezoidal towers, a vast oblique terrace, propylaea. Next to it a section of wall some 120 feet high. What was that wall? . . . There are columns but not from temples: votive, or at least isolated, columns, enormous ones. We come back to the central mass: a tall oval tower, more enclosing walls, buildings with massive angles that make one think both of Chaldea and of Robert Mallet-Stevens;[9] another rather low, oblong building thrusts before it, like the pyramids, three flat walls oriented like the spokes of a wheel. Beyond the ruins are numerous nomads' tents. On those dark spots small flashes appear; we are being fired on. But again, it seems, with antiquated firearms.

Beyond the walls, or between two walls only one of which is standing, we make out, as well as the temples, monuments full of mystery—things whose purpose we cannot make out. What is the meaning of that H lying flat on the highest terrace of the tower that dominates all the ruins? Is it part of an observatory? The reinforcement of a hanging garden? There are still many such gardens in upper Yemen; thirty miles from here, all the house roofs are covered with clumps of hemp. Can we imagine the Sabaean woman lying here in a hanging garden of hashish and gazing with the eyes of an Old Man of the Mountain on the landscape that in those days teemed with perfume trees?

Here and there, outside the walls, down below, we again see some abandoned Muslim houses. And within the city itself, like Palmyra, like so many others, the ruins have been occupied by successive villages, which in turn have been abandoned; perhaps the wells have dried up. Here and there,

[9] French architect, born in Paris (1886–1945), with a somewhat monumental style.

half-effaced traces of fields, for the field does not vanish more quickly than the house. Muslim houses are red, but what are the gutted white buildings, in the center of the ruins, which look like the nests of gigantic birds? Some of them, simply houses, warehouses perhaps. This whole region derived its wealth from the spice trade; between some now abandoned sections of wall the trappings of all the forms of worship of the ancient world were accumulated over the centuries. Veneration was piled up in those holes and that debris. . . . City of magician-queens and astrologers, how good to see you draw your fortune from the gods and to imagine still in the smell of your sand something of the fragrance of sacred substances! . . .

We go on circling. Over there, far back, a caravan making its way west comes into our field of vision. Loaded with what? Myrrh is still harvested today, and the camels that bring it to San'a carry back in exchange heavy packs of small padlocks; men here hardly worship any longer, and the price of religious perfumes has dropped. This city used to be considered one of the richest in Asia because it was the world's market for perfumes, because this bazaar, now completely destroyed, was the only one in the world to have enormous baskets of the seven essential perfumes: male incense, otyrax, frankincense, soud of India, rose-scented lebanon, myrtle, and lunar coriander.

How did that other ruin, with concentric walls, bristling with angles, serve the living men who bestirred themselves there, not, like ourselves, to dream, but to act? Was it an observatory? I have seen no ancient observatory; but the observatory of the Mongols in Delhi has those strange angles sticking out among the violet asters and the daisies, just as these do in the sand. If we were to land, would we find, engraved on those stones, calculations and trajectories of stars? Oh, if one could bring to each of one's friends a stone broken off around a horoscope, an unknown destiny signed by the Sabaean stars. . . .

It is too bad that it is impossible to land. A small tribe of blue and green lizards is probably bringing one of the world's most beautiful legends to an appropriate end here.

Instead of climbing in a spiral we gain altitude straight ahead of us, to the south, where there is another ruin, small and of little interest. It is five and three-quarters hours since we left; we have only four and a half hours of gas left in our tank. If the wind, which reduced our speed and which now should increase it, has not died down, if we reach the coast directly, all will be well. . . .

Here is the end of the desert, the place—eroded by its sand, glued to the core of the earth like a suction cup, with its flat and menacing force, with its blue-tinged or dazzling hollows—where it breaks against the ridges of the steppes.

Here the human landscape reasserts itself; here ends the planet made for other eyes than ours, for those of the red eagle of which we see only the shadow that follows our plane's shadow, for those of the fly, the queen of these solitudes where even time seems to burn as it trembles in the heat. Here are a few trees, something else, in short, besides those gigantic sand flowers and that fauna of animal skeletons.

And suddenly an immense sacrificial dagger appears, composed of volcanic rocks—curved, sparkling with black facets by the hundreds, like the obsidian knives of the ancient priests: the Valley of the Adites, where, according to legend, are buried the kings of Saba who are not in Marib. The crevices in those rocks, epic in their desolation, have for thousands of years accumulated dead kings and their warriors; their small slate tombs glitter in square flashes like the windows of a city in the setting sun. . . .

Half-sunk in the pallid steppes like a snake, this valley is attuned to man, like despair, like dirge music, like the Muslim songs that hundreds of thousands of camel drivers are singing at this very moment in the heat riddled with mirages and with flies. Many Arab travelers and a few whites, including Joseph Halévy, have seen these tombs at a greater or lesser distance. There are said to be treasures beneath those black cubes that surmount the bodies of kings, warriors, councillors, all kinds of rich men. No doubt they are deeply hidden, like those of the grandees of Egypt, and the unresourceful Bedouins have not yet found their way to the sepulchers.

For all those who have come, as for us who fly over it and can touch nothing, this valley of Tantalus remains mysteriously guarded, yields neither its precise spirit, inscriptions, and documents nor its heart of dreams, the key to the legends with which it is gorged as it once was with blood.

91

Tombs! All Asia is tombs. As though they had been sown across the desert and the steppes from this seed accumulated beneath us, I again see the tomb of Jahangir, in Lahore, where, behind a ravishing marble court covered with arabesques and full of squirrels, the arid clay mosque swells beneath its drowsy vultures—and central India is nothing more than a garnet tomb covered with cupolas, unceasingly washed by the endless rains of summer. And I see the tomb of Hafiz with its basins, its mulberry-colored grapes, and its opium smokers, and the tombs of Persepolis, and how many others! . . . Tomb of Tamerlane; tombs of the Chinese emperors with their innumerable doors, their monsters, and the whole guard of their sacred wood lost in the solitudes; endless rivers, full of ice or clay, where are hidden the bones of the Mongol emperors; and, not so far from here, in Damascus, the modest tomb of Saladin, where in a small garden gone wild again the finest figure of Islam is buried beneath the sweetbriers.

We have turned to get a better view of the tombs; suddenly a great bank of reddish mist appears before us, moving against the hostile wind; and it seems as if the sand, all at once lifted up like a hawk in midflight, wings outspread, rends all those rocks, crushed in its invisible talons.

But the wind drops down like a sail; here are the black stones again. Under those cubes swarm the dreams of ten centuries, enigmatic until some mission is able freely to examine the tombs. What truth lies hidden here, like the serpent of Balkis's coffin? And you, Queen, has your crypt been ransacked by the ravishers of tombs and does nothing remain of your bartered mummy but a fallen eye, bone and lapis, like the eye of the pharaoh's wife in the Cairo Museum, which was found in a tomb stairway full of mummies of alligators and of huge-eared cats? Five hundred million Christians and two hundred million Muslims have dreamed of you for centuries; shall we ever find the thin impressing that covered your face, with the clumsy hollow of the metal indented by the thumbs to keep the imprint of your still warm eyelids? Or perhaps some poorly incised trapezium like the one at the museum at Athens that bears the dusty and solemn label "Mask of Agamemnon"? . . .

Corniglion-Molinier takes up the story with his own record of the return flight:[10]

> The mysterious city of Queen Balkis has long since disappeared, but the vision of it still dances before our eyes. The sandstorm becomes almost red and the Valley of Kings is completely obliterated.
>
> Maillard leans toward me, showing the levels of the gas tanks:
>
> "We've got to turn back right away, captain. . . . We've been too lucky. It can't last. . . ."
>
> But what do the buffets of wind, the air pockets, the swirls of sand matter now! My arms play with the squalls and when our plane lists, makes a dive, or rears, I often "give her her head." I feel grateful to her for having behaved so well and enabled us to live this dream, and I leave her free to play as she likes with the capricious wind.
>
> Not since the war, I think, have I had so completely the sensation of the bond that unites the pilot to his plane, the sensation of the mysterious coupling that prolongs the balance, fingers and feet applied to the controls. These wings are not separate from me, they are extensions of myself, a part of me. I know, of course, that every pilot has something of this feeling, that he loves his plane with the love of every man for what enhances him. But today more than ever the plane that lists to the right touches my right shoulder, the plane that dips her nose tugs at my chest. It has not been sufficiently realized that the plane is the only craft that catches man by several of his senses: hearing, which warns the pilot of the slightest misfiring of the engine; sight, in all directions, for the plane advances, tips right and left, forward and back, and bears in herself the strange vulnerability that suddenly tranforms this hawk into a simple stone; touch, for the relation between the stick and the air is ten times more subtle than that of the wheel and the road, the wheel multiplies and the stick divides; and, more than anything else, the strange sense of equilibrium by which the pilot participates in the currents and the resistances of that russet mist.

10 From his unpublished diary of the expedition.

93

Meanwhile my fingers tighten on the controls, for the sandstorm flares up again and our gas supply is running low. . . . The duel of the mountains and the human mind continues tirelessly, more intense since we have succeeded, since we are no longer in passion but in absurdity; what would be the sense of a crash now? The fascination that drew us on is dead; we are in emptiness, in the determination to return with this single-engine plane, which, if it fell, could not even give the position of Saba by radio, since it has no transmitter.

A short break in the clouds enables me to calculate our drift approximately. The wind is in our favor. . . . A few last rifle shots to salute our departure, and I at last catch sight of the plain that precedes the Red Sea. At the same time certain vibrations worry me, but the tachometers are reassuring, and besides, the danger of the hostile mountains has disappeared. We now have only to fear the fanaticism of the Muslim warriors.

Through the windshield on which oil and sand have drawn a lunar, tormented landscape, a caricature of the one we have just overflown, I try to make out the coast. How long it takes to approach!

I keep turning around. From the back of the fuselage, Maillard, who has his eyes on me, cocks his head questioningly: "Can you see the shore?" "No, not yet"—and yet the wind cannot have turned.

We don't see the coast until we are right above it. I can at last signal to Maillard that we are leaving Arabia. A broad smile, and Maillard passes me, on a small card, a few strong and Rabelaisian words of congratulation. I have forgotten to tell you that the mechanics of the Djibouti squadron had briefed Maillard on certain customs of the Yemenite warriors, who can marry only after having demonstrated their bravery. The victor brings to his future father-in-law certain proofs of his victory that Maillard definitely had no inclination to furnish. . . .

I tell Maillard not to rejoice too soon, for the Red Sea is full of sharks.

The time appears very long. My body begins to ache and I no longer know what posture to assume to avoid the cramps that I get in this narrow cockpit. I envy Maillard and Malraux,

94

who can move and change places. . . . At last the far shore appears. We have hardly any gas left. Should we try to reach Djibouti? No, it is safer to land at Obock.

I arrive over the landing field and, no longer feeling my fatigue, my cramps, and my pains, I subject Maillard and Malraux, clutching their seats and smiling, to a fanciful descent—falling, propeller blocked, like a dead leaf, with sideslips and upside-down turns.

We extricate ourselves painfully from the fuselage and, a few paces from one another, looking up to the sky, we thank the gods for their benevolence, and bring our feeble contribution to the future fertility of this desert spot. . . .

The "viceroy" of Obock, who happens to be a former sergeant in the colonial service, presently arrives in great pomp, escorted by his personal bodyguards, a handful of Somali or Arab prisoners. He communicates the irrepressible gaiety of the Midi in his accent, in his gestures, in his hospitality, in his "You'll take a glass of *pastis!*" and, as we leave, the guard of honor, by main force, puts a live gazelle in our plane.

He is the only white man who lives in Obock when Henry de Monfreid is away. He goes to Djibouti two or three times a year, but it is seventeen hours by boat.

He is, in fact, quite happy. Sometimes he shouts and rolls his eyes fiercely. The prisoners' only response is a friendly smile. When I comment on this to him, he replies, "You understand, *mon capitaine,* I feed them well, much better than when they are free. . . . And you have seen the prison, how gay it is—all painted red, white, and blue!"

In Djibouti the day had passed unusually slowly for the members of the French Somali Coast Squadron. There was real anxiety among the staff at the base. Malraux, Corniglion, and Maillard were liked by all of them. A close comradeship had developed, and the adventure undertaken by the three explorers involved considerable risks. Esparre and Gambert awaited their return impatiently, hoping to see them come back safe and sound.

Its tanks once filled in Obock, the Farman made the short flight back to Djibouti without incident. Esparre, Gambert, and the whole squadron went to the airfield to meet the three adventurers.

"The expedition was completely successful," Corniglion told the delighted group as the explorers got down from the plane. The victory of the "Malraux expedition" became a victory for the whole squadron. Malraux and Corniglion immediately sent off the following telegram:

DJIBOUTI, MARCH 8, 7 P.M.
HAVE DISCOVERED LEGENDARY CITY OF SABA TWENTY TOWERS OR TEMPLES ARE STILL STANDING AT THE NORTHERN LIMIT OF THE ROUBAT-EL-KHALI HAVE TAKEN PHOTOS FOR IN-TRANSIGEANT.

Paul Gambert recalls that later they went strolling on the beach to relax. Malraux left the group to walk alone by the water's edge. A light sea wind ruffled his untidy hair. He was far from the others, but farther away in mind than in person, seeming to ponder and digest the events of the day, the remote wastes and the lost city over which he had flown. Gambert remarked on his abstraction to Corniglion, who simply replied, "Let him be. That's his way."

"His Majesty, the King of Kings, my august master the Emperor of Ethiopia, will be very happy to receive you," said the consul general of Ethiopia to Malraux and Corniglion the next day, "since the city you have discovered was the capital of his ancestress."

Seen from the sky, Addis Ababa was heralded by some blue lakes set in reddish mountains; then suddenly the capital appeared between its stone cliffs, forming a blue green spot on the ground, like a lake.

Its name means "the new flower." It is a flower planted at an altitude of seventy-five hundred feet, in limpid air, in a grandiose and fertile country where the nights are mild and the water abundant.

Horse-drawn sulkies crisscrossed the streets of the city instead of taxis. A broad avenue climbed toward the center. Police officers regulated the traffic at the crossings, which included donkeys loaded with sacks. Some Ethiopian women in tight, printed dresses and perched on high-heeled shoes had defrizzed hair. Others kept the traditional costume, a draped robe that leaves one shoulder exposed, bare feet, and the tall headdress surrounded by a veil. The men wore white trousers that fit the calves so tightly that, according to legend, they are never removed. They too draped themselves in a white toga, the *chama*. There were storekeepers or civil servants in European-style business suits, in contrast to the country dignitary mounted on a mule, sporting a black cape and a large saber, who was attended by a file of personal armed guards and servants.

The city is full of palaces and villas smothered in flowers, of earth hovels, and open-air markets where squatting women still spend a day trying to sell three bananas or a couple of eggs. Famished-looking dogs, flocks of goats, and camels roam freely, and hyenas slip in at night.

Addis Ababa is also a twenty-five-thousand-acre forest of eucalyptus trees. The fine fragrance that rises in the evening, the blue smoke whose wisps dissolve in the pure sky, is the smoke of eucalyptus wood burning in thousands of homes where the *ongera* is being cooked—a griddle cake on which will be served *wat,* the national dish, cut-up chicken in a highly spiced sauce.

At six o'clock every evening the bells of all the churches in town peal forth. Traffic in the streets comes to a standstill, all passersby turn in the direction of the imperial palace, the Gulbi, and observe silence. This is the daily homage to the emperor. It lasts two minutes.

The imperial palace is an Eden—large trees, lawns, fountains, an avenue of mimosas, and wonderful flower beds, in a country where flowers are abundant and beautiful. The geraniums grow to a height of seven feet. At the entrance to the park a magnificent lion with a black mane walks about dragging his chain. The emperor collects lions, Abyssinian lions, which are the world's finest, and they sleep in a row of cages in the palace garden.

A lion in effigy—immense, wearing a crown—stands on a square in Addis Ababa. It is the lion of Judah, one of Haile Selassie's most honored titles.

"It took us two hours and fifty minutes to reach the capital," Corniglion-Molinier has recalled. "As we arrived above the airfield, which is also the racetrack, we discovered that it is a decidedly many-purpose field, for today it was being used as a polo ground.

"The Minister Plenipotentiary of France and Madame de Reffye welcomed us and took charge of us, while the head of the Ethiopian air force, a compatriot of ours, Sergeant Major Correyer, took the rest of the crew in his car.

"The reception given by the minister for foreign affairs of Ethiopia was conducted with great dignity and took quite a scholarly turn. The minister was, in fact, his country's chief historian, and Malraux proceeded to ask such precise questions that the minister, flattered to find a

European showing such interest in his work, dwelt at length on the bonds of friendship that united Ethiopia to France.

"We were received in His Majesty's small palace. One of the king's great daily ceremonies involved his going from the grand palace to the small palace or from the small palace to the grand palace. At those times the wide road connecting the two palaces is filled with dignitaries on horseback followed by their men-at-arms, and two to three thousand persons accompany the imperial automobile, of French make, which moves slowly at the pace of a man walking."

Haile Selassie is the 255th monarch of the world's oldest dynasty, and the grandeur of his lineage required considerable protocol from those who came to visit him.

"It is very regrettable," the minister plenipotentiary of France told the explorers, "that you have no cutaways or top hats, for the protocol for several months now has required them for audiences with His Majesty."

The cars bringing Corniglion and Malraux arrived at the palace by different roads, "the guard that was to do the honors dividing into two camps of differing persuasions," as Corniglion explained it later. "One favored the minister's car because of the top hat, the other chose the car in which Maillard and Correyer, by their imposing stature and their uniformed driver, gave off an undeniable importance.

"We entered the throne room. The king cut an impressive figure, seated on his settee raised on a small dais to which three steps gave access. He welcomed us, all smiles, and said to Malraux:

" 'French is for me a second mother tongue.'

"The French minister introduced us in a charming manner, making lavish use of hyperbole in accordance with the best Oriental traditions. If, as he said, I was one of the greatest pilots of modern times, Malraux for his part had received awards from all the academies, and Maillard was engineer-in-chief of the expedition. As for Esparre and Gambert, who had flown in with us, they noted with a certain pride the importance their two old Potez planes could assume far from Djibouti.

"His Majesty, after some words of congratulation, told us he was by no means surprised by our discovery, for he had always been sure of the existence of the city where his illustrious ancestress was buried.

"We left the palace with the same court formalities that had attended our arrival and, accompanied by the French consul, visited the city. When I expressed my surprise at the number of doors on which hung a curtain with a red cross, I was told that this insignia indicated neither hospitals nor drugstores, but courtesans' abodes.

"Malraux created something of a stir in the French and other European circles of the city. His recent Prix Goncourt had made him known even here. He bought several strange paintings, with iridescent colors, by Ethiopian painters. He seemed to know all about the figures, and explained their meaning, revealing their beauty, to his friends."

Then came the moment to leave Addis Ababa. The engine of the light Farman was not meant to develop its full power at such an altitude. The runway was short, the ground heavy. As he took up position at the end of the runway, Corniglion-Molinier, at the controls, shouted to his companions to come forward and press themselves against him, consolidating their weight at the front of the plane. There was a hump on the ground as sole indication of the end of the runway, "and I knew that all the eucalyptus trees had names—those of the pilots who had crashed into them."

At the very last moment, Corniglion lifted the plane off the ground, just missing the hump and the trees, then opened the throttle and took on altitude. "We were all shoulder to shoulder, watching the maneuver," Paul Gambert reports, "and Malraux, without being a pilot, impassive in the face of danger, behaved like a true airman."

Two days after their return to Djibouti, the guests of the squadron bade their comrades farewell and returned to France. Malraux handed over to Captain Esparre for safekeeping several lengths of film on which could be clearly seen the tiered structures of the ancient city, so different from those now found in Arabia and in the Middle East. Thanks to this precaution, even if the English authorities were to search the plane during their stopover in Egypt and confiscate the remaining films, the evidence that their expedition had been crowned with success could still be brought back to France by boat.

"Via Massaua and Port Sudan, Tripoli, Tunis, Bône, Algiers, Fez, Barcelona, and Lyons," Corniglion wrote in his diary, "with wind, hail, snow, mist, and rain vying for the honor of escorting us, our return was a difficult one. . . ." In his *Antimémoires* Malraux has told at length of the terrible storm that beset them on the last stages of their return trip. He called it "the experience of a lifetime." But they came home safely after all.

"Not with impunity will the gods of Sheba let themselves be aroused from their long sleep," wrote Malraux on his return to Paris. The very day that the first photographs of the lost city appeared in

MALRAUX

L'Intransigeant, ibn-Saud's army marched on San'a. Malraux's analysis of the situation follows:

Not much is known in France about this little sultan, who has something about him of a prophet or an ancient conqueror, who set out with his puritans to capture the holy cities, and presently all Arabia. Today he controls more than half of it and he seems to be the only one who could attempt to unify it. . . .

The last dispatches tell us that after having taken Hodelda, he has just been brought to a stop in the mountains that we overflew and that have stopped the Turks for so long. But he can attack San'a from the north, and this he will not fail to do.

If he is defeated, Saba will remain what it is; the present Imam [of Yemen] will be all the less disposed to undertake an expedition in the desert, for the honor of archaeology, as his relations with the dissidents seem to be those of a benevolent hostility. If ibn-Saud is victorious, on the other hand, it means the end of dissidence; his well-armed troops, partly composed of Bedouins, will transform the dissidents into vassal tribes. Will Arabia then open up? It is possible. I doubt it, however, for ibn-Saud's strength reposes in part on the purity of his faith; it is more probable that some Anglo-Arab agreement will transform Arabia into another Tibet. And Saba will remain a forbidden city. But perhaps a mission—if not English, and infidel, at least Indo-Muslim, formed in Delhi or in Calcutta by Western scholars—will be able to go and read the inscriptions and bring all that neglected mystery into history.

What can be expected of this?

I do not wish to begin a discussion that can be of interest only to specialists. Let this suffice: on the one hand the exploration currently being carried on in Yemen is bringing us knowledge of the history of several Sabaean kingdoms and of a land of Saba, almost nothing of which remains, other than present-day Marib; on the other hand, legend and the Arab historians and geographers assure us that a Queen of Sheba did exist and that her city lies abandoned in the desert. The transfer of the name of a city to another is in fact not rare in this region. Whether it is called Ubar, Saba, or Raiz, this is the

100

city. The queen who, according to the Bible and the Koran, visited Solomon can moreover only have reigned in the tenth century B.C., at which period no queen reigned over the Sabaean cities that have so far been explored, all of which were governed by kings.

It is up to a future mission to read the inscriptions that will either modify or preserve the history of the kingdom of Saba. As for us, what we expected from this city, beyond any questions of archaeology, was a fine human adventure, and this it has given us.

We are told that disciplinary action might be taken against Corniglion (it is more difficult to take such action against me, who am neither an officer, nor decorated, nor a pilot—and consequently do not have to ask for future overflight permits) for having overflown Yemen without the country's authorization. I refuse to believe it. There are and there can be no such things as overflight permits for Yemen, where France has no diplomatic representation and which is not a member of the League of Nations. We were flying on our own responsibility without any official status, not even informing the governor of Djibouti of our project. If we had crashed, so much the worse for us! And it could not be otherwise. Finally, Saba is in dissident territory and not under Yemen's authority. Are we also expected to ask for overflight authorization of all the independent emirs of the peninsula? So much for that. . . .

In India, from which the mission that will bring Saba into history will perhaps set out, I have passed through Amber. It is an ancient Mongolian city. From Jaipur, the rose-colored limestone city where hundreds of melancholy monkeys seek coolness by moving with the shadow round the Palace of the Wind, an avenue leads to Amber, which has been without water for two hundred years. The temple, the red marble palace, and those roofless houses in which tufts of wild flowers grow in the corridors—everything reverts to nothingness amid a profusion of plant life, with grotesque stone masks on the walls swept by the branches of palm trees, with the monkeys sitting on the window ledges and the flight of peacocks suddenly overwhelmed by the silence. I thought of Amber as the shadow of a hawk glided away from that city of Saba about

MALRAUX

which the ancient geographers used to say that one stepped
into its luxury and its perfumes as into the sea. Babylon,
Nineveh—sterile mounds; Persepolis—scattered columns where
the wasps buzz! Saba will probably have to return to the desert
like those great buried names, and those fleshless monuments
will be once again forbidden to almost all European eyes. . . .

"Saba, or Marib, whatever one likes to call it," wrote Malraux in
his *Antimémoires,* "is still in the hands of the dissidents. They held
out against the emirs, against the Yemenites, against the Egyptians, and,
what was still harder, against the oilmen, whose expedition quite recently failed."

"I find it quite astonishing," Malraux told me last summer, "that
thirty years should have passed and, to my knowledge, no expedition
has even tried to reach Marib. We shall speak of it someday."

NOTE BY FRANCOIS BALSAN OF THE
SOCIETE DES EXPLORATEURS

The places over which Malraux flew were already quite well known
to land explorers. In 1589, Fathers Paez and Monserrate, captured on
the coast of the Hadhramaut, were brought to the Imam of Yemen, and
on their way traveled through the dead cities and saw the Temple of
Balkis in Marib. In 1843, Théodore Arnaud was the first to investigate
the two ancient capitals of Marib and Kharibah (Sirwah); he brought
away fifty-six inscriptions. Joseph Halévy visited Marib in 1870, and in
1884 Edward Glazer worked there fruitfully.

André Malraux and Corniglion-Molinier have to their credit the
first overflight of the territory, which gave them a perspective of the
area, an achievement the more remarkable because a forced landing
among those savage tribesmen would have exposed them to great perils.

It was not until August, 1951, that real excavations began, with the
expedition led by Wendell Phillips. The Temple of Balkis (an ellipse
330 meters in circumference) was cleared from the sand and splendid
statues of stone and bronze were revealed. But everything came to an
abrupt and violent end in 1952, after countless demonstrations of bad
faith by the Yemenite authorities and, finally, outright menaces of death
on the part of the tribesmen. Abandoning all the fruits of their expedition, the party managed to escape to the Aden Protectorate in the last of
their trucks that were operable, hotly pursued by askaris on camelback.

102

6.

Spain: A Revolutionary Ideal

Nineteen thirty-four was for André Malraux a triumphal year—large printings of his books, money, notoriety. The notoriety brought by the Prix Goncourt is often a fugitive one. For one Marcel Proust how many prizewinners have fallen back into obscurity! But Malraux's achievement was already sufficiently outstanding for his work to have taken its place in the century. He had forged a lyrical style.

André Gide, who was of Protestant origin through his father, the jurist Paul Gide, and Catholic through his mother, already exerted a considerable influence over the French intelligentsia. He immediately "adopted" Malraux. Admiration being contagious, Gide's followers— who constituted the most "closed" group in the Paris literary world—also adopted Malraux.

The history of the Gide-Malraux friendship, with the literary climate of the *Nouvelle Revue Française* as its background, might well be the subject of a whole book. It could be said of the two men that they were constantly being brought together by what separated them.

No writer of this century (except perhaps Drieu La Rochelle or Hemingway[1]) has been so attached to women as Malraux. With this difference, however, that Malraux has never committed himself to writing a romantic novel, whereas the other two have given women the place of honor in their work.

While Gide was a knowing and sensitive observer of women, he was not sexually attracted to them, and became instead prophet, theoretician, and practitioner of homosexuality. An age difference of thirty years separated him from Malraux, who could have been his

[1] Drieu, that country gentleman whom François Mauriac characterized rather summarily as "the most depraved young man in Paris," wrote a preface to *Farewell to Arms* that introduced Ernest Hemingway to French readers with masterly insight and skill.

son—a son of whom Gide would have been very proud. While Gide loved men, Malraux preferred all humanity, and his relations with men took the form rather of a "virile fraternity" that he has eloquently evoked in some of the most vibrant passages in his books, from *Les Conquérants* to *Antimémoires.*

Gide secretly suspected Malraux of "erotic misogyny," no doubt because of his prefaces to the French editions of D. H. Lawrence's *Lady Chatterley's Lover* and Faulkner's *Sanctuary* (which, we must not forget, is the clinical but nevertheless romantic account of a rape); or because of his study on Laclos and *Les Liaisons dangereuses,* which was included in the *Tableau de la littérature française du XVIIIᵉ siècle.*[2]

Gide's homosexuality did not disturb Malraux. The two men had several grounds for a meeting of minds—diffidence, style, political views, and moral rigor—and their friendship remained steadfast through the years.

Malraux did not pull the wool over Gide's eyes, he fascinated him, and Gide made many references to the fact: "Every time [Malraux] opens his mouth, genius speaks. . . . Oscar Wilde used to claim that he had put his talent into his work and his genius into his life. Malraux puts his genius into everything: into his life, to begin with, and afterward into his work. . . . Ingres used to say, 'With talent one does what one can. With genius one does what one wants.' With his genius Malraux does what he wants." A book would be needed to collect Gide's laudatory comments on Malraux.

The unanimity of praise for Malraux, in fact, ranged from *L'Humanité,* the Communist daily, to *L'Echo de Paris,* the rightist bourgeois paper. The reservations were mainly social and political. The critics were enchanted by the writer, but disturbed by the man.

L'Humanité wrote: "His frenzied individualism asserts itself by finding its stimulus in the movement of the masses, but is completely indifferent to these masses, to their suffering, to their hopes."

And François Mauriac, in *L'Echo de Paris:* "Imagine a man who since his adolescence has taken his stand against the laws and for whom to live is to be in opposition. . . . Shall we see him climb, one by one, the rungs that the astute old world has placed beneath the feet of young

---

[2] Published by Editions Gallimard (*NRF*) in 1937, with an introduction by André Gide. If Malraux's study dealt with Choderlos de Laclos, Drieu La Rochelle drew a portrait of Diderot as "the first journalist of modern times" and the father of the literature of current events, in which individuals as different as Hemingway, Dos Passos, Sartre, Camus, Simone de Beauvoir, and Drieu himself were to distinguish themselves.

conquerors and shall we someday see that tragic face expand in the smile of the satisfied man?"

One could almost believe it, for a new woman had appeared in André Malraux's life. He met her in the offices of Gallimard, his publisher. She was a young and attractive novelist named Josette Clotis, whose first book, *Le Temps vert,* was published by the *NRF* in 1932.[3] The manuscript, according to Malraux, was sensitively written, evoking wild fruits with an acid taste, in which youth—radiant, feverish, tense—burst from every page. We know that Malraux could never do without women. Henceforth a woman, Josette Clotis, could not do without him and his presence, which she described as "a permanent and paradoxical enchantment."

When she had come to Paris from the country, she had been taken on by the women's magazine *Marianne.* There she initiated a column that she called "Under the Lamp," because as a little girl she had been charmed and fascinated by an enormous oil lamp that used to stand on the dining room table at the home of her best friend, Edith.

Her first reporting assignment for *Marianne* was to go and interview Yvette Labrousse, who had just been elected Miss France—and was, some years later, to become the Begum Aga Khan.

"What can I say about her?" Josette lamented. "She is so beautiful!" For Josette beauty was a mark of nobility. She herself was not conventionally beautiful, despite her gray green eyes and shining chestnut hair. Her features were regular but strong; they gave her face great character and charm. She was tall, about Malraux's height, and enjoyed buying attractive clothes, especially tweed suits, which she wore with an air. She was extremely feminine, however, and had indulged herself at Lanvin's one day by buying a model dress because it was named "Béatrice," after Beatrice Portinari, the beautiful Florentine whom Dante celebrated in *The Divine Comedy.*

"I shall get married," she used to say, "and I shall have children, a girl I shall call Corinne, like Madame de Staël's Corinne, and a son, Guillaume, like Apollinaire."

Colors were very important to Josette. She loved blues, all blues, and detested what she called aggressive shades. In her room she had blue curtains hung up at the windows, like fishing nets. "In that way I see the sea," she said, "but not just any sea. Mine. The Mediterranean." She liked everything beautiful, but was allergic to music. And yet, if

[3] Malraux wrote a preface for the book.

in a book she had read there was a verse or a refrain of a song, she would buy the record and play it again and again, because it reminded her of the book.

"I first met her as a child," her best friend, Edith Tissier, relates. "She was ten years old, and I was eleven. Her mother was from Montpellier, her father from the Pyrénées-Orientales. He was a civil servant, working in the tax office of Chevilly, in the Loiret, when we met. Her mother, who was partially crippled, had difficulty in keeping up with the household chores. That is why Josette went to boarding school in the Orléans *lycée*. Very much alone, she had a doll that she worshiped, and that she called Edith. When we met, in the boarding school, we became friends. As my name was Edith, too, Josette almost immediately abandoned her doll.

"Already at ten she thought only of 'the other side of the wall.' Her imagination was boundless. She lived in a dream. When she liked something, or when she was attracted to someone, she would invent all kinds of stories around that object or that person. These, she said, were 'moonlight tra-la-las.'

"She would say to me, 'Why do you do your math lessons, Edith? You don't understand anything. Neither do I. Do as I do, hand in a blank paper,' and I obeyed her, for she liked and knew how to command, and she liked to make decisions for others.

"Three times, for instance, she took me to the movies to see the same film, *Anna Karenina,* with Greta Garbo.

"Her French teacher told her one day that she didn't know how to write, that she had no talent. Josette was furious, and told me, 'When I leave the *lycée* I'll write a novel and I'll send that professor my first book.' Which is just what she did.

"Later, when we were young girls, we would go to Banyuls,[4] close to the Spanish border, for our summer vacations. I remember Josette often saying, 'Friendship must not be a tyranny. You go walking in the woods because you like to, and I go and dip my feet in the water. There must be no constraint. Each one must be free. That is what friendship, true friendship, is. The boys, too, must forget that we are women. We must not be that kind of a problem to them.'

"She was romantic and sentimental, and all men fell in love with her. She needed to be sought after, she liked to feel herself desired, but she had no preferences.

"She had one passion, which was literature. She loved life, she

[4] A coastal village near Perpignan.

106

loved to be on the go, to travel. She needed to wake up with a suitcase within arm's reach. She had mastered the art of making the unreal live, of making it real."

At the age of fourteen Josette had read Jeanne Sandelion's *L'Age ou l'on croit aux Iles* ("The Age When One Believes in Islands"); it was a romantic novel, which so impressed her that in order to get the full impact of what it was like to live on an island she actually went to the Balearic Islands to do so.

It was understandable that this imaginative young woman immediately fell in love with Malraux; he fascinated her by his intensity, the pitch at which he lived and cared about life, smoking incessantly, making speeches at leftist rallies, traveling widely—the sales of *La Condition humaine* had made him rich—writing and talking with a brilliance that amazed his audiences. His tales of adventure dazzled her. So did what she later described as "his combination of intelligence warring, sometimes, with egoism and a hypersensitive susceptibility."

And Malraux, won over by her air of timidity, her womanly grace, by the delicate perfection of her face, her lips, still fresh as an unripe fruit, could no longer do without Josette, whom he called his *source vive*—his living spring.

In October, 1935, a little more than a year after Malraux's visit to Ethiopia, Mussolini's tanks and planes invaded the country without any previous declaration of war. Addis Ababa, the capital, had already fallen when Haile Selassie presented himself before the League of Nations, on June 30, 1936, to plead his cause. It was on this occasion that he spoke these prophetic words:

"Outside the kingdom of God, there is on this earth no tradition superior to others. . . . Are the states [of the league] going to create a terrible precedent by yielding to force? It is international morality itself which is at stake."

The emperor aroused admiration by his presence and his sincerity, but he pleaded in vain. The League of Nations was unwilling as well as unable to take effective action. Ethiopia was annexed by Italy; Haile Selassie went into exile.

Malraux now figured on all the antifascist committees, and took a leading role in them, along with André Gide, who shared many of his sympathies. But events were to call Malraux beyond the Pyrenees, to resume his role of revolutionary fighter.

By the end of 1935, the Spanish center-right party that had been in power since the general elections of 1933 could no longer hold the country together. New elections were held in February, 1936, and the Popular Front—so-called after a similar French coalition led by Socialist Léon Blum—won by a substantial majority. It comprised a large group of left-wing parties and trade unions, which included Syndicalists, Socialists, and Communists, who had banded together to ensure electoral victory for the Left. Manuel Azaña, who had become a popular hero and the pivot of progressive hopes, emerged as their leader, and in May he was elected president of the Republic.

Soon, however, fresh disturbances began, on an even larger scale than before. There were uprisings by peasants, who seized landholdings from absentee landlords and stubbornly refused to move off them. There was rioting in the cities, with many cases of arson (directed principally at properties owned by rightists and by religious organizations—which in Spain were often one and the same) and even of outright murder. The new premier, Santiago Quiroga, simply could not cope with such chaos.

It was understandable that the government's feeble attempts at reform made little impression—the country was ripe for rebellion. In such conditions it was also understandable that the Spanish fascist movement, the Falange, greatly increased its strength, rallying to its cause many who were weary of extremist violence and anxious to restore some form of law and order at almost any cost.

One of these was General Francisco Franco, the ex-chief of the Spanish general staff, who tried without success to get the Republican government to proclaim a state of emergency. The government not only refused, but exiled Franco to a remote post in the Canary Islands. Rightist opposition then began to group under the leadership of General José Sanjurjo y Sacanell and of José Calvo Sotelo, chief of the Monarchist party.

On July 13, Calvo Sotelo was assassinated. Five days later, the troops of Spanish Morocco mutinied, and the garrisons in Spain rose up to join what rapidly became an insurrection. Franco immediately issued a manifesto, flew to Morocco, and put himself at the head of the troops. Civil war had broken out.

Malraux was to fling himself recklessly into the battle of the republic assaulted by fascism. Several of the leftist Spanish leaders were his friends, notably the Socialist leader, Francisco Largo Caballero. He flew at once to Spain, perceived the crippling shortage of planes and pilots in the Republican air force, and set himself to build up a foreign air squadron. He knew two French government ministers—Pierre Cot and Léo Lagrange—well enough to hope that he could persuade France to release planes to Spain "unofficially." For pilots, he would have to rely on volunteers and on mercenaries.

A couple of weeks after the rebellion broke out, he ran into Captain Jean Esparre, who had just been assigned to an aerial observation group in Toulouse. Esparre reports:

"On a fine summer afternoon, two aviators in flight dress, parachutes dangling from their belts, came into my office—Corniglion-Molinier, followed by Malraux. I had not seen him since the Djibouti expedition and thought he looked tired. They had come to ask me to have the mechanics at the center check the planes they were convoying to Republican Spain. To my great regret, the orders that I had received prevented me from rendering them this service. The Léon Blum ministry had decided to adopt a nonintervention policy. And yet Malraux and Corniglion had my full sympathy—if not political (the army did not engage in politics in those already distant times), at least my human sympathy.

"I offered them my personal car to reach Toulouse. But they refused the offer and went to join their small squadron, which flew off in the direction of Republican Spain."

In September, Malraux's friend Largo Caballero formed a war ministry composed of Socialists, Republicans, Communists, and, later, Anarchists.

A month later, the Nationalist "defense junta" in Burgos was supplanted by Franco and his "technical junta," and Franco was named chief of state. The Nationalist forces consisted of the regular army, which included a large part of the navy, the Falangists, the Monarchists, and the Carlists. They had the support of Germany, which was to send its Condor Legion, and of Italy with its Blackshirts. The really considerable help given Franco by his fellow dictators was ultimately to be responsible for his success.

In the Republican camp, the motley assortment of Socialists, Communists, Trotskyists, Anarchists, Socialist and Syndicalist trade unionists, members of certain liberal middle-class parties, and Basque and Catalan nationalists was supported by the Soviet Union, which sent men and planes, and by the volunteer International Brigades. These were created seven weeks after the outbreak of civil war, and idealistic young Europeans and Americans flocked to Spain to join them. Malraux was to become the chief of the International Flying Squadron in support of Spain, a kind of private foreign legion whose pilots he recruited and for which he somehow managed to find the planes.

That October, Gaston Vedel, the director of Air France in Barcelona, saw a whole French squadron fly in, six or seven brand-new observation and bombing planes. Their commander was André Malraux, lean, gaunt, eyes flashing. He had come to fill his planes' gas tanks.

"As I was getting one million liters a month and I only needed a hundred thousand liters to keep 'my' planes flying, nine hundred thousand liters went to the Republicans, who had my support.

"With their tanks filled, Malraux and his squadron could take off for Madrid, where they were heading to join the Republican forces."

The following month Largo Caballero and his government transferred their headquarters to Valencia, leaving the besieged Madrid in charge of a junta presided over by General José Miaja.

In the course of convoying planes to Madrid, Malraux made several landings in Barcelona. On his way back to Paris he used to take the regular Air France flight.

A former French pursuit pilot has given me a fascinating account of what it was like to serve with Malraux in Spain. He was one of the very few survivors of the bombing squadron, which sustained severe losses of men and matériel:

Having asked for and obtained leave without pay from the French air force, I reached Albacete on November 7, 1936, via Toulouse and Alicante, and placed myself at the disposal of the commander of the bombing squadron there, *Coronel* André Malraux.

The personnel of the squadron, including the *patron,* was lodged in the Regina Hotel, the lobby of which was darkened by the smoke of innumerable cigarettes and the air redolent with the powerful smell of Spanish olive oil.

There Malraux and his men—Frenchmen, Swiss, Czechs —lived in perfect community.[5] The meals, of which the menus were composed of local dishes, were eaten round an immense table, which was also used for briefings and all our meetings.

The day I arrived, lunch was already being served when I

[5] Mercenaries outnumbered volunteers in Malraux's little command. Incidentally, his close associates were all French and of similar political sympathies.

presented myself to the *coronel,* who simply said, "Sit down. You're going to eat."

Although Malraux kept us to a familiar, almost familial discipline, which contrasted with the immense disorder that prevailed in the Spanish Republican air force and with the harshness in the Soviet squadrons—where the base commanders went so far as to kick their men in the buttocks, including the pilots, as I personally witnessed—we all said *tu* to our *patron.* And even in the heat of the inevitable bawlings out, Malraux was never ill-natured and carefully refrained from humiliating or hurting feelings. On the contrary, he impressed us as kind and fair, and we obeyed him eagerly.

He was always friendly, and while he liked to chat with us, he never broached literary subjects. Literature, to be sure, was for most of us the least of our worries. On the other hand, apart from the briefings and the usual work of the squadron, we constantly argued about the future of the Spanish republic, events in France, the future of the Popular Front. We did not understand the policy of nonintervention being practiced by the government of Léon Blum, who was himself the head of the Socialist party. Nor in fact did we understand the policy of England, which had also decided not to intervene.

Malraux quite lucidly anticipated World War II. How many times I have heard him say, "War is inevitable."

Once, though, Malraux brought up the question of my political affiliation.

"Are you a Communist?" he asked me.

That day André Marty, the French Communist deputy and general commissar of the International Brigades, had made a speech to the volunteer troops, saying among other things that "the internationals who turned around and ran would be shot on the spot."

When I answered no—in fact I belonged to no political party—Malraux said to me, "That so-and-so Marty! . . . Why doesn't he start by shooting the Spaniards who turn around and run?"

That day I became firmly convinced that Malraux was not a Communist, notwithstanding the accepted belief that he was, which had existed ever since the affairs that he had been mixed up in in China and that he never spoke of.

For that matter, among the Frenchmen in the international air force very few belonged to the Communist party. Most of them undoubtedly had leftist views, like myself; but most of the fellows were there because they loved a brawl. There were also those who had signed up because of the money—those we today would call *les affreux* ("the hideous ones").

One of these was a former pilot of World War I, who had enlisted at seventeen and came out with seven authenticated victories to his credit, the son of a fine family, who had made and lost a fortune in the United States and later became a car thief. He enlisted in our ranks on his release from prison.

He was a real daredevil, whom no one could match in dive-bombing—it was he who sank the cruiser *España* in one single swoop. He also used to convoy planes between France and Republican Spain. Sometimes he would fly three planes in a single day from Toulouse to Barcelona. For each plane transported, he got a premium of twenty-five thousand francs, which enabled him to get back on his feet and buy a hotel a short time later near the Porte Maillot in Paris. But once again he lost all his money, and finally he committed suicide in a hotel room on the rue Pierre Charron—just on the eve of coming into a big inheritance.

He committed suicide, but most of my other comrades in the squadron died in combat in the sky over Spain or elsewhere in the course of World War II, and I do believe that of the Albacete squadron Malraux and I are today the sole survivors. . . .

A fact that I consider symptomatic of Malraux's attitude toward communism is the choice he made in detaching two of his pilots to a Soviet squadron: one, a Swiss, was a strictly orthodox Communist; the other, myself, was not.

This choice, I was convinced, was deliberate, because it enabled him to introduce into the mysterious and hermetically sealed world of Russian aviation an observer who had no Marxist allegiance, and he could thus freely study the men's daily lives, their weapons, and their tactics. After spending a month there, I had a good insight into the iron discipline that prevailed in Alcantarilla and was able to note especially the characteristics of their planes and arms, which were greatly superior to ours. Their firepower was prodigious: four machine guns in the wings firing at an extraordinary rate—two thousand rounds a minute—ten vertical bombs and four fifty-kilo bombs under the wings. But the very morning of the day planned for an operation in which I was dying to participate, the Russians, ever suspicious—and for good reason—decided to send me back to my squadron. My Swiss comrade, even though a Communist, had no better luck, and bitterly reproached me. "It's because of you," he said, "that we've been sent back."

Of course I gave Malraux a report on everything I had seen, from the civilian outfits, "brightened" by red, pink, or green shirts with matching neckties, to the training of the pilots, who had to be able to drill out a plate of sheet iron in a single passage of their machine guns.

Our squadron was a bombing formation. It had five or six French Potez 540 planes. Malraux had already participated in bombing missions on the Madrid front, when he was stationed at Alcalá de Henares—at Medellín a section of General Asensio's column was almost entirely decimated by the Malraux squadron—and he allowed no one else to lead his men in combat.

Although he knew nothing about piloting, and his qualifications as a navigator and a bomber were rudimentary, he assumed the role of flight commander with a bravery that amounted to heedlessness.

One day, when his group had been moved from Albacete to a makeshift base situated between Valencia and Madrid, he ordered me to take up a pilot with dual controls.

"Take this guy," he told me, "and let him take the controls."

After circling a bit, I realized that this guy, who didn't even have a pilot's license—which he finally admitted—was almost hopelessly incompetent. Having landed, I said as much to Malraux, who ordered me again, "I'm telling you to let him take over, you have to let him take over! He has to be ready this evening to go and bomb Saragossa. What is more, I am the aircraft commander and I'm going with him!"

My arguments and pleas had no effect. I had to let the *type* take over. Before he left with Malraux that evening, I nevertheless took the precaution of having the olive trees that barred the end of the airstrip torn up. Unfortunately there was no way of removing the huge water trough that "closed" the end of the runway.

Malraux and his novice pilot flew off in the night to carry out their mission. The colonel dropped his bombs by sight— the plane had lost its bombsight—and somehow or other they managed to head back to the field, where I was anxiously waiting to see the outcome of the mad escapade of a pilot who could hardly fly and a flight commander who knew nothing at all about piloting an aircraft.

When they finally appeared in the distance, fortunately ignored by Spanish, Italian, or German pursuit planes, I gave a sigh of relief—too soon, though, because the plane landed full on the stone water trough that I had been unable to remove. Without harming the crew, fortunately, but with considerable damage to the aircraft.

"You see," Malraux said to me, as he squeezed his way out of the smashed-in cockpit, "you see, he not only got there but he came back. He really shows promise."

Typical Malraux!

In combat his face was a mask of courage and coolness. "Fear," he said, "must be stripped of its powers. If a chief shows that he is afraid, his men are terrified. That leads to panic, from which nothing good can come."

He was living at that time in a castle; its owner had been shot by the Republicans, but his widow had been allowed to remain there. It was a poor sort of castle, though, where the colonel slept on a camp bed and feasted, like his men, on the regular mess diet—chick-peas, rice, and heavy Catalonian wine.

Was he already thinking of writing *L'Espoir?* Quite possibly. That may have been what he was working on when he scribbled at odd moments. He always had some loose sheets of paper handy.

His relations with the Spaniards were excellent, although the Spanish flyers were not too fond of us. As for the Russians, we never saw them. They kept very much to themselves. We didn't see too much of the International Brigade volunteers, either. I remember, though, witnessing the landing in Albacete of five thousand men of all nationalities who, without being given the order, formed ranks in the station court and then, falling into step and singing "La Marseillaise" in all languages, marched to their barracks. We were not used to so martial a spectacle. The Spanish Republican troops made a rather poor showing most of the time. The Spanish aviators were not much better. The best pilots, and their officers, had stayed with the Nationalists.

In February, 1937, my leave was up and I returned to France, though I did see Malraux subsequently several times when he was convoying equipment between Paris and Barcelona, via Toulouse, Graúlhet, or Lézignan.

On the Nationalist side, Franco was proclaimed *caudillo* in the month of April, 1937, and the various parties were united under his leadership.

Among the Republicans, on the contrary, there was constant trouble between Largo Caballero and the Communists. Fights broke out in the streets of Barcelona, with government supporters on one side and Trotskyists and Catalan Anarchists on the other.

Between the French-Spanish frontier and Barcelona there was a whole succession of roadblocks. These were guarded by Republicans from different political groups, Marxist-Leninists, Anarchists, Communists, and others, and sometimes they would fire on one another. If a car succeeded in passing the roadblock guarded by the Communists, the Anarchists would stop it, and so on. There was, however, one infallible open sesame, and Gaston Vedel, the Air France director in Barcelona, knew the secret. Every week he was sent from Paris huge rations of tobacco, of which the Republicans were deprived. "In this way I never had the slightest difficulty in traveling between Barcelona and the frontier," he explains blandly.

"One day I saw General Weygand arrive in the airport. He had come incognito to inform himself what was happening, and stayed only a few hours. When he left he said to me, 'I'll tell you something. I'm a man of the Right. Well, if they would listen to me in Paris, France would get into this war. We would support the Republicans and we would win it with them. And do you know why we ought to support them? To avoid a subsequent war, which might well turn into a world conflict.'"

In May, 1937, Juan Negrín succeeded Largo Caballero at the head of the Republican government. But he in turn came up against the hostility of the Anarchists and the trade unionists and the internal difficulties of the Socialist party, in which those who favored and those who were hostile to unity of action with the Communists were in perpetual opposition.

Early that spring, Malraux, acting as a kind of unofficial minister of propaganda and foreign relations, left for the United States on a lecture tour to collect funds for Spanish medical aid. Josette Clotis accompanied him.

In the New World, Malraux's reputation as a romantic young leftist writer and as a revolutionary adventurer had spread far beyond the circle of readers of his two most famous books, Les Conquérants and La Condition humaine. He was also recognized as the organizer and commander of the volunteer squadron. He had recently been wounded, and this further added to his prestige.[6]

After several speaking engagements in New York and other large eastern cities, Malraux and Josette left for California. In Hollywood they were put up at the Hollywood Roosevelt Hotel as the guests of Donald Ogden Stewart. Here Malraux was met by the man who had translated his La Condition humaine ("Man's Fate") and Le Temps du mépris ("Days of Wrath"), Haakon Chevalier,[7] professor of French at the University of California in Berkeley and a friend of J. Robert Oppenheimer.

Chevalier acted as his interpreter. Malraux and the German left-wing poet Ernst Toller addressed a crowd that filled the immense Mecca Temple Auditorium to overflowing. Malraux was asked to countless receptions, cocktail parties, dinners. All Hollywood wanted to meet him, and money for his cause flooded in. Reuben Mamoulian, Miriam Hopkins, William Saroyan, Clifford Odets, Lillian Hellman, Lionel Stander, and many other actors, screenwriters, playwrights, novelists, and directors heard Malraux speak to them about the Spanish Republicans but also about the art of the motion picture, in which he was deeply interested.

He visited several studios, and turned up at MGM at the time of the shooting of a bedroom scene with Marlene Dietrich and Herbert Marshall. Miss Dietrich was wearing a more or less transparent night-

---

[6] The fiercest battles between the Republicans and Franco's troops took place at Teruel. Malraux was shot down while returning from a bombing mission over Teruel, and crashed close to Valencia, headquarters of the Republican government. He was fortunate enough to be pulled from the wreckage of his plane without permanent injuries.
[7] Chevalier's translation of La Condition humaine was published by Random House in 1934, that of Le Temps du mépris also by Random House in 1936.

gown, and in the breaks between takes she would go over and talk with Malraux. "During this scene," according to Haakon Chevalier, "all the studio personnel were avidly watching, not Marlene Dietrich, but 'the young Frenchman who had been fighting in Spain.' "

Then Malraux left for San Francisco. On the day of his arrival, he spoke at a large luncheon at the Sir Francis Drake Hotel, chaired by Haakon Chevalier, with violinist Yehudi Menuhin and the French essayist Julien Benda as guests of honor.

The following Sunday morning Chevalier organized a breakfast at the University of California Faculty Club to have Malraux meet some of the prominent faculty members. Malraux on that occasion spoke not on Spain but on art, and fascinated his audience of some two hundred professors by giving a foretaste of some of the ideas and material that he would later incorporate in his books on art. Chevalier had invited Oppenheimer, but he was unable to come, and the meeting between the father of the atom bomb and Malraux was to occur only in 1953, in Paris, again at the initiative of Chevalier.

Malraux's American tour produced an avalanche of checks, some of them very large, and the gift of a number of ambulances.

In October, 1937, the Spanish Republican government moved to Barcelona. It had published a charter of unity of action, finally, in the month of August. But the Italian and German intervention on the side of Franco was becoming increasingly powerful. Malraux continued to live like a kind of Lord Byron in the service of the *dinamiteros,* like the hero of Ernest Hemingway's *For Whom the Bell Tolls.* He had found time, somehow, to produce a novel, based on the notes he had taken on his Spanish experience. *L'Espoir,* one of his finest books, was published by Gallimard in December of that year.

In April, 1938, Franco's troops reached the Mediterranean, slicing the territory of Republican Spain in two. Negrín formed a new government. The Russians intensified their backing, and Malraux retired from the armed struggle to devote himself to collecting funds.

When he brought Juan Negrín the money he had collected, the head of the Republican government told him, "If some day you would like to put on a show or a play that could be used as propaganda, let me know. We are ready to help you."

L'Espoir had been published the year before. President Manuel Azaña said after having read it, "Stirring and authentic. But those

Frenchmen are extraordinary! Really, having a commander of the civil guards talking philosophy is going a little strong!" For a Spanish notable, even a republican one, a civil guard of modest social standing could not have that level of intelligence, nor of culture.

Malraux decided to make a film based on certain scenes in his book, hoping thereby to stir up greater concern in the United States about the fate of the Spanish republic.

L'Espoir, like all Malraux's novels, is a succession of significant scenes that unfold in a way reminiscent of the structure of a film. In a motion picture the spectator is no longer motionless, as in the theater, where the distance between him and the actor never changes. Thanks to the miracle of the cameras, he can move about among the actors, close up or at a distance, at the will of the director. This is a technique that Malraux has used in his novels, the writing of which depends on the action, as the action depends on the writing.

Malraux had an extremely precise vision of his film, which was particularly helpful in preparing the screenplay. He had already secured the services of Max Aub, who had spent some time fighting in Spain and spoke the language fluently, and Denis Marion, a young writer who was to help him with writing the script. But he needed an editor to help him compose the scenario, and when one day he watched a documentary about railroads, he immediately announced, "I'm going to ask the chap who did this to work with me." And he did.

A few days later Boris Pesquine, the author of the documentary, came to Barcelona to get an idea of the nature of such a collaboration. The port had just been violently bombed. Great clouds of black smoke rose in the sky. "It's a funny idea to come and shoot a film here," said Pesquine to his friend Louis Page, the cameraman for the film.

"After our plane landed," Pesquine remembers, "an airport employee came to us and said, 'Please wait. Monsieur Malraux will come and fetch you.' We sat down on the ground and we waited in the open field. Malraux arrived in a small car that the Spanish government had put at his disposal. He struck me as very young—tall, lean, hair tousled. He immediately created a mood of friendliness. And yet meeting Malraux impressed me enormously. His books summarized the problems of my generation. It was an encounter that I shall never forget."

Pesquine continues:

Malraux wanted us to work with him and we hit it off because the idea appealed to us from the start. He took us in his car and we went for a ride through the region around Barcelona, passing through towns and villages, to spot locations for the film. Then we went and visited the studios situated on a hill above Barcelona, in Montjuich. Those studios were the sole vestiges, somewhat run-down, of an international exposition. There were streets with houses built in the different styles of the provinces of Spain, an old palace transformed into the principal stage. That was where we were going to shoot. It hardly lent itself to the movements of the camera. The four thick columns supporting the roof made it hard to take distance shots.

On a nearby and smaller stage some Spaniards were shooting a surrealist film. We watched the shooting of a rather far-fetched scene—a young man, astride a broom handle, suddenly arriving in the midst of a crowd of people wearing strange costumes. . . . It impressed me to see these people engaged in so unexpected an artistic activity in a country at war, in a city that was often bombed. It was undoubtedly their way of meeting the tension under which they were living. Malraux found it very appealing. He had, to a certain extent, the point of view of the young *contestataires* of today, of the leftists. But the world at that time was different from what it is today, its consumer society did not yet exist. . . .

I stayed two days in Barcelona, and then I went and set myself up in France, near the frontier, in Banyuls, not far from Perpignan. My wife—we were newlyweds—acted as my secretary and did the typing. Malraux, with Josette Clotis, and his team, Denis Marion and Max Aub, would come from Barcelona to work with me on the script. We did this almost from day to day according to the sequence that he wanted to shoot. We had very sharp discussions. He was very meticulous, wanted to know everything in the smallest detail. I confined myself to making technical objections. From time to time, in reading my script, he would change my draft, correct my style. This was a writer's mechanical reaction, and it amused me. He was fascinated by the cinema, understood it perfectly, and hit upon the most telling images almost instinctively. He would say, "I am not a technician, but I think I have a visual imagination." Unfortunately, the circumstances were such that the director could not always follow the script. Besides, when Malraux and his team arrived from Barcelona, they reacted

119

as do all people coming from a country at war to a country at peace. In Barcelona they had left rationing, wretchedness, bombs behind, whereas in Banyuls or Perpignan there was everything, it was a feast.

In the evening, after work, we used to dine in the restaurants of Perpignan and eat the grilled mullets of the region, or Catalan bouillabaisse. And we drank good wine. Malraux, who is a gourmet, asked for the detailed recipe of the Catalan fish soup, while my wife, who is from Marseilles, sang the praises of *her* bouillabaisse, which she said was superior to all others. And so we would argue until midnight or one in the morning. We talked mostly about movies. Malraux's favorite directors were Erich von Stroheim, René Clair, and especially Eisenstein, with whom he had worked. Eisenstein had wanted to film *La Condition humaine* in the USSR and got as far as making tests, but the project did not materialize for political reasons. As the sequence in which prisoners are thrown into a locomotive boiler was impossible to film, he had had the brilliant idea of using shadows and projecting the scene against a background of smoke.

Malraux was also fond of Charlie Chaplin, but not sufficiently so for my taste. "I am not too good a judge," he would say. "Comedy is not my strong point. . . ."

We spoke little of politics. I remember that he was anti-Stalinist. He respected the early Marxism. The communism that Russia had adopted, a rigid Stalinism, depriving the individual of all possibility of expression, appeared to him wrong. And while he sympathized with a certain Communist ideal, he has surely never been a member of the party. When he discussed politics he quickly became satirical, mordant, and bitter. His expression always remained serious even when he laughed, which was very rare. He was never gay, but so alive and animated that he radiated an impression of gaiety.

On the evening of July 14, in Banyuls, we met Ilya Ehrenburg and his wife in the street. Malraux and Ehrenburg shook hands warmly, and we all went and danced in the outdoor *bal populaire,* under the colored lanterns. . . .

At the end of July the shooting began, and so did the difficulties. Everything had to be made from scratch. There were no arc lights and one had to be fetched from Valencia. Alerts were frequent. The Italian pilots based in the Balearic Islands bombed the port of Barcelona regularly. One day the studio was transformed into a regular sieve; bomb splinters even fell into the paintpots.

Louis Page, *L'Espoir*'s cameraman, still recalls it vividly:

We were short of almost everything, so we had to use our ingenuity. Every scene presented a problem that we had to solve.

For example, we had to shoot a scene in which *dinamiteros* take to their heels in the countryside after climbing over a wall. The militiamen are firing with machine guns. The bullets have to be seen in bursts ricocheting on the crest of the wall. We had neither a simulator nor machine guns to produce such an effect. We gave guns to the best shots among us, asking them to aim at points six inches apart to imitate a burst.

One morning we were on a hilltop. The Nationalist General Mola's cavalrymen were supposed to arrive at the bottom of this hill and we had to send a car full of explosives into their midst to stop them. We had asked the artists' union to send us their best stunt man. Malraux, with the help of Max Aub, his interpreter, explained the scene to him. "You get the car started," he said, "and when it has taken on speed you jump off and let it go." The "stunt man," dismayed, blurted out, "But I'm a ventriloquist!" As there were fewer and fewer men available, the artists' union had just sent the first one they could find.

We often found ourselves without an electrician, and when we left the studio in the evening at six we were never sure of finding the same people there the next day. In the course of the night they would receive orders to leave for the front, which was in fact getting dangerously close. We once hired a poor, underfed old man of eighty who no longer had the strength even to handle his projector!

Then one day we needed a plane in the studio. Malraux asked a man named Bergeron who had belonged to the España escadrille, whom he had known when he himself was commanding the foreign volunteer bombing squadron, to build us a life-size set of a Potez in the studio. Bergeron, an excellent

pilot, who had been badly wounded in combat, was conva-
lescing in Barcelona. Having been a specialized mechanic with
Bloch, the big aircraft manufacturer, he knew all the details
of a plane. With the spare parts that he found in an airplane
"graveyard," he built up a Potez for us, which was hard because we wanted to be able to dismantle it in order to place
the camera at various angles without too much difficulty.

But in order to give the illusion of the plane in flight, we
had to have clouds moving past. We had no transparency. . . .
So I painted with a spray gun sixty-five feet of "sky," which
was to turn on a drum. Alas, the drum would not work. So we
placed the sky on a cart and had it move slowly past the plane.
That's how we made *L'Espoir*.

Louis Page remembers that Malraux seemed to be fascinated by
death. After the bombings to which Barcelona was so constantly subjected, he would often go to take stock of the damage on the spot. He
was fearless and seemed to court danger. His usual garb was a leather
jacket, a rough-spun Catalan shirt and trousers, and Catalan sandals,
and nothing about him betrayed the soldier or the firebrand.

"Malraux's life and work are all of a piece," says Max Aub, "which
can also be said of Camus or of Mauriac. This welding of the two is
not indispensable, as, for instance, with Montherlant, Claudel, or even
Aragon. It has little to do with the quality of the work, but it does
count in an absolute way. . . .

"The definition of Malraux's work can be found in one of his
lines—'to attempt to give men an awareness of the greatness in themselves
of which they are not conscious.'"

"One day," Max Aub continues, "we were flying in an old Potez
with the machine gun taken out of the forward turret and a camera
put there instead. We were going to film a village from which *guer-
rilleros* were going to emerge to attack the fascist tanks—we never got
to film this scene, for some real tanks appeared and prevented us! Three
Messerschmitts appeared, flying very high. The pilot of our plane made
an about-turn and sneaked off, at low altitude, in the valley, following
its windings. The Messerschmitts did not see us, or perhaps disdained
us. I went into the forward turret and there I found Malraux reciting
Corneille. . . ."

The great sequence of *L'Espoir* is the descent from the mountain.

SPAIN: A REVOLUTIONARY IDEAL

A Republican plane has just been shot down. The bodies of the wounded and the dead are carried down by men from the nearby village, accompanied by its whole population, in a heroic and grief-stricken procession. "This," Louis Page remembers, "was one of the most difficult sequences to make. We needed five or six hundred extras to produce the effect of a mass of people. Only the army could supply so many. We had to do a lot of negotiating in order to get them. After all, we were making the picture in a country at war, and even for a picture being done by Malraux and intended for propaganda purposes the military chiefs hesitated to divert hundreds of men from their sole mission, which was to fight."

On the day they were at last able to shoot the scene, the crew learned that Malraux had decided to have it accompanied by an Aragonese *jota,* the native chant which is improvised upon a particular set theme. Accordingly, he had asked a *jota* singer to be present while the sequence was shot. That evening, at an inn, the singer gave a first hearing of his improvisations. All the actors in the film were present, and they broke into a chorus of revolutionary songs. One of them recited some Verlaine poems, and Malraux spoke to them about Victor Hugo and Chateaubriand.

"Our Spanish nights were drawing to an end," Louis Page takes up his story. "One evening—it was in the beginning of January, in 1939—Malraux told me that some Republican soldiers back from the front had seen scribbled on some German tanks, 'Nach Toulouse—Paris!' and, showing me a newspaper, he said, 'You see, Hitler has just named his ninetieth general in the Luftwaffe. If there are generals, there are also squadrons, *and we know what they are for.'*

"On January 25 the film was finished. That very evening we learned that General Mola with his army was very close to Barcelona. At four in the morning we headed for the French-Spanish frontier in two cars, driven by soldiers, put at Malraux's disposal by the Ministry of Information. At ten in the morning the city fell and General Mola entered the capital of Catalonia.

"The Franco general was ahead of schedule—unlike the actors in our film. Constantly, when we planned to start work at nine, they would turn up around noon and say, 'Well, how about a little food? It's time for lunch.' Malraux never got angry. He would just smile and call them scatterbrained. He has always made allowances for people. For him this was just an experiment—which in fact he never repeated."

In Spain events took an increasingly rapid turn. In March, General Casado, in Madrid, engineered a *coup d'état*. There were bloody combats in the streets between Franco followers and Communists. Negrín left Spain for France. By April 1, 1939, Franco had entered Madrid. The joint intervention of Italy and Germany had ensured his victory.

Back in Paris, Malraux set himself up in the studios in Joinville to shoot some connecting scenes and begin the cutting of the film with the collaboration of Marguerite Monot, a professional cutter.

The front part of the Potez plane set that Bergeron had built in the Barcelona studio reached Joinville without incident, while nearly all the rest of the equipment was lost in the course of the exodus. All the film they had shot, however, miraculously escaped destruction en route from Spain to Joinville.

There is a particularly dramatic sequence when the small Potez crashes into the mountain.

"We had already shot this," Louis Page told me, "by setting up our camera in the cabin of a *téléférique*[8] near Montserrat, in Catalonia, that lifts almost vertically. In certain places the cabin nearly touches the wall of the mountain. We shot this approach to the mountain by increasing the speed a little, which gives the sensation of crashing directly into the rock wall.

"We shot all the transparencies and the shattering of the forward part of the Potez in Joinville. Before he crashes into the mountain, the pilot of the Potez sees a pursuit squadron in his rearview mirror. There was no pursuit squadron in Barcelona, so it was impossible to film the scene. There were, of course, a few pursuit planes on the airfield, but they were otherwise occupied! Back in Paris, Malraux managed to find a Japanese pursuit squadron in the film library. The fact that the planes were Japanese did not matter, for the planes at that period were all more or less alike and we made the double exposure in the laboratory."

"In Malraux's books of action there are remarkable details," says Max Aub. "The lens comes close to the reader and gives to a leaf, to a drop of water, to an ant the same magnitude that the sky, for instance, might have in the scene in Tolstoi's *War and Peace* where Prince Andrei, lying wounded in the field after the Battle of Austerlitz, looks up at the clouds in the night.

"In *L'Espoir,* when the planes, hidden in the woods, are about to fly out on a mission, the pilots remove the tarpaulins that cover them. As he takes his place in the cockpit, one pilot sees a large ant going

[8] The French term for an aerial cable car.

round and round his compass. We completed this scene in Joinville using a transparency shot to show the ant on the compass."

Such a scene, even in a motion picture context, is typical Malraux. In his work these symbols have at times as important a place as the characters whom they define or to whom they add an important facet in a decisive moment of their destiny. The ant, not knowing where to turn on the unfamiliar contraption—a hunter probably doomed to destruction—may well be meant, in Malraux's imagery, to evoke man's destiny. In its obstinate, blind circling, finding no way of escape, the ant symbolizes the Malrauvian hero who wages a hopeless battle but will not capitulate until defeated by main force.

Malraux's work is rich in these symbolic evocations. In *Le Temps du mépris,* Kassner, the antifascist incarcerated in a Nazi prison cell, gauges his chances of escape by staring at the crevices in the moldy wall. "The wall sweated destinies," Malraux writes. The same symbolic evocation recurs, again and again, as in *La Lutte avec l'Ange*—the French soldiers, crowded together like cattle in Chartres cathedral, ringed round by German machine guns, become conscious of their forfeited destiny, of the war they have lost, of the defeat which they must assume—for defeats, in Malraux's view, have to be assumed, like victories.

During the shooting of the film, Malraux often spoke to Max Aub of his experiences in the service of the Spanish Republican air force. Much later, he was to sum up his feeling about this period of his life. "In fighting with the Republicans and the Communists, we were defending the values that we considered—and that I consider—to be universal."

Max Aub also remembers "as though it were yesterday that afternoon when we heard about the Ribbentrop-Molotov meeting. 'Revolution at *that* price? No!' Malraux said to me."

7.

The War Begins

The signing of a German-Russian nonaggression pact in Moscow on August 23, 1939, gave Hitler the free hand he needed to attack Poland. On September 1, at dawn, without bothering to make a formal declaration of war, his armies invaded Polish territory and the Luftwaffe bombed the main cities. Britain and France sent Hitler an ultimatum demanding the immediate withdrawal of all German forces from the territory of their ally. The Führer coolly ignored their demand, and his refusal to respond led them to declare war on Germany on September 3. World War II had begun.

"German squadrons, without any previous warning, have bombed Warsaw, Krakow, and other Polish cities," announced *Le Journal,* the big Paris morning daily. "General mobilization in France and Great Britain. A state of siege is declared throughout the country."

André Malraux was just finishing the cutting of *L'Espoir.*[1] When the mobilization call went out, he tried to join the air force but was turned down "like a bad student," as he put it. Instead, he was assigned to a tank regiment and went to war in Flanders in a Renault tank.

With Russia as his ally, Hitler had no great anxiety about his Western enemies. Despite their superiority in men and equipment, the French and British armies under General Maurice Gamelin limited themselves to occupying the fortified positions of the Maginot Line, and Hitler was able to crush Poland in less than a month. He annexed

---

[1] *L'Espoir* was first shown to Premier Negrín, and was passed for public showing by the government of France. Unfortunately for the film, however, the outbreak of war intervened, and all movies were submitted to review a second time. Malraux's film failed to pass the second test, and accordingly was only shown privately in 1939–40. During the German occupation, the film was put for safety in the storehouses of the Pathé-Natan studios and saved for posterity thanks to the vigilance of Henri Langlois, the director of the Cinémathèque, the French film library, one of the most extensive in the world. The film was again shown publicly in 1945 and won the prestigious Prix Louis Delluc, the cinematic equivalent of the Prix Goncourt. It was reissued in 1970.

a part of the vanquished country and made another part into a protectorate. Meanwhile, in accordance with the agreements signed between Germany and Russia, the Red Army invaded Poland's eastern provinces.

Shortly after this the Russians imposed their "military assistance" upon the Baltic countries, absorbing Estonia, Latvia, and Lithuania in quick succession. The Soviet Union had expected to obtain military bases from Finland. When the little country refused, its giant neighbor promptly invaded. The Finns, aided by wintry conditions, fought heroically, but were forced, in March, 1940, to yield the Karelian Isthmus and the Hangö peninsula.

In April, 1940, in order to secure the Baltic and his shipping routes, Hitler occupied Denmark without combat, and parachuted invasion troops into Norway. The Norwegians, doomed, put up a fierce resistance, and the British and French sent troops to aid them. Pockets of resistance held out for a few weeks, but it was a forlorn hope. In early June, the last small Allied expeditionary force evacuated Narvik and abandoned Norway to the Germans.

Since the beginning of the war, the French armies and the small British expeditionary force had undertaken no major operation, limiting themselves to waiting for the adversary behind the Maginot Line. Those long months of inaction demoralized the troops and made them susceptible to defeatist propaganda, of which there was a great deal. The "phony war," as it was called, became quite accepted in France. The situation seemed unreal but stable in its unreality. "We were looking for four-leaf clovers," as Malraux put it. Like their predecessors in the trench warfare of World War I, the soldiers were bored and wrote home to families and girl friends, saying so.

Two letters survive that were written by Josette Clotis during this time to Stany Cordier, a childhood friend of whom she was very fond.[2] They are charming, friendly communications, full of the sensibility that made Josette so appealing. The first is dated late November, 1939:

> *Mon petit* Stany, excuse me for not having answered your letter sooner. It gave me so much pleasure. It isn't right to let our warriors down.
>
> When I received it I was thinking of something much nicer than answering it . . . I was thinking—have thought for a month—that I would be going to Rouen. So you can imagine! What a joy to be able to tell you: Come quickly to the

2 Stany Cordier survived the war and is now a television producer.

Hôtel d'Angleterre, so I can see and hear you, instead of saying, I am well, thank you, and you? Did you know that the whole *NRF* staff has settled in Normandy? But the days have gone by and I am not in Rouen. And I'm not going to wait for the end of our thirty years' war to tell you how touched I was that you should think of writing to me. I wish you could stay in Rouen and grow old there. In any case, if you pass through Paris, be sure to let me know. . . .

I am glad you have dropped motion pictures to resume your medical career. The cinema is a vocation that leads nowhere. But I should have preferred, of course, to have you drop it for something other than war. And what about your lab? How fickle you are! And ungrateful, too, for after all it is your lab that gives you a privileged military job—but for which, as a movie director, you might be polishing boots, as so many of our illustrious friends are fated to do. . . .

Mon cher Stany, write me, and above all come and see me. Genuine good wishes. One has no inclination, this year, to offer them lightly.

Yours,
Jo Clo

The second letter is dated January, 1940:

I am happy, *cher* Stany, if my letter can have had one-tenth of a second of interest in a life which you tell me is monotonous; yet I wish all of you any amount of this monotony rather than the liveliness that a greater danger would bring you. I wish it as it is hardly possible to wish anything—fists tight, with thumbs turned in, as on examination days. Did you do that too? No, that must be a girl's trick. . . .

Everyone says, "All lights out at eight in the evening!" and that seems so sad. But why? Would you think human beings got so much pleasure out of lighting? You know that for years—about three now—I have lived in blacked-out cities.[3] But that never made me either happier or unhappier. Being in lighted cities after dark cities did not surprise me, or increase my happiness, or have any effect at all—but I am perhaps sentimentally nearsighted, and then, after all, since every-

[3] A reference to her life in Spain, especially Barcelona, with Malraux.

one complains of the dark, perhaps it is because if it wasn't dark people would be happier. They would be happier, but because the return of light would imply something else, other things . . . it seems to me. Anyway, it's a personal point of view. . . .

I didn't think you would leave M. (She didn't either: "He can't live without me," she used to say.) I am glad you did it, for it is what you wished and if you hadn't done it it would have been out of weakness; I would understand your writing me that you are happy and a thousand times chained but not that you are chained and detest your chains. It is true that it suits you to be solitary. I know no one who can build himself a pink and blue solitude as you can. I don't think of you as a very mysterious character, or as a phenomenon, either, but in Banyuls, where everything was so luminous and so transparent at the same time, you were a kind of prince. What dream solitudes you built yourself, alone with your sails, alone with your ropes, your knots, and your little knives!

I am sorry we didn't go to the Canary Islands, to Madeira, as we said we would. We were not very rich, but so what? We should have gone two or three thousand francs more into debt at that time, and we would have had the voyage.

And we will never have the chance again! When shall we be as young? Together we should not have been alone (and I don't like solitude as you do) and we should have seen landscapes, new lights, faces, images, and that is so important. A trip is something you acquire permanently—it has no counterpart, no obverse side. In my life I have gotten nothing without bitterness except opening my window and seeing the Arno, in the early turquoise green dawn, or coming upon the completely mysterious arcades of Padua in the middle of the night, or not understanding why the pine trees are so dark at nine in the morning on the Stockholm station square during Christmas week. . . .

Why didn't we do it?

Now I should be afraid of leaving André . . . [so] I shall never know Tenerife, except in the form of a little dog.[4]

So long, Stany! I often, very often get notes from young

[4] A breed of curly-haired terrier, usually white. Josette is, of course, punning on the name of the largest of the Canary Islands.

soldiers who, even though they don't know me, write to me: "Be my godmother!" I don't know what it is to be a godmother to an unknown, I should in fact be incapable of being anything whatever, but it gives me pleasure always to have news of you, to tell you affectionately that I think of you.

Jo Clo

"Malraux was happy during this period," Boris Pesquine told me. Josette contributed to this happiness. The two loved each other. They were a united, inseparable couple. She had followed him in Spain during the Civil War. She would follow him later in the maquis of Corrèze. In 1939 she gave birth to a boy—Gauthier—and Malraux's joy was complete, despite the war.

With his Scandinavian offensive completed, Hitler abruptly ended the state of "phony war" on the French front. Only a thin fringe of German troops was stationed opposite the Maginot Line, while Gamelin's divisions were spread across the whole front from Switzerland to the English Channel. The bulk of Hitler's forces, his air force, and his armored tanks were concentrated on his right wing. That was where he would strike. His offensive was planned in two stages—a kind of pincer attack.

On May 10, 1940, without declaring war, he invaded Holland, Belgium, and Luxembourg, all three of which had observed the strictest neutrality. That was the first stage.

In the second, he flung an armored and motorized army through the Ardennes and over the Meuse, which was poorly defended because it was considered difficult to cross. The fast-moving columns pierced the French lines like a wedge and descended the valley of the Somme to the sea, thus encircling the Allied troops fighting desperately in Belgium. The Belgians capitulated. The British and the French succeeded in holding out for a while around the port of Dunkerque in June, 1940, but despite the heroic efforts of the hastily organized ferry system of naval and civilian vessels, only a remnant of the expeditionary force was ferried across the Channel to safety, and almost all their equipment was captured.

The best divisions were disorganized. General Maxime Weygand replaced General Gamelin in the course of the battle, trying, without conviction, to stem the German advance. The Nazis swept on, occupied Paris, took the Maginot Line from behind, reached Lyons, and marched on Bordeaux. On June 10, Italy declared war on France. Events were moving quickly.

The French government hesitated. Should it cease an unequal combat while there was still time to gain some concessions from the enemy? It was an agonizing decision.

On June 16, 1940, President Albert Lebrun asked Marshal Henri Philippe Pétain to form a new government, replacing that of Paul Reynaud. In this moment of defeat, France turned to the veteran marshal, the eighty-five-year-old hero of World War I, whose name still represented victory although his attitude had long been defeatist.

On June 17 Pétain asked for an armistice. His task was to secure the best conditions he could, with his country in a state of almost complete disorganization and military collapse. Hitler dictated his terms in the forest of Compiègne, in the very railroad car in which Marshal Foch, in 1918, had received the German delegation on a similar mission.

By the terms of the armistice, Pétain's government was left in charge of the French fleet and colonies, and was allowed to maintain an "armistice army" of no more than 100,000 men at home. France was divided into two zones: the northern part and the entire Atlantic coastline remained under German military occupation; the southern part and the Mediterranean coastline were under the direct administration of the French government.

On June 18, 1940, fighting thus ceased upon the demand of the old marshal, who had put himself in contact with the enemy. That same day, at six o'clock in the evening, a forty-nine-year-old French brigadier general broadcast on the BBC from London a call for resistance, for a continuation of the fight, calling upon the French people to rally round him. "I, General de Gaulle, at present in London, ask all French officers and soldiers now on British soil, or who should find themselves on it in the future, with or without their arms . . . to get in touch with me."

Free France was born, headed by an almost unknown man whose name, an envoy told Churchill, was a good one because "it sounds like a trumpet blast." Frenchmen in Britain flocked to join de Gaulle; Frenchmen escaped from France, singly or in small groups, to swell his forces.

André Malraux was not among them, however. He was wounded on June 14 and taken prisoner four days later. With thirty-five hundred companions in misfortune, he was penned in a prison camp in the cathedral town of Sens, in conditions of great privation and misery.

Outside the barbed wire, life went on. The French, as has often happened in the course of their history, were torn by two opinions: one of weakness and consent, which was that of Marshal Pétain; the other of daring and combat, that of General de Gaulle.

On July 10, the National Assembly, specially summoned at Vichy to ratify the terms of the armistice, granted Pétain emergency powers until "a new constitution" could be promulgated.[5] Pétain made himself chief of state, with Pierre Laval as his vice-premier.

In November, 1940, Malraux succeeded in escaping from the prison camp, disguised as a carpenter and wearing a pair of shoes that were agonizingly too tight for his feet. He managed to cross into the unoccupied zone and made his way to Roquebrune-Cap-Martin on the Riviera by December. Here he found refuge in a villa, La Souco, which belonged to his good friend the painter Simon Bussy and his wife. "Long before my stay there," Malraux remembers, "La Souco had been lent by its owners to Rudyard Kipling and to André Gide. . . . The caretaker used to tell me that Kipling was the funnier of the two, 'because he used to whistle when he took his bath.' "

In early 1941, de Gaulle and the Free French movement had few followers. The resistance was not yet organized into a maquis. For two years there was understandable confusion; networks of resistance had to be created.

"There was plotting, but there was no fighting," says Malraux. "My first experience in the active resistance was in Toulouse, in 1941, where, together with Emanuel d'Astier de La Vigerie, whose pseudonym was Bernard, and Corniglion-Molinier, we blew up a German munitions train. We did not know at the time that what we were risking was the extermination camp. No one at the time, not even people like Picasso or Fernand Léger, believed that such things as death camps existed.

"I spent the first half of 1941 in Roquebrune, the other half at Cap d'Ail. I had rented a house, the name of which I have forgotten. . . . I remember, though, that it had belonged to Oustric, the financier who had been involved in a sensational swindling scandal.

"During this period I lived like a writer who does his job. . . . I wrote *Les Noyers de l'Altenburg,* in particular, which I was unable to

---

[5] The "new constitution" was never promulgated and on November 13, 1942, France's territory was fully occupied by the Germans.

publish in France because of the German censorship, but which appeared in Switzerland in an edition of one thousand copies."[6]

In Roquebrune and in Cap d'Ail, Malraux was joined by the faithful Josette. They received the visits of a few reliable old friends, including Louis Page and Boris Pesquine, who had found their way down to the Côte d'Azur, and Raymond Maréchal, also a devoted friend, who had fought with Malraux in Spain. In *L'Espoir* Maréchal played the role of the aviator whose plane crashes into the mountain. Earlier in 1941 he had been in Toulouse. Sought by the Gestapo there, he succeeded in reaching the Côte d'Azur and became assistant to Louis Page, who was working in the Victorine studios in Nice.

On Sundays they would go see Malraux. They had begun to speak of resistance in general terms—of contacts to be made, of plans for action—but there was nothing precise or immediate.

In early June, 1941, Malraux left the Côte d'Azur for Commentry, in the Allier, to pay a visit to his childhood friend Louis Chevasson, who had taken over the management of a machine tool factory in that region.[7] Boris Pesquine, who was an engineer by training, later managed it for him for some time. Both men were living in a nearby house. Malraux spent a week with his friend Chevasson and talked a lot to Pesquine.

"We spoke at length at that time about the problems of anti-Semitism," Pesquine recalls. "Malraux had been the founder and president of the League Against Anti-Semitism and the Front of Anti-Fascist Intellectuals. He was thoroughly familiar with the Jewish question. My father, of Russian Jewish origin, had been struck by Malraux's generous, liberal attitude on these problems."

On June 22, 1941, without declaring war, Hitler suddenly launched his armies upon the conquest of Russia. In the course of the summer the Germans had swift successes. But the early winter of 1941–42, the aggressiveness of the Soviet armies, the stern defense measures that mobilized the whole population in resistance to the German advance, forced Hitler to mark time before Moscow and finally to draw back

---

[6] The Swiss edition was titled *La Lutte avec l'Ange*. After the war this work was republished by Gallimard as *Les Noyers de l'Altenburg*. It is now out of print, but some passages have been reproduced in the *Antimémoires*.
[7] The factory had belonged to Jews of Polish origin. Chevasson had taken over its management to protect the factory from being confiscated by the Germans.

with heavy losses. In December, 1941, after the Japanese attack on Pearl Harbor, the United States entered the war.

By 1942 the situation had begun to change. The armies of the Axis powers no longer had the initiative. Their economic reserves had shrunk. The Western Allies pushed back Rommel in North Africa; in the bloody ruins of Stalingrad, the Russians would inflict the first decisive defeat on the German armies.

In France circumstances were changing too. The German occupation had become more oppressive and more brutal. In November, 1942, it was extended to the whole country. Food was rationed, war prisoners were being liberated only in dribbles, while workers were being requisitioned in increasing numbers for forced labor in Germany. In order to escape this, more and more young men took to the maquis. Networks of resistants were organized, deliberately encouraged by the Allies. Supplied and equipped by parachute drops, which were rather sporadic in the beginning, these units were frequently covered and even helped by the local police and administrations. From London, Free France gave instructions by radio.

But the repression by both the Vichy mercenaries and the German occupation troops grew more and more bloody. There was increasing recourse to deportation, to the execution of hostages, to torture.

The war once again called Malraux to action. He abandoned the life of a "plotter" for that of an underground soldier, and in 1943 became an official combatant in the maquis. That same year Josette bore him a second son, Vincent.

With a regular army officer, now a chief of the Secret Army, Lieutenant Colonel Pierre Jacquot, André Malraux was appointed to organize the maquis of Corrèze, in the foothills of the Massif Central. The faithful Maréchal went with him, to act as his deputy and handle the youth. Malraux also took command of the maquisards of Dordogne and the Lot area, an active minority chiefly composed of men from Alsace and Lorraine who had fled from the Germans.

On the Mediterranean front, the American, British, and French troops drove the Italian and German forces out of Tunisia, invaded Sicily, and landed in the south of Italy. A succession of Italian defeats led to the fall of Mussolini, but the Allies had to battle every step of the way north up the Italian peninsula, which was bitterly defended by the Germans.

In Russia, Stalin's armies launched one offensive after another, reconquering the ground they had lost in 1942 and advancing into German-held territory.

In retreat on all fronts, Germany faced growing difficulties in the occupied countries, particularly Yugoslavia, Norway, Poland, Belgium, Holland, and France, in which the resistance movements were becoming stronger and bolder all the time.

8.

Resistance in Black Périgord

"Radio Paris lies, Radio Paris lies, Radio Paris is German! . . ."

The slogans that the BBC broadcast to occupied France were assuming a more resolute tone, and a quiet assurance had begun to supplant the extravagances of propaganda and the promises that were often unkept. The Normandy landings of June 6, 1944 (that "longest day," which it had seemed never would come), had revived the confidence of 80 percent of the French people.

The underground fighters, soldiers without uniforms (or formal graves), took count of themselves. How many of them were there? Sixteen thousand, scattered over five departments, Corrèze, Cantal, Lot, Lot-et-Garonne, and Dordogne, in an area known as Black Périgord.[1] But could this improvised patriot army face the enemy in actual battle? And, to begin with, could this cosmopolitan assemblage of men, which included a large proportion of exiled Spanish Republicans, really be called an army at all?

Various political loyalties divided them at this touchy turning point when the maquis was becoming official, when the partisans were about to enter the history of World War II. Apart from a few tiny groups for whom resistance and pillaging were synonymous, these irregulars were essentially composed of the AS (*l'Armée Secrète*—"the Secret Army") and the FTP (*Francs-Tireurs et Partisans*—"Snipers and Partisans"), the latter wholly controlled by the all-powerful Communist party— *le Parti des Fusillés* ("the Party of the Executed")—which for a long

---

[1] Black Périgord is an area some sixty miles long and twenty miles wide in places, which borders the River Lot, covers a part of the Lot-et-Garonne, and extends over a fraction of Dordogne. It owes its name to its forests, which chiefly consist of chestnuts, beeches, and elms. Its geographical opposite, White Périgord, is given over to wheat fields and other arable cultivation.

time had sought to turn its acts of daring, as well as its victims, to advantage.

All this was communicated to General de Gaulle, in London, in the spring of 1944. There were uncontrolled elements, outcroppings of terror, anarchy. Some kind of order must be brought into this disorder. A way must be found to unify this anti-German insurrection, which the orthodox Stalinists dominated both by their discipline and by their numbers. The FTP must, willy-nilly, be incorporated into the FFI (*Forces Françaises de l'Intérieur*—"French Forces of the Interior").

To this difficult task of unifier, of military and political catalyzer, André Malraux was to devote himself. A few days before taking on this responsibility he went to Montluçon, in the Allier, where he met an emissary from London.

When Malraux took "the affair in hand" he was barely forty-three, but he had experience.

"I wage war without liking it," he wrote once and for all, as though by these words he was signing his testament as an adventurer of the advance guard. He had only one war to his credit, that of 1939. But revolutions abounded in his memory, from the China of 1925 to the tragedy of the Spanish people.

"I wage war without liking it." Doubtless that was why he waged it so well.

"He is aware of danger like a wild animal who senses the presence of hunters stalking in the savanna," Hemingway said of him in Madrid in 1937.

And Arthur Koestler: "I salute this intellectual who has the courage to lay down his pen to pick up a machine gun."

For Malraux, "thought kills action." At the end of spring, 1944, in order to succeed, he needed precisely that—vigilant thought to back up his action. For this fighter who undertook to "harmonize" the resistance, to make the tricolor fly higher than the hammer and sickle, was tackling a powerful adversary. However carefully he verified his information, however scrupulous his investigations, what he was up against was a solid mass of obscurity.

Those whom he had to bring into line were sometimes his political adversaries, even though the fact that they fought for the same cause and shared the same ideal—liberation of the national territory—had muted the violence of former quarrels.

It was no longer a time of polemics among the intellectuals of the

Left. Nevertheless, the orthodox Stalinists had not forgiven Malraux his defection, or certain reservations that he had formulated during the Spanish war about the Soviet general staff—"The Russians did a lot but could have done more." Nor, finally, could they overlook his unequivocally definite position at the time the German-Soviet pact of 1939 was signed.

"Genius is the sense of resourcefulness." Malraux was to give real meaning to this maxim of André Gide's during those decisive summer weeks of 1944.

To carry out the task with which the head of Free France had entrusted him—to unify the resistance from Limousin to the Pyrenees—Malraux (who was known as "Berger" for underground identification[2]) had only a narrow margin of time. Events were pressing. He must act quickly, with authority and tact.

It is hard to describe this resistance—official or "marginal"—that Colonel Berger was assigned to take in hand. It was a confused mosaic of forces scattered throughout the five departments of Black Périgord; the agents of the Abwehr called it "the gangrene of the southwest." The poorly welded amalgam included not only the groups already mentioned but others of such diverse allegiances as the ORA (*Organisation de la Résistance de l'Armée*), apolitical maquis units, and various marginal groups—originally just armed bands—which had won their place in the ranks of the resistance through exploits that were often spectacular. From the shock group organized by "Tarzan" (now the well-known journalist and film producer, Armand Gatti) to that led by an ex-convict known as Soleil ("Sun"), the "gangrene of the southwest" included a good thirty of these foolhardy fractions, which often paid a high price for their love of freedom.

Taking his role as war chief seriously, Malraux decided to set up his headquarters in the geographical center of the "terrorist zone" that was surrounded by a heavy red line on the enemy staff maps. From his command post at Saint-Chamant, in Corrèze (where he usually left his faithful companion, Josette Clotis[3]), he went down into the valley of the Dordogne, where old medieval ramparts and rocky cliffs and buttresses rose above centuries-old forests.

Dordogne boasts something over seventeen hundred châteaus.

---

[2] He chose Berger as his pseudonym after an old Alsatian family, Berger de Reichbach, which had chosen the side of France after the Germans annexed Alsace and Lorraine as victors' spoils from the Franco-Prussian War. He had written about the family in *Les Noyers de l'Altenburg*.

[3] Josette also lived for some time at the Château de Fayrac, in Dordogne.

Malraux chose the one that seemed to him the most inaccessible: Urval. It was a fine sample of classical medieval fortress architecture, and it became the center and rallying point for the heads of the maquis groups.

Urval was at the entrance to the Black Périgord region, whose forests were such an ideal refuge for clandestine groups that it might almost be called a paradise for illegal activity. But at the moment it was no paradise. The Brandenburg SS troops had spread terror throughout the area by lining up twenty-six of the most stalwart men of the village of Frayssinet-le-Gélat and shooting them out of hand. The corpses were exhibited in front of the church, to the sobs of the bereaved mothers, children, and wives. The massacre had taken place on May 19 but the maquisards had not moved to retaliate. They had neither the organization nor the arms; it would have meant sheer carnage.

The underground fighters in the southern part of Black Périgord were Soleil's men, and wholly devoted to him, more from terror than because of his powers of leadership, however. Soleil was a figure whose legend had spread far beyond the region. Twenty-six years old, a *méridional*, lithe and supple as a cat, he had done time in Les Baumettes prison in Marseilles, and was foolhardy to the point of total indifference to danger. On June 19, at Mussiden in Dordogne, his group made a surprise attack with grenades on the heavily armored train of the elite Das Reich Division, which was moving up toward the Normandy front. The Germans were engaged, but neither halted nor decimated. Soleil's group, on the other hand, although it was the best trained of the maquis units for such surprise assaults, suffered heavy losses in the operation.

Such reckless exploits, far too costly in human lives, exasperated Malraux. There was no need to ask him for whom the bell tolled. For him the death of every man was a tragedy. He planned to end the waste of men and matériel in rash uncoordinated movements. As soon as he arrived in the area he began making arrangements, assisted by Colonel Jacquot, the regular soldier who was his second-in-command, to convene the maquis leaders of all persuasions at the Château de la Poujade, at Urval.

The undertaking might have appeared a forlorn hope to anyone but him. The obstacles seemed insurmountable. He had to make contact with some forty chiefs scattered across a hexagonal territory that embraced three ancient provinces. Once he got them to Urval, he would then have the well-nigh impossible task of getting his heterogeneous henchmen to implement his combat plan—unity in action. He would worry about that, however, in due course.

Kept remarkably up-to-date by his informers, Malraux successfully made contact, one by one, with the various "responsible" people. In Cazals, a canton of the Lot that has been called the Tuscany of France, he went to see the local notary, Maître Brouel, and his younger brother, Captain Marcel Brouel, who later would be killed in a minefield at the Pointe de Grave. The elder Brouel was the brains of an autonomous but committed group in the Communist party. Malraux presented his plan in inimitable style. A witness to the meeting, Lieutenant Dieudé, a World War I hero, affirms that Malraux began by pulling out a Communist party card and tossing it on the table. "You see!" he exclaimed. "I'm one of you—and this proves it!"

There is nothing surprising in this. Malraux, despite his repudiations of Stalinist tyranny, had behind him twenty-seven years of Marxist dialectics. While he never belonged to the Communist party—having limited himself to being a fellow traveler—his half brother Roland, who was a journalist with *Ce Soir,* the Communist daily, was a militant member of the powerful political machine. The party card might have been his. Or it might have been a false one. Besides, in 1944, did the end not justify the means?

Screening the membership of the Secret Army, on the other hand, and the local groups that had rallied to it, was really for Malraux little more than a formality. It was notoriously a body in which the more conservative noncommissioned and commissioned officers of 1939–40 had resumed service in uniforms that had been scrupulously put away in mothballs. Because of this, Soleil's roughneck maquisards referred to them contemptuously as *napthalinards.* There were certainly no Communists or Communist sympathizers among that "mothball fleet."

(Malraux himself used to wear a simple uniform for the formal maquis meetings. But a uniform can get one into trouble, especially if it is cut from the battle dress of the British army. From this to making Malraux-Berger an agent of the British Intelligence Service was only one step. From Beaulieu-sur-Dordogne—where he admired the Romanesque church, which would later illustrate his *Le Monde Chrétien* —from Souillac to Montauban—Ingres's birthplace—a calumny spread, propagated by a few individuals jealous of Colonel Berger's status: Malraux had "demanded" that his colonel's pay be given him in pounds sterling. "As in the time of the Spanish Revolution," these detractors said, "when he recognized only one currency—the dollar." Malraux either knew nothing of this at the time or paid no attention to it. His most important task at this point was to make contact with the groups under his command.)

Soleil's men, however, were in quite another category. Some of them, those called upon to carry out punitive tasks, affected the showy elegance of the Marseilles gangsters. With equal aplomb, they would sack post offices, rob banks, empty the tanks at gas stations, disarm hesitant gendarmes, or, after a mass, arrest a village curate whom they considered too much attached to the image of Marshal Pétain and to the dying myth of the national revolution. They lived off the native population and would kill a suspected collaborator as lightheartedly as a hunter would a grouse.

A bare trio composed Soleil's general staff: *L'Astre du jour* ("Day-star"), a slum leader now turned Communist, seconded by a more level-headed giant, *Double-Mètre* ("Two Meters"), and by a gangster-film Negro, Michel, who went by the inevitable name of *Blancheneige* ("Snow White").

Whatever one's judgment of them, such men were not to be neglected. And Malraux's slogan was: no one is ruled out. He was concerned to keep alive the spirit of revolutionary fraternity that he had known in Spain among combatants of all countries. ("You don't ask a fellow who is going to blow up a viaduct whether he has a clean police record.")

Malraux, accordingly, went to see Soleil, on his own territory, on the borderline of the Lot and Dordogne where he had set up his command post astride the converging cantons of Cazals and Villefranche in the Black Périgord. "People don't summon me, they come and find me," the Marseillais boasted. Malraux came to him, but in the role of inspector of the chestnut-grove battalions, as a coordinating mission-ary. He was quite aware of the danger of venturing, at night, on the roads leading into the Brel-Bas forest, where Soleil had his encamp-ment. According to an extravagant rumor that circulated briefly at the time, Soleil had been assigned to "physically liquidate" Malraux and do away with the corpse of the author of *La Condition humaine*. Mal-raux was an experienced commander; mistrustful, quite naturally he took his precautions. Among the trees surrounding Soleil's command post, with his acute sense of clandestine strategy, he stationed lookouts who were crack sharpshooters—just in case. That Malraux should be-come Soleil's prisoner was unthinkable. The fact that the encounter was to take place had been made known in advance in high places.

141

The meeting of Malraux and Soleil has remained an indelible episode in the history of the Black Périgord resistance for all those who witnessed it. On that day—June 25, 1944—two legends confronted each other: that of the man who by proxy was the voice and the eye of London, and that of the young man who had pushed his way to the front rank of the maquisard hierarchy. The Brouels had warned Malraux, "Soleil hates authority no matter where it stems from, but he will nevertheless listen to reason if pressured by the professional military. And his reputation does not do him justice. Since we gave him to understand that, in the general interest, he was not to encroach on our territory, he has observed the rules of the game."

When the combatant-writer walked up to the boldest of the extreme-left resistance chiefs, the latter was dumbfounded. Malraux, accompanied by several members of his staff (his *francs camarades,* as he used to call them), presented himself, held out his hand, and simply said, *"Salut!"* It was a luminous approach.

"He impressed me," Soleil admitted, after Malraux had left. "For the first time in my life I felt like springing to attention."

"You should have," Double-Mètre replied. "He's a great guy, who puts the resistance above politics."

It had taken five minutes for them to recognize Malraux as *le patron.*

Jacquot had been busy also, arranging rendezvous with the chiefs of the different groups, sending messengers to confirm the date and time of the vitally important meeting at the Château d'Urval. Like the Brouels, Colonels Georges and Veni (who headed a liberal group) and the other "responsible" leaders responded to the call. By morally disarming Soleil, meanwhile, Malraux had succeeded in making the other dissident hotheads of the rebellion toe the mark. What had seemed impossible to bring about—the round table conference over which Malraux would preside in the hall of the château where troubadours had once entertained the lords of Urval and their guests—had become an accomplished fact.

This did not mean that there were no problems. Jacquot was on tenterhooks because of the magnitude of the risk. Had there been a leak or an indiscretion or even a traitorous denunciation, the entire group could have been captured and killed, and all the maquisard resistance in the region would have been wiped out at one blow. Normally, such conferences were limited to the minimum and kept as short as possible. But the Château d'Urval meeting was so crucial that the risk simply had to be taken. There were some thirty-seven units under Colonel Berger's command; every one of the leaders was present that night.

When Malraux rose to address them, on the evening of July 17, 1944, he showed no nervousness. His was the firm, clear language of the *patron* on whose shoulders a whole infrastructure rested—about one-fifth of the French national resistance.

He said to them: "You are all chiefs here. I shall confirm you in your commands if you pledge yourselves to attack and to fight when I give you the order. Only then. I shall have those who do not obey executed." Henceforth the slightest of his messages was heard, listened to, and obeyed in Périgord and far beyond. Chiefs of opposed ideological tendencies—like the Marxist Ravanel—paid tribute to his lucid realism, to his serenity in command, to his bold anticipations.

As soon as Malraux had finished speaking, the fidgety Jacquot hastened to put in a word. "There, *messieurs,*" he said briskly, "now you know what we expect of you. The meeting is ended." During the entire evening, he had kept reassuring himself that his automatic pistol was ready to hand at his side.

"When it comes to war, real war, a theory is worthless if it is not put into practice, into movement," says Malraux. "When the largest armored division of the Third Reich is in your area and must under no circumstances get to Normandy—that is war. It is also the obligation to take responsibilities for oneself and for others. And if one has made a mistake, it is a duty to accept comments from no one."

First and foremost, however, this gifted warrior was a man. Where fear prevailed he reassured. Where disorder was rife he restored a sound control. The enemies were the Germans. Liberating France was more important to him than punishing "collaborators," Frenchmen who had supported Vichy through misguided motives, whether of the heart or of the head. "A life is worth nothing," Malraux has written, "but nothing is worth a life." There had been too much bloodshed, too many summary executions, too many fratricidal settlings of account.

"Better to kill one innocent than to let ten guilty get away," one rabid resistant had urged. But Malraux was firm. The innocent were no longer going to pay for the guilty. And the guilty would no longer be judged on the run—with two bullets in the back of the neck. Methods changed. People could breathe freely once more, the Republic could again be glimpsed on the horizon, with its three words on the pediments of its city halls: *Liberté, Egalité, Fraternité.* Malraux was there, and from the Château d'Urval he was giving a new dimension to the battle on the home front. It was resistance on a human scale.

"Every man needs to find his lyricism," he wrote in *L'Espoir*. Malraux had found his lyricism, and with him provinces previously torn asunder were now hopefully working together for peace.

Clara Malraux with her five-week-old daughter, Florence, in May, 1933.

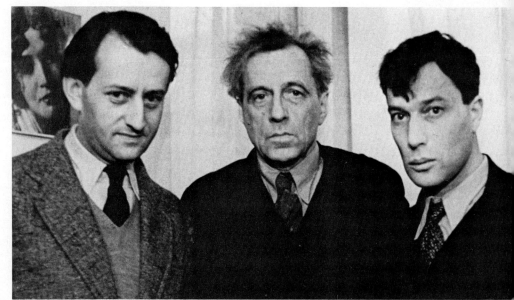

In a photograph (left) taken around 1935, André Malraux, aged about thirty-four, stands next to his good friend, writer Marcel Arland; seated at right is Paul Valéry, the great poet and essayist, then in his sixties; directly behind Valéry is Jean Paulhan, who was responsible for setting Malraux on the road to success by publishing his work in the *Nouvelle Revue Française*. Above, visiting Russia in August, 1934, Malraux poses with Vsevolod Meyerhold, director of the Moscow Revolutionary Theater, and writer Boris Pasternak (right). This photograph was presented to Malraux, when he revisited Moscow thirty-four years later, by the Soviet writer, Constantin Fedin.

February, 1934: About to set off in search of the lost capital of the Queen of Sheba, the three comrades in adventure joke on a French airfield in front of their Farman 190. Pilot Edouard Corniglion-Molinier is at left, the mechanic Maillard at center, Malraux—with the inevitable cigarette—on the right.

The Nocetto house, the palatial establishment that the French air squadron in Djibouti used as its headquarters, where Malraux and Corniglion-Molinier stayed while making ready for the Saba expedition. The squadron offices were on the ground floor, the living quarters on the floor above, with windows open to catch the least hint of any sea breeze to relieve the furnacelike heat.

Commandant Jean Esparre

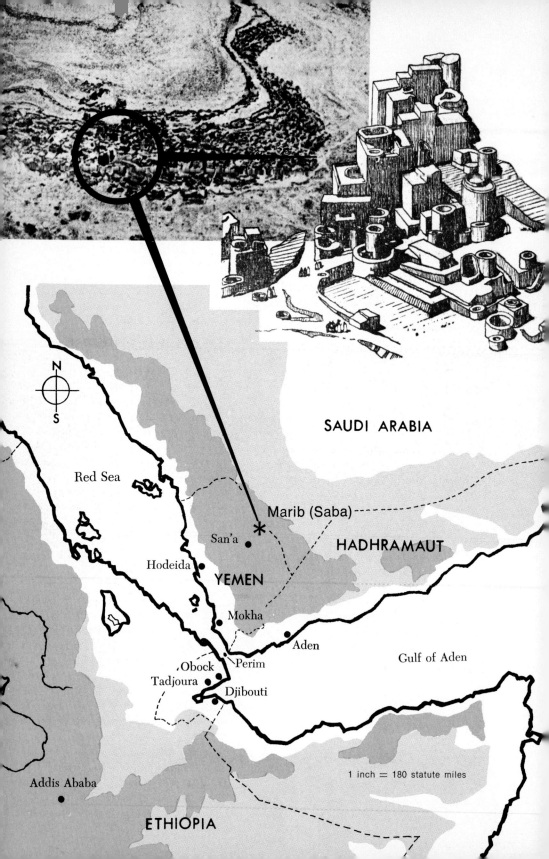

SAUDI ARABIA

Red Sea

Marib (Saba)

San'a

HADHRAMAUT

Hodeida

YEMEN

Mokha

Aden

Gulf of Aden

Obock

Perim

Tadjoura

Djibouti

Addis Ababa

ETHIOPIA

1 inch = 180 statute miles

The map at left shows how Malraux and Corniglion had to fly from Djibouti, at the mouth of the Red Sea, almost to the eastern border of Yemen, in southwest Arabia, before they found the city they were seeking, which it now seems likely was Marib rather than another lost capital. One of their photographs of the hillside city of "Saba" is inset at top left, and an architect's suggested reconstruction of one of its principal buildings at top right; both pictures are from the account of the trip published by Malraux in the French newspaper *L'Intransigeant*. Below, Malraux and Paul Gambert, one of his hosts in Djibouti, set off for Addis Ababa to receive the Emperor of Ethiopia's congratulations on the daring expedition to the capital of his ancestress.

Commandant Jean Esparre

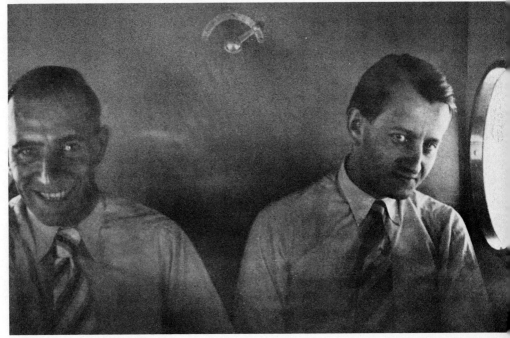

Josette Clotis, the able young writer who became Malraux's second wife in all but name, is seen here in Victorian costume. She bore him two sons, Gauthier and Vincent, before her tragic death in a railroad accident in 1944.

Coronel André Malraux of the International Flying Squadron supporting the Republicans during the Spanish Civil War stands in a flying suit beside one of his planes. He regularly joined his men on missions, acting as bombardier.

Hat in hand, Malraux arrives in Los Angeles during his United States tour in 1937 as unofficial spokesman and fund raiser for the Spanish Republicans.

At a Hollywood restaurant, the visiting Frenchman sits between director Robert Florey and author Clifford Odets (right), then a movie scriptwriter.

At Saint-Chamant in Corrèze, the district where he was in charge of maquis activity, Malraux takes a moment out from war with his elder son, Gauthier.

André Gide (left) and Malraux were old friends, despite the considerable dis-
parity in their ages. The great writer had a profound respect for his younger
confrere. "Every time Malraux opens his mouth," he said, "genius speaks."

Ex-tank corpsman Malraux, after his escape from a German POW camp in November, 1940.

ICI FUT ARRÊTÉ
LE 7 JANVIER 1945
PAR LA 1ᴱᴿᴱ D.F.L. ET LA
BRIGADE ALSACE-LORRAINE
L'OFFENSIVE ENNEMIE SUR
STRASBOURG

Memorial to the Alsace-Lorraine Brigade's achievement in the battle to prevent Strasbourg from being retaken by the Germans: "At this spot, on January 7, 1945, the First Free French Division and the Alsace-Lorraine Brigade halted the enemy offensive against Strasbourg."

At Stuttgart, with the war nearly won, General Jean de Lattre de Tassigny, commander in chief of the French First Army, presents "Colonel Berger," commander of the Alsace-Lorraine Brigade, with the Croix de Guerre. Malraux was honored with this decoration four times in the course of his unusually distinguished war service.

Old comrades-in-arms reminisce: In the tranquil setting of his book-lined study, Malraux entertains his former second-in-command in the resistance and in the Alsace-Lorraine Brigade, former Colonel, now General Pierre Jacquot.

In the spacious studio of his Bois de Boulogne home, Malraux works on the complicated task of laying out the illustrations for one of his books on art.

Maurice Jarnoux, Paris-Match

At his writing desk, with his eldest child, Clara Malraux's daughter, Florence.

André Malraux collection

The men of the family inspect a troop of Indian figures. The boys, from left to right, are Malraux's younger son, Vincent, his elder son, Gauthier, and his nephew, Alain, the son of Roland Malraux, who was killed during the war. Madeleine, Roland's widow, subsequently married André Malraux, and the three boys, who were very close in age, were brought up just like brothers.

Malraux and his wife, Madeleine, at the bedside of Gauthier, aged eighteen, who had fallen seriously ill during a vacation in Italy and was in a hospital.

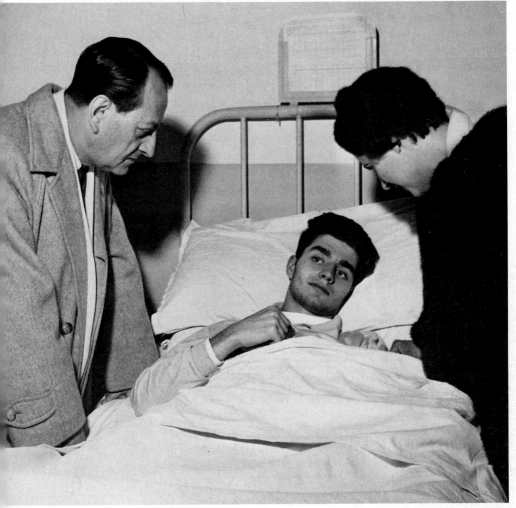

Three years later, in May, 1961, a grief-stricken Malraux enters the hospital at Beaune, near Dijon, in eastern France, where the bodies of Gauthier and Vincent had been taken after the car accident that cost them both their lives.

What more suitable setting for a minister of culture than the eighteenth-century elegance of the Palais-Royal, in Paris? Malraux, who never sits for photographers, agreed to pose for Philippe Halsman because Halsman had taken one of the only two pictures of him that the critical Malraux ever liked.

Spokesman for Gaullism: A born orator, full of brilliance and passion, Malraux ends a speech on behalf of General de Gaulle—whose poster dominates the platform—his face an eloquent tribute to the intensity of his emotion.

Jack Garofalo, Paris-Match

Paris-Match archives

At one of President de Gaulle's rare press conferences, Malraux shares the front row with Georges Pompidou, the general's heir-apparent. "I would always have this brilliant friend at my side," de Gaulle wrote of Malraux. "The image of me that this incomparable witness reflected continuously fortified me."

Malraux and Pompidou, in the latter's office, 1965. Malraux's relationship with Pompidou lacked the basis of personal friendship he had had with de Gaulle, and he quit the government when the general resigned, in May, 1969.

Jack Garofalo, Paris-Match

Jacques de Potier, Paris-Match

Walter Carone, Paris-Match

Malraux greets American author William Faulkner, whose work he has always admired (he wrote a preface for the French edition of Faulkner's *Sanctuary*). At right, Malraux talks to François Mauriac, one of France's most distinguished novelists (and winner of the Nobel Prize in 1952). Mauriac, who respected Malraux's ability but feared both his agnosticism and his early far-left sympathies, once described the younger man as a "bird of prey with magnificent eyes."

Novosty

At home and abroad, Malraux is constantly in distinguished company. At top left, he is welcomed by Prime Minister Nehru during his 1958 visit to India. Their intimate and free-ranging discussions form a fascinating section of Malraux's autobiography, *Antimémoires*. At top right, Malraux meets Russian officials in the Kremlin, in 1968. Premier Aleksei Kosygin is opposite him, with Malraux's Soviet counterpart, Minister of Culture Ekaterina Furtseva.

Paris-Match archives

With Jackie Kennedy—and the Mona Lisa—on the occasion of the Malraux-
arranged loan of the Louvre's most famous painting to the United States in
1963. Also present are President Kennedy and Madame Madeleine Malraux.

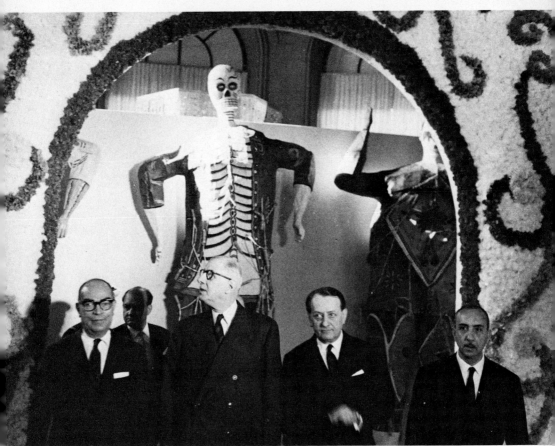

Philippe Le Tellier, Paris-Match

Malraux and President de Gaulle at the inauguration of a Mexican art exhibition in Paris on August 22, 1962. Malraux calls this an extraordinary picture because of the coincidence that the figure of Death lowers directly above de Gaulle's head. A few hours later, the president narrowly escaped an OAS assassination attempt as he was driving back to his country home at Colombey.

Reporters Associés
Agip

Malraux, the *amateur* of fine art: at left, at a showing of sculptures by Giacometti; at right, with an antique statuette of one of his favorite cats. Below, as minister of culture, he visits the prehistoric paintings at Lascaux, which he first saw while hiding resistance supplies in the caves during World War II.

Lagrange

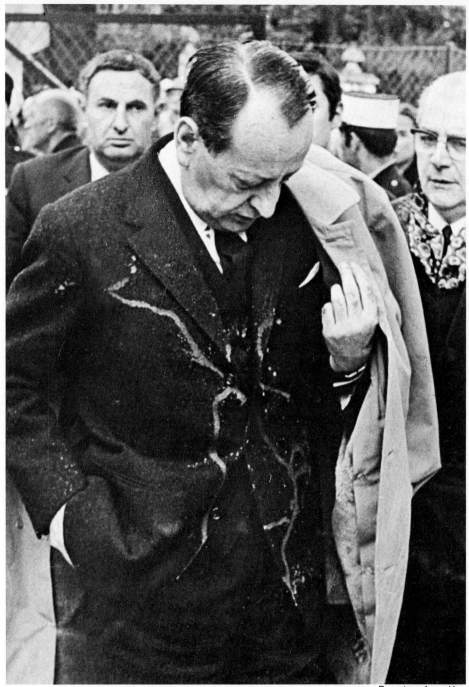

Above, on a visit to Nice in 1969 to lay the foundation stone of the building that will house one of Marc Chagall's most distinguished paintings, Malraux was splashed with paint by an enemy of Chagall's work. The minister seized the paint can and doused his attacker in turn. "Simply an aesthetic disagreement," was his comment as he examined the damage done to his suit.

Malraux's favorite Parisian restaurant is also one of the most exclusive: Lasserre, on the avenue Franklin Roosevelt. When in Paris, he eats there almost every day. Above, he lunches with Greek actress Melina Mercouri.

A peaceful cigarette with Louise de Vilmorin, the last of his loves, in the Blue Salon at her country château of Verrières. They are seated in an unusual *causeuse*—so-called because it allows three people to chat in comfort.

André and Louise, the lovers of Verrières, stroll in the gardens of the château.

9.

Resistance on a Human Scale

With Malraux at the helm, a sense of security gradually took the place of fear.

War had to be waged, subversive war, the war he knew best, the one he preferred, one might say, for it was the kind of warfare that most resembled revolution. Resistance was an active revolution, often improvised, which depended on harassing tactics and on surprise attacks.

What sort of action was it, precisely? The task was to delay, by sabotaging rail and road communications, the northward movement of German reinforcements to the Normandy front. The sabotage of the Souillac viaduct, for instance, in the Lot, on the line between Paris and Toulouse, cut the Germans' route to the third European front and prevented their retreat. Malraux's men also had to be prepared for actual battle, and many of them were undisciplined soldiers who all too often confused actual resistance to the enemy with the intoxication of uncontrolled power that being "in resistance" brought with it. Illegality had to be brought under control and integrated into clandestine legality.

Action thus consisted of instructing the new, inexperienced recruits and in inculcating a fresh approach upon the old—a new spirit to replace the outworn conceptions of 1939–40. The handling of a Sten machine gun can be learned in two minutes. What takes longer to learn is the rejection of the past in favor of a future on which a civilization will depend. Whereas training is a matter of pure technique, the transformation in the latter case is purely psychological.

"To transform experience into a consciousness—that is what it means to be a man," exclaims a Malraux character in one of the key chapters of *L'Espoir*. In the same book he has justified his title in these

145

words: "Hope is the force of the Revolution." These two quotations, inspired by two years of the Spanish Civil War, explain Malraux's attitude as maquisard in chief.

A chief commands and anticipates. Already Malraux was thinking about the future, about the "pockets," the blockhouse retreats prepared by the enemy to sustain long sieges, which were part of the famous Atlantic Wall.[1] The whole coastline from the Gironde to Brittany was one long succession of beaches bristling with barbed wire that was punctuated by a succession of imposing and lugubrious-looking block-houses. The Pointe de Grave, La Rochelle, Royan, Lorient (where Soleil, in April, 1945, would conduct himself heroically after receiving a bullet in his head) were the advance bastions of that fortress-ringed sea front.

Malraux's plan was to build up large hidden stores of weapons, and this required an intensification of parachute deliveries. Allied planes landing on narrow country airstrips brought machine guns. The supplies had to be stored in secret locations; many of these were the ancient caves that honeycombed the Dordogne area. It was on such storage missions that Malraux first saw—by the beam of a flashlight—the prehistoric wall paintings at Lascaux and Les Eyzies.

Action was not limited to these danger areas (for the Germans and militiamen kept the roads leading to the "hot points" under constant close surveillance); it also had to be pursued behind the front lines. A disunited France must be reunified, with a view to welcoming in a Fourth Republic that would replace the precarious French state Pétain had tried to build under the threat of the German guns, and which was already collapsing.

Lenin had a theory about the propagation of the ideological microbe: wrong-thinking people (even if they are not actually harmful) can in no case be assimilated with right-thinking people.

For Malraux there was such a thing as an offending *opinion,* but mistaken loyalty was not necessarily an offense. In the eyes of the maquisard in chief, the French who were opposed to General de Gaulle could be divided into two camps, those who served an idea and defended a cause (attachment to Marshal Pétain), and those who had betrayed France. In short, the camp of the passive and the camp of the active. It was only on the basis of this shade of distinction that a purge could even be conceived.

[1] This enormous reinforced concrete structure was wholly built by compulsorily recruited French laborers, under the direction of German engineers.

RESISTANCE ON A HUMAN SCALE

"I want no French blood on our hands, except in cases of outrage to the fatherland." Such words were often heard on Malraux's lips. The man shrank from punishing. He chastised only when it would have been cowardly not to do so.

How did he operate, in those days when impunity triumphed, when the only judge for the leader trying the guilty had to be his own conscience? He would convene a council of wise men, a kind of round table of local notables that would be attended by the mayor, the town councillor, the parish priest, the subprefect, the brigade commander, and such leaders of opinion as the schoolteacher or the doctor.

The man who faced a death sentence for committing a crime would be executed only after a trial behind closed doors and after having been given a chance to defend himself.

A secretary would take down the judgment of the notables (from the priest to the schoolteacher) regarding the defendant who was on trial. The evidence—for the prosecution and for the defense, on which the innocence or guilt of the suspect or traitor depended—would be typed in several copies, one for each juror in this exceptional court of exception. At the bottom of his declaration each juror affixed his signature; he was then asked to keep the document.

Collected to constitute a file, these sworn affidavits were to be sent, in triplicate, to the high authority of the clandestine hierarchy, the CNR.[2] Malraux for his part kept three copies of these declarations in a steel filing cabinet that he buried deep in the ground.

Why he took all these precautions will be readily understood. It was not in order to flee responsibilities, to be protected against possible future backlashes of history, to exculpate himself, as the man who made the decisions, behind those who pronounced judgment.

To Malraux it was of prime importance not to commit the gross error of confusing the victims and the guilty. If man is born to fight, he is not born to kill in cold blood.

What may be surprising—during this period that extends from the D-day landings in June to the moment when the Alsace-Lorraine Brigade went into battle the following October—is the absence of outstanding exploits that can be chalked up to the credit of an essentially spectacular man who has "put on a show" wherever he has passed.

Malraux, as we have said, has more than a life: he has a destiny,

[2] The *Conseil National de la Résistance*, which was headed by a Christian Democrat professor of history, Georges Bidault. He had succeeded Jean Moulin, one of the great figures of the resistance, after the latter's arrest and death under torture.

MALRAUX

a destiny that progressively affirms itself. To this destiny is grafted his
legend, which has followed his footsteps since the age of twenty. On
this score, we must quote Pierre Laval's remark when, referring to the
Franco-Soviet discussions of 1933, he said, "Stalin felt a decided liking
for two Frenchmen, Malraux and myself."[3]

Malraux the maquisard gave to an incoherent rebellion its patent
of nobility—order, tolerance, honesty. Like Lawrence of Arabia,[4] he
harnessed himself to those "obscure labors that prepare dazzling victories."

Hardly any of the labors that Malraux accomplished in the shadow
of those resistance days are known. To save the treasures of the Louvre
from Hermann Göring's greedy hands[5] (or from the no less rapacious
German Bureau of Artistic Property), the bulk of the masterpieces had
been given shelter in the Ingres Museum of Montauban, which seemed
a perfect haven at the end of the interminable exodus of June, 1940.
André Chamson, who would later accompany Berger in his Alsatian
crusade, and René Huygues were the chief curators of those two
museums whose combined treasures were literally beyond price. Youths
doing their compulsory training in the Vichy-sponsored *Chantiers de
la Jeunesse*[6] were made responsible for watching over these treasures.
When times became more uncertain, a safer hiding place had to be
found. Chamson and Huygues immediately called upon Malraux for
his advice and knowledge. With his complicity, the Mona Lisa, the
Botticellis, the Vermeers (some two thousand canvases) were taken
by truck to the Château du Montae, in Saint-Cére, close to Corrèze,
where Anatole de Monzie was living in half-enforced retirement. De
Monzie, who had served twenty-two times as a minister in the Third
Republic, had been an admirer of Malraux's work since the publication
of *La Tentation de l'Occident*. There was a rumor, at the time of the
liberation of the Lot, to the effect that if the ex-minister had been

[3] This remark has been confirmed by Josée Laval, now Madame René de Chambrun, the
daughter of "the man in the white tie" who, starting out as mayor of Aubervilliers (a
working-class suburb of Paris), found himself the actual leader of the French state of
which Pétain was the symbolic head. For a quarter of a century, Laval was one of the
great political figures of France. It is interesting to realize that Malraux, as always
precursor and prophet, was personally acquainted with Stalin as early as 1932.
[4] T. E. Lawrence's memoirs, *Seven Pillars of Wisdom,* so impressed Malraux that he
wrote a lengthy study of Lawrence during his stay at Roquebrune, which was published after the war.
[5] The head of the Luftwaffe always had a weakness for good painting, without regard
to schools. "A great Bonnard is worth a genuine Cranach," he used to say.
[6] From the time of the 1940 armistice until the liberation of France, all French youths
of twenty, instead of being drafted for military training, had to undergo an eight-month
training course in these youth camps.

148

neither arrested nor robbed by the maquisards, he owed it to his connection with Malraux.

Events were moving fast. On July 23, 1944, on the road between Gramat and Labastide-Murat in the Lot, where he had gone to arbitrate a dispute between two rival maquis units, Malraux and four of his men were trapped by a German ambush. They abandoned their car and ran across a wheat field, their one hope of escaping the enemy. The Germans opened fire. Malraux fell, wounded in the leg, and was captured; the others were killed. Colonel Berger was wearing a field-service tunic without stripes. The men of the Abwehr, in the lobby of the Hôtel de France in Gramat where he was taken for questioning, thought they had caught a terrorist.

He was first subjected to the ritual psychological conditioning. He was brought from the barn where he had been taken on a stretcher and stood up against a wall before a firing squad; the soldiers aimed; Malraux stared at their bent heads. Then an officer shouted, "At ease!" and they lowered their weapons, looking disappointed. If his life was being spared, Malraux realized, it was in order to obtain valuable information from him. He was well aware of the methods.

There followed the dreary stages of a too well known itinerary, worked out in detail like a theatrical performance. But with Malraux, destiny (or the gods) always leaves the door ajar for the unforeseen. In this case, it verged on the absurd.

The officer conducting the questioning did not dare to believe that Malraux was telling the truth when he admitted, quite freely, who he was; it would be too fine a catch. The man who called himself Malraux was bluffing, was lying. The journey to Toulouse, the successive interrogations by a German general and by the Gestapo, the hostages who were tortured in order to "impress" the next "client"—nothing was spared, save the unforeseen end. Malraux has told in the *Antimémoires* how he was, in fact, saved by a confusion of identity (an analogy of given names) with his own brother Roland, whose case history was supplied to the Gestapo instead of that of André himself.

From Gramat through the Abwehr, the military police, and then from Cahors through the Gestapo, the Malraux record (because of his importance as a figure) was communicated to Paris for verification. The delays in the mail, the dismantling of the railroad network, the general confusion prevented the corrected Malraux record from reaching Toulouse before the city was liberated.

Less than a week had passed between the "summit" meeting in

Urval and July 23, the day on which Malraux fell into the hands of the Germans. This meant that the liberation of the territories that he was assigned to free had to be carried out without him. But Colonel Berger had taken his job as military leader seriously and had made provision for his succession "in case of trouble." His adjutant, Colonel Jacquot, replaced him, and it was to Jacquot that the German garrisons of Brive and of Tulle handed in their surrender on August 15.

The tide was beginning to turn, though the fates had determined that Malraux would not be on hand when, from August 14 to 23, the yokes of the Wehrmacht, the Feldgendarmerie, and the Gestapo burst in Agen, Périgueux, and Cahors. On August 24 he liberated himself and his cellmates from the Saint-Michel prison in Toulouse by smashing the door of the cell with a piece of heavy timber. Elected by popular acclaim as the leader of the motley crew of prisoners milling in chaos around the prison building, which the Germans had abandoned in their haste to leave Toulouse, he quickly established some kind of order that would permit them all to get away safely.

Once again Malraux found himself free and whole, while the Germans, emptying their last cartridges before their exodus, cracked the skull of Jean Cassou[7] with their boots and the butts of their guns, leaving him—as they thought—dead in front of the railroad station.

Losing no time in renewing the necessary contacts, in making a lightning descent upon his deputy, Malraux again took his men in hand.

"It is always difficult," says Malraux, "unless one is the incarnation of vanity, to speak of one's feats of war. But it was we who obtained the first surrender of a German unit to one in the resistance. The ways and means of surrender were worked out by Colonel Jacquot, my successor, since I was a prisoner. We had no buildings in which to lodge the officers who had just surrendered, nor camps in which to confine the men. My comrades ran the risk of being shot an hour later. . . . But it was essential to attend to what was most urgent—the surrender."

At Autun, in the Charolais, the Wehrmacht battalions, decimated by the Americans ascending the Rhône Valley from Provence,[8] joined with the units that were fleeing before the FFI. The resistance was becoming outright warfare; it was shedding its skin.

---

[7] The resistance writer, painting enthusiast, and distinguished authority on Spanish literature, whose knowledge of the arts subsequently won him the directorship of the Paris Museum of Modern Art.

[8] The landing in Provence that created the second French front took place on August 15.

To those who did not want to continue with him to Autun, Malraux gave free choice. Men would be needed to clean up the "pockets" on the Atlantic. The maquis of the southwest split in two. Malraux continued in pursuit, carrying the war back to the country whence it had come. To his chauffeur, Roger Bouyssou (then a mechanic, now a butcher), Malraux said, "If you don't feel that soldiering is your vocation, go back to your work, but drive me to where I must go."

Inevitably Malraux had become Berger, and he intended somehow to carry through an idea that now obsessed him—to form an Alsace-Lorraine Brigade from among the many Alsatians who had served under him in the maquis, which would take an active part in the deliverance of a province he had come to feel specially attached to.

In Saint-Chamant he stopped off to embrace Josette Clotis, who had shared with him good days and bad.

"A joyous period," he was to say later, banteringly, of the days he had just lived through. He would not forget them. He would forget nothing. Twenty-four years later, he had a sumptuous spray of flowers placed on the grave of the proprietress of the Hôtel de France in Gramat, on the day of her funeral.

Between two of his questionings by the Abwehr, she had brought him, with defiance in her peasant's eyes, a steaming cup of *café au lait* with slices of buttered bread right out of the oven.

THE RESISTANCE IN CORREZE, DORDOGNE, AND THE LOT

Colonel Jacquot, today a reserve army general, who with André Malraux was one of the men most responsible for the successes of the French Forces of the Interior, has passed on to me his notes on the resistance in Corrèze, Dordogne, and the Lot. Their style is all the more eloquent for being coldly military. The bulk of them were written in September, 1944, three months after the landing of the Allied armies. General Jacquot has added a brief summation:

The action of the armed units of the interior French resistance made it possible to liberate the whole southwest of our country without any assistance from the regular armies. The combats waged in this vast region, at the time of the landing on June 6, 1944, in Normandy, retarded the entry into action on the main field of battle of particularly formidable large units like the Das Reich Division. The collapse of the local German garrisons that followed the capitulation of Brive on August 15, 1944, likewise facilitated the advance of the Franco-American army group that landed in Provence by eliminating any threat to its western flank.

This brief but effective participation in the carrying out of the Allied strategic maneuver is not the only one to be noted. The action of the saboteurs who paralyzed road and rail transport and laid ambushes for the enemy sector troops contributed appreciably to the disorganization of the German plans and to the demoralization of the Wehrmacht. Independently of its real force, the maquis, by its very existence, represented a permanent and elusive menace, which the blind repression carried out by the Gestapo, the passing German troops, and the French Vichy militia only reinforced and hardened, regardless of the losses the maquis suffered.

It is important to specify what these units were and what they were able to accomplish, despite the fact that external aid was both belated and limited.

The fiction of the French Forces of the Interior: The appellation "French Forces of the Interior" given to the armed units of the resistance operating on national territory corresponded neither to moral nor to material reality. The maquis in fact belonged to various social and political horizons. The *Armée Secrète* (AS), reinforced by the career soldiers assembled in the ORA (*Organisation de la Résistance de l'Armée*), was composed of various shades of republican opinion, from socialists to conservatives; the partisan *francs-tireurs* (FTP) were under Communist leadership; finally, numerous maquisards obeyed the orders of independent chiefs whose authority and prestige were sufficiently great to enable them to subsist in the margin of the larger groupings. Holding together men who had very different concepts of what the social structure of France should be after the departure of the enemy was a considerable gamble. . . .

The forces and armament: The maquis forces remained rather weak until the landing in June of 1944. The stocks of weapons and munitions at their disposal did not allow any considerable increase in the number of clandestine volunteers. Had the forces been too numerous, they would only have increased their costs and their dangers, and would have created even greater weaknesses. A mass uprising makes no more sense and is no more effective in an insurrectional war than in a conflict between regular armies. Numbers do not in themselves

constitute a force. The decision reached by the Free French authorities in Algiers, after the June landing, to link up the ranks of the
maquis with the declared forces complicated the task of the local chiefs,
in fact, more than it strengthened the power of the insurrection.

Constitution and structure of the maquis: The first maquis unit
appeared in Corrèze in the early summer of 1943. The threat hanging
over all able-bodied young men of being deported to serve as forced
laborers in Germany greatly contributed to its increase in numbers.
Hope of an Allied landing on French territory in the fall of 1943,
hinted at by the London radio, likewise brought many volunteers into
the maquis.

In early October, 1943, when the hope of an imminent landing
collapsed, the local chiefs realized they were going to have the heavy
responsibility of seeing those who had volunteered prematurely through
the winter. It was out of the question to send home those who could
not be armed. It would have meant handing them over to the Gestapo.

It was a severe ordeal, but patriotic faith won over hardship. De-
sertions were few despite the meager food supplies. As the spring of
1944 approached, the numbers began to grow once more, under the
double stimulus of the hope of a forthcoming landing and the man-
hunt being conducted in the towns by the Vichy French militia and
the German police.

The major problem remained the supply of arms and especially
of munitions. Parachute deliveries, repeatedly promised, often did not
materialize and were always insufficient. Messages sent out by London
radio were far from being uniformly honored. Yet at each announcement courageous men took serious risks to provide ground lights, and
arrests were proportional to the number of sorties. Many angry words
were heard in the various resistance groups.

When the national insurrection broke out on June 6, 1944, the
arms that the maquisards could lay their hands on were utterly inade-
quate, made up mostly of hunting rifles and automatic pistols obtained
commercially. In lower Corrèze, however, a number of French Lewis
guns had been captured, with their ammunition, from the Forty-first
Infantry Regiment barracks in Brive, before the town was occupied by
the Germans in November, 1942. These automatic weapons and the
unparalleled valor of the insurrectional chief who had captured them
were the secret of maquis power in the Brive region.

In Dordogne and the Lot the situation was unfavorable. Rumors
that certain units were systematically favored [on arms drops] as com-

pared to others appear to be without foundation, however, for the shortage was general and affected the AS as severely as the FTP. It was to continue in all three departments until the large-scale parachute deliveries of July 14, 1944, which radically transformed the situation.

The battle of June 6, 1944, and the following days: This difficult situation was further aggravated on the day of the Allied landing in Normandy by an erroneous call from London radio for general and immediate insurrection throughout the territory.

That night, while the German militia and garrisons were entrenched in their billets, the saboteurs went methodically to work and obtained unhoped-for results. By dawn the railroad system was full of torn-up tracks and many of the main highways were cut. Groups of resolute men left the towns, with no attempt at dissimulation, to join the maquis, where they confidently expected to be given arms. The resistance chiefs were thunderstruck when they saw this human flood arriving, because all their weapons had already been distributed and their units were all set to go into combat in an attack on the German forces about to pass through the region on their way to Normandy. The subsequent rectification by London radio limiting the field of the immediate insurrection could do nothing to alter the situation. These men now had to be fed and protected; otherwise they would be handed over to the Gestapo or the militia.

Such was the additional problem that this London radio error, hard to excuse, brought on the chiefs of the maquis on the day that they were going to involve their troops all-out and thereby participate in an exceptional action in support of the landing forces.

With the strategic sense for which he was known, General Revers, who commanded the ORA, had for a long time advocated opening a barrage of fire on the Dordogne, flanked to the north and to the south by a deep network of ambushes. This well-conceived idea was adopted by most of the maquis chiefs; it implied the acceptance of heavy losses and the certainty of exhausting the available ammunition in two or three days of combat, but it had the great advantage of bringing the maquis forces of the Lot, of lower Corrèze, and of Dordogne out of the local role and having them participate in the main battle.

Chance gave a special luster to this combat because the first big German unit to appear was the Das Reich Division, on its way to the Normandy front.

The conduct under fire of the volunteers of every political allegiance was exemplary. At the Bretenoux bridge, some thirty partisans were wiped out after having held up tanks and infantry with their barricades and machine guns for nearly an hour. In Noailles, in Sarlat, the young maquis troops fought with notable heroism. The Das Reich Division lost nearly forty-eight hours of its planned schedule between Cahors and Limoges. Its chief finally decided to follow an itinerary farther west, avoiding the foothills of the Massif Central. The RAF, alerted by our network's secret sending stations, attacked it near Angoulême, and thus relieved the maquis.

By June 9, the munitions had run out save for the strict minimum needed for the units' security. The maquis heads decided to break off combat until fresh ammunition supplies could be brought by parachute. A commando unit continued to harass the enemy on the roads, however, and the sabotage of the railroad system was kept up.

This lull continued until July 14, on which date a huge parachute drop was carried out in broad daylight from ten o'clock till noon. Its twelve hundred containers full of arms and munitions brought to the maquis of the three departments what they needed to resume active combat against the local enemy forces.

The resumption of battle and the destruction of the enemy forces: Colonel Berger, alias André Malraux, decided immediately to intensify the guerrilla activity and to undertake to roll back the local German forces in the direction of their garrison towns.

Colonel Berger's idea was to distribute the territory among the different maquis chiefs and make them responsible for the effectiveness of the ambushes and the breaks in the rail and road connections in the sectors for which they were responsible. This plan . . . was worked out technically by Lieutenant Colonel Jacquot, Colonel Berger's second-in-command, and accepted by the maquis chiefs as a body at a meeting held on July 17 at the Château d'Urval, in Dordogne. Colonel Berger, at the end of the meeting, emphasized that every maquis chief would answer with his life for any insufficiency in the action of his forces in the zone for which he had assumed responsibility. It never came to this, but the warning was a salutary one for one or two who tended to take their responsibilities a little lightly.

On July 23, 1944, Colonel Berger was wounded and fell into the hands of the Germans. In his Citroën bearing the cross of Lorraine insignia, he had traveled on a main road in order to gain time, instead of taking the small side roads, and had run into a German patrol.

Lieutenant Colonel Jacquot succeeded Colonel Berger and took over his responsibilities. The rare sorties of the German garrisons became costly and demoralizing operations. By early August the maquis controlled almost the whole territory of the three departments with the exception of the towns of Brive, Tulle, Ussel, Périgueux, Bergerac, and Cahors. The enemy showed growing signs of weariness. The unsuccessful plot against Hitler caused clashes between the Wehrmacht command and the SS.

The resistance chiefs decided to carry the combat to the very gates of the cities still held by the Germans.

On August 13 and 14 the commander of the German troops in Corrèze engaged in negotiations through various channels. The subprefect of Brive, M. Chaussade, facilitated their conclusion by bold and skillful interventions. Lieutenant Colonel Jacquot, at the request of the local chiefs present, consented to draw up and sign the acts of capitulation.

A general convention for Corrèze and a special execution convention for the Brive garrison were signed on August 15 at 9:15 P.M., to go into effect in Brive at 11 P.M. A convention for Tulle was drawn up on August 16, late at night, going into effect on August 17 at 8 A.M. The FTP and AS chiefs were present and affixed their signatures to the documents.

The garrisons of the two towns surrendered in accordance with the international conventions governing prisoners of war. Virtually all their equipment fell intact into the hands of the maquis. In the week that followed, the other garrisons fell or escaped after several battles. . . . On August 25 the total liberation of the three departments was an accomplished fact. It was the work of the maquis and of it alone.

An uncertain period was to succeed the combat phase. Certain volunteers considered their task terminated. Others thought only of continuing the struggle. The first conception had honorable advocates—men of a certain age, semi-invalids, civil servants bound to their posts. There were also those who felt that the time for material or political advantage had come. For the younger resistance chiefs, and in particular for those who had belonged to the army, there was no problem. Their duty was to lead those volunteers who wished to continue to serve, to constitute marching units and lead them to the fighting wherever it was going on.

By the first week of September, the Secret Army brigade of Corrèze had boarded the train for the east. Several sniper and partisan battalions set out westward for the "pockets" still held by the Germans on the Atlantic seaboard. The men from Alsace and Lorraine who had sought refuge in the southwest, reinforced by local elements, formed the independent Alsace-Lorraine Brigade and started out by road in the direction of Dijon to participate in the liberation of their two provinces.

The sequel is no longer the history of the resistance but that of the collaboration with the French First Army of the units that came from the maquis. It is another adventure, complicated but not devoid of greatness, which led, in accordance with the government's wish, to the progressive integration of the insurrectional bodies into the regular army. General de Lattre de Tassigny succeeded in bringing about this amalgamation while avoiding any unnecessary slights.

The interior armed resistance had had its day. It has often been attacked by those who had reasons to be systematically hostile to it. It has been attacked also by others who deplored too many excesses committed after the liberation of the territory. The climate of the period explains, without justifying, the violences committed. These in no way detract from the patriotic character of the national insurrection.

General Eisenhower has spoken in moving terms of what he felt he owed to the army without uniforms that rose up at the time of the landing. It had required the great blast of the French Revolution of 1793, or the pathetic appeals of Gambetta in 1870–71, to bring together an equally great number of volunteers. France can be proud of all her men who fell in the maquis, or who died in the horrors of the deportee camps, thereby giving a national character to the liberation of their country.

10.

Colonel Berger and His Brigade

The men from Alsace and Lorraine had made a bold decision: to go home, weapons in hand, forcing their passage as dramatically as they had left—rather than with suitcase and railroad ticket.

Bernard Metz, a native of Strasbourg, who is today a professor in the faculty of medicine of that city, was made responsible for regrouping the Alsatians among the maquisards of the southwest. He and Father Pierre Bockel, today dean of the cathedral of Strasbourg, jointly had the idea of forming an autonomous unit. They needed a chief to lead them. Colonel Jacquot suggested that the Alsatians take Malraux as commander of their unit. He would continue to be known as Colonel Berger. The men who would be his subordinates were quickly won over to the idea, and when Metz made his proposal, Malraux was enthusiastic and at once replied that the adventure appealed to him.

It was now necessary to obtain authorization to create an autonomous brigade, because all the FFI had automatically been integrated into the French First Army. Malraux and Jacquot went to Limoges to visit the regional military delegate, who opposed the project and refused to relinquish the best battalion—that of Major Paul Diener-Ancel. Malraux and Jacquot acted with dispatch. Accompanied by Bernard Metz, they instantly went to Toulouse to appeal to General Chevance-Bertin, who had full powers over the FFI of the southern zone.

By chance they caught sight of the general in the street, as he was riding through on a motorcycle. They called out to him, he stopped, and Malraux and Metz at once engaged him in conversation. Jacquot, meanwhile, left them and went directly to the general's office.

158

There he found his adjutant, Colonel Pfister, an Alsatian and a friend, who received Jacquot warmly and immediately told him, "There is nothing to prevent me from signing the paper regularizing the creation of the brigade." The trip had paid off handsomely.

Malraux immediately named his new command "the independent Alsace-Lorraine Brigade." The name was a kind of echo of the Spanish war. "We liked it," says Bernard Metz, "and we were delighted to see the corrosive effect it had on certain staffs and offices."

Colonel Berger decided to continue to wear the black Basque beret of the Spanish Republicans, a beret loathed by the Nazis because they saw it as a continual reminder of the presence, in occupied Alsace, of France and the French.

For Malraux this adventure was to be, in the highest degree, both an undertaking of liberation and a symbol. It appealed to the adventurer in him, to the lover of fraternity and human freedom, and to the artist.

After having been Indochinese with the Indochinese, Catalan or Basque with the Catalans and the Basques, he now became an Alsatian with the Alsatians, in order to reconquer and liberate that province of which the spire of Strasbourg was both the main objective and the symbol.

But his intent was not only to free a people and a province from tyranny and oppression. He wanted the adventure to be, for the men whom he led to combat, an opportunity for them, the humiliated, to reconquer a "liberty of free men."

Nevertheless, certain officers did not have confidence in Malraux, whom they considered to be above all a partisan. Others, who like him were authentic members of the resistance, raised their arms to heaven when they learned that Colonel Berger was to lead them to battle and to the Rhine. They had not forgotten the visit he paid in May, 1944, to the "Alsace-Lorraine Legion," a maquis unit of the Secret Army. He was wearing a colonel's uniform and had saluted the unit flag with a raised fist.

But in September, 1944, when these officers made contact with Berger, they found that he had exactly the same basic ideas as they about the future of the country, and that he gave evidence of the strictest patriotism now that he was at the head of the Alsace-Lorraine Brigade. "As a mattter of fact," Malraux said, "in Spain my worst enemies were the Communists."

Father Bockel, who became the brigade's chaplain, gives us his impressions of his first contact with Colonel Berger:

159

Somewhere in Corrèze in a huge school playground—an oddly recreational atmosphere. The joyous cries of school-children were replaced by the virile hubbub of a troop from which burst orders and curses with a background roar of motors, the rattle of arms and mess cans. The Metz battalion of the Alsace-Lorraine Brigade, en route to the Vosges front, was preparing to bivouac. But then something happened. The deafening din vanished as if swept away by a wave that spread across the playground. Colonel Berger! Someone was calling me. Overcome both by curiosity and awe—this was a first contact—I hurried to the spot from which the silence had spread. I came to attention. "My respects, colonel. . . ."

An odd kind of colonel. To be sure, he wore his uniform with perfect elegance and, except for that legendary "irregular" small black beret, nothing in his dress would have distinguished him from any other officer. And yet there was nothing about his face or his manner—if the military will forgive me for saying so—to suggest the traditional type of a "regular." Beyond the young, drawn face, constantly moving, shaken by incessant tics, behind the serious glance that conveyed both courage and lucidity, behind the tragic face, it was easy to recognize Malraux. The conversation was brief, laconic, cold. I was still standing at attention, in perplexity rather than out of discipline, when the colonel's car disappeared. This first appearance had a shock effect on me. I understood then the remark I was told André Gide had made: "When you are in front of Malraux, you no longer feel very intelligent."

We met again a few days later before General de Lattre's headquarters in Besançon. It was there, as we paced back and forth in the rue du Lycée, that I really got to know Colonel Berger and was able to rectify the somewhat severe impression of the first contact. I was very quickly put at my ease by his friendly manner, and it was not long before we felt ourselves in mutual "complicity," to use an expression that he is fond of.

This meeting was the beginning of a friendship.

I could guess what the Alsace-Lorraine Brigade meant to him. Of course it represented an opportunity for a great adventure, which was a logical sequel to that of the underground . . . and so many others. And this adventure had two choice features: a great objective—Alsace and Lorraine—and

excellent material to work with—all those young people who had
managed to escape and then had become underground fighters, impelled by a fierce determination to return to their homes,
to participate, at whatever risk, in the liberation of their
soil, of their families, of their friends. But beyond the adventure
itself, it may be worth saying that two considerations chiefly impelled Berger. Both of them had to do with men from Alsace
and Lorraine, those men back home who were awaiting the end
of their enslavement and those who, along with him and
under his command, had decided to pay the price of liberty.

The first must be given back their freedom; the others,
those of the brigade, must be given the opportunity, through
a heroic adventure, to become free men through the consciousness that they were serving, of their own free will, a cause that
was greater than themselves.

It was getting late. Berger took me to dinner in a small
restaurant in the town where we ran into other officers of the
brigade. I had a first taste of the colonel's mess. An odd kind
of mess, which, with Berger, Colonel Jacquot, who was the
second-in-command, and Major André Chamson,[1] was a kind
of combination of a drawing room, a circus, and an amphitheater.

Berger charmed everyone at the meal. He liked to chaff
and a good-natured smile would often light up his serious
face. He enjoyed a brigade joke or the story of a somewhat
savage exploit of one of his men. He liked, in fact, the reputation his unit had of being a little wild, everything that
marked it off from the too "regular" type . . . probably because this sense of the picturesque and of humor expressed
in its own way a sense of freedom.

These meals, begun in the hubbub of many exchanges,
would often end in a scintillating monologue. Berger liked
to pick up a sentence in midair, as it were, and complete the
idea that another had started to express, and would then develop it with amazing lucidity and astuteness. Only a few
words were needed to launch him on a theme, which he would

---

[1] The distinguished writer André Chamson served during the war as curator of all the
national museums, which of course included the Louvre. He was on the staff of General de Lattre de Tassigny, commander in chief of the French First Army, but was
currently serving as liaison officer with Malraux's brigade.

sometimes explore in its worldwide implications, and he had a knack for recognizing and seizing in the present the signs that prefigured the future.

From every event, Malraux could trace extraordinary and impressive lessons; he also had the art of drawing random but profound parallels, as, for example, in the Dordogne, when he was talking one day with Professor Fontaine, dean of the faculty of medicine at Strasbourg, who was posted to the hospital at Clairvine. Malraux gave the dean a stunning discourse on psychosomatic medicine and the magical acts performed by the shamans among certain tribes in North America, Siberia, and the far north of Asia. With André Chamson, he would talk with equal brilliance about art, music, painting, theology, the form of French law, or palmistry. He had a very broad idea of Mediterranean culture and civilization. He believed that Europe could bring the United States and the Soviet Union a sense of the values of the Christian West. As Father Bockel puts it, "He has always had a sense of adventure, in the noble sense of the word."

Action in the maquis of Corrèze had been for Malraux a complete episode. An adventure. He had been a perfect *guerrillero*. He considered this chapter ended with his escape from prison in Toulouse. He was now beginning a new adventure, the Alsace-Lorraine Brigade, to which he would apply the classical rules of the military art, rules he seemed to understand instinctively.

The brigade at first included Alsatians who were deserters from the Wehrmacht, a Belgian captain, and a few other foreigners, all wearing American uniforms. When the brigade became attached to the French First Army, it became necessary to weed out the "foreigners." Colonel Berger let them go only in the last extremity and with great reluctance.

He had two concerns, to obtain the intelligent participation of his men, and to see to it that they were provided with at least the normal means of combat. Those concerns certain services of the regular army did not always understand. Malraux, who was very relaxed with his officers, sometimes seemed a bit timid in the presence of private soldiers; they admired him nevertheless, even without understanding him, and swore by him.

For those twenty-two hundred men Malraux was a familiar enigma: a chief who treated his subalterns as buddies, who asked about their children, who looked at the snapshots they showed him. It is not the number of men that matters—it is the stuff they are made of. Malraux went about fashioning "his" brigade with a reasoned enthusiasm, combined with remarkable psychological insight, making one think from time to time of Trotsky organizing his crack battalions for the Red Army.

In his discussions with his officers, Malraux refused to speculate on France's political future. He had only one objective, inherited from the revolutionary tradition—to drive the enemy from French territory. In staff conferences he would generally opt for the most direct—and least ·orthodox—solution to a problem. He conceived the command of his unit only in the spirit of traditional courage, and consequently was always in the front line.

One day, after having briefed his officers and men on what was going to happen, he concluded his speech by calling upon all the assembled soldiers to stand at attention. "I am counting on each one of you," he said, with a wholly military absence of emotion, "to perform the henceforth sacred duty of liberating Alsace, and I salute, gentlemen, those who tomorrow will fall on the field of honor!"

He exposed himself deliberately. In the course of the first engagements in the Vosges, he said to André Chamson, "Ah! how fine it would be to die here, on this soil of Alsace!"

During the Sundgau offensive he and an officer cadet set off alone to blow up a viaduct.

During the fighting in the Mulhouse region, General Schlesser asked Colonel Berger for a detachment to neutralize an armored train that was giving trouble.

"Never mind, I'll go myself," Berger replied—and he did.

When Altkirch was taken, brigade headquarters was set up in the only available room in one of the few buildings still standing. The windows directly overlooked the enemy lines. "Never mind," said Malraux. "Let's get to work right away."

Jacquot tells the story of how a regular officer "came to us one day to say that he considered it out of the question to order his men into battle without their having had sufficient military training. We answered that he was surely right, but that circumstances were dramatic enough for the units of the First Army we were reinforcing to force us to take this risk.

"He then asked to leave. We had him pass before a commission, which informed him that he was relieved of his command."

163

One of the commission members proposed that the officer be court-martialed, but Malraux at once broke in:

"In the Alsace-Lorraine Brigade we don't court-martial our men. Take him to the station at Luxeuil and let him take the first train. *Ainsi soit-il!*"

Father Bockel, the brigade chaplain, has vivid memories of Malraux as an intrepid commander:

While the battle was raging, nerves sometimes weakened and fear or despair seized one or the other of us. It was then that the silhouette of Colonel Berger would appear on a knoll or on the edge of a forest. A cigarette between his lips, he would give a brief order, then silently gaze in the direction of the adversary with a look that we knew to be charged with something completely different from hate, because Malraux has always scorned hate as much as he has despised war. "Ah! if only victory would rest with those who wage war without liking it," he wrote in *La Lutte avec l'Ange.* That silent and dignified presence—"Dignity," he wrote, "is the contrary of humiliation"—was enough to revive faltering courage, because it was both an example and a symbol: the symbol of our common will, which he incarnated.

Was he looking for death? We might have thought so from the way in which he exposed himself to danger and also because we knew that such a death was to him the supreme act of freedom—the giving of one's life for the life of others is the ultimate means by which man both liberates and transcends himself.

This was felt deep down, at least in a confused way, by each of Malraux's soldiers, each of the "partisans." It was sometimes necessary to reveal it to them in explicit terms, to reveal them, in fact, to themselves: why they were fighting, these freedom volunteers—for we were only volunteers—and how from this free giving of themselves to a cause that transcended them because it was shared by others, was the cause of a whole people, of man himself, in short, they would acquire a new dignity and a fresh dimension, the dignity of free men.

Death was often the key word for Colonel Berger. But it was obvious that for him death thus assumed an absolute and transcendent value. An agnostic, he was perfectly aware that at that level his thought and his commitment expressed values that were shared by the Christian majority of his unit. You could even say that this passionate love of man and liberty revealed new depths of faith in us. He knew this and secretly delighted in it. To such a point that certain anticlerical spirits humorously christened our unit "Colonel Malraux's Choirboy Brigade."

While Malraux continued to court danger, to push every encounter to the limits, Josette remained in Saint-Chamant in a comfortable house where a locally recruited *gouvernante* helped her look after her two little boys, Gauthier and Vincent. In the icy maquis of upper Corrèze she had shared his bed and his life. She had given him what no other woman had given him—two sons. His marriage to Clara had produced only one living child, his daughter, Florence, born in 1933, who was being brought up by her mother, apart from Malraux by necessity. The fact of having two vigorous, healthy boys was for their father a compensation for the past and a complete happiness, despite the torments of the war.

11.

Tragic Destiny

On November 8, 1944, in a Corrèze now liberated, but which was still suffering from its wartime wounds, Josette Clotis was taking her mother to the tiny station at Saint-Chamant. Madame Clotis had come from the Var, where Josette's father was mayor and treasurer of the small town of Hyères, to spend some time with her daughter, and especially to find out when the father of her two children would make up his mind to marry her. But Malraux was still fighting in Alsace. They planned to get married after the victory. If he had not yet married Josette, it was because he did not want to divorce Clara, a Jewess and a German, in the midst of the Nazi occupation.

The small departmental train came into the station. Josette climbed into the compartment with her mother to kiss her good-bye. She stayed till the last moment, when the train was just about to leave, and then hurried out. She was wearing shoes with wooden soles, the only kind obtainable under the occupation—soles that were too thick, too stiff, too heavy—and as she stepped down she tripped, missed one of the steps, and fell. She was crushed beneath the wheels of the train.

A tragic accident—so uncalled for, so unfair! Once again fate, sparing Malraux himself, had struck someone near and dear to him. He was not even vouchsafed the time to give his name legally to the woman whose life had been so intimately linked with his, with whom he had shared tenderness and passion in the shadowy period of the resistance. So that, despite the love that had united them, it was not Madame André Malraux, his legitimate spouse, but Mademoiselle Clotis—the mother of his two sons—whom he came to bury in the clay of the Limousin countryside.

Colonel Berger obtained leave to attend the funeral, which was conducted in accordance with the simple and fervent tradition of the region. One can only imagine the depth of his affliction as he accompanied the being who was dearest to him to her resting-place in the Brive graveyard,[1] and the utter solitude that he must have felt—despite the many messages of sympathy he received—during those three somber days of November, 1944.

"One suffers alone, one dies alone, suffering and death cannot be shared," Malraux has written. This is one of the great Nietzschean themes of his work. Nor can anyone boast having seen the author of *Le Temps du mépris* weep in public.

He had probably never felt so intently the need of a family, of some intimate presence, as in that dreary late fall of 1944. The Malraux family, of which he was the head, was hopelessly scattered. His brother Roland had been working as an active member of the resistance in Corrèze in the spring of 1944 when he was arrested by the Germans and deported to a Nazi concentration camp. Claude, a dashing twenty-two-year-old, had been carrying out daring sabotage activities in the Normandy ports when he too was arrested by the Gestapo, in March, 1944, the same month as his older brother Roland. No news had been heard of him since; it subsequently became known that he had been shot by the Gestapo in Rouen soon afterward.

Roland's wife, a professional pianist named Marie-Madeleine Lioux, whom he had married in 1943, was living in Toulouse, making her living by giving piano lessons. On June 6, 1944, she had given birth to a son, whom she named Alain-Montgomery, in honor of the victor of El Alamein, who had just set foot on French soil. It was she who now took care of André's motherless children, herself the mother of a son who would never know his father.

Roland had been imprisoned briefly in Paris, and before leaving for the deportee camp in Germany he had been able to get a message through to his mother. In it he requested that Claude's fiancée, Catherine Escudier, see Pierre Drieu La Rochelle, the editor of the *Nouvelle Revue Française,* and ask Drieu to intervene with the Germans in his behalf. Under Drieu's aegis, the magazine had been frankly collaborationist, following its editor's own increasingly fascist sympathies, but, because he was one of André's oldest and best friends, Roland hoped he might agree to exert some influence.

"I was received by Drieu," Catherine relates. "I found him wonderful, but utterly dejected. When I told him of Roland's request, he

[1] The burial was a temporary one. Once France was again at peace, Josette's body was transferred to a cemetery in Paris.

said, 'I have hardly any more influence. The little I have left will be for André in case he should find himself in difficulty.' Shortly after this Drieu committed suicide. . . ."

After Josette's funeral, Malraux, in the company of his sister-in-law, Madeleine, visited Paris on his way to rejoin his brigade in Alsace. One of their objects was to seek news of Roland at the Hôtel Lutetia, which had been requisitioned by the French Army Ministry to serve as a receiving center for homecoming deportees and a clearinghouse for information about them. Prematurely, they were told that Roland had died in deportation.[2]

That evening André Malraux turned up in Gide's apartment on the rue Vaneau for an impromptu dinner. One can understand his need for the warmth of friendship. At Gide's home he was one of the family. He appeared at the door with a ham under one arm, his fore-finger to his lips. This meant, "Not a word about the catastrophe that has crushed me but left me still standing."

Gide was absent. He was in Tunisia, where he had been since the liberation of Paris some months before. Malraux was being received by the "family."[3] He immediately made himself at home.

"Is Camus here?" he asked. (No, Albert Camus, the editor-in-chief of *Combat,* the daily that had set itself the program of passing "from the resistance to the revolution," was still in the newspaper office writing an editorial.[4] Gide had lent him his room in the apartment.) "And so Gide is idling in Tunisia?" said Malraux when later they had all sat down to table. The mountain ham he had brought constituted the *pièce de résistance* of the meal in that time of rationing. "I suppose he is basking in the sun. He still has that hankering for Africa!"

"He is rewriting the myth of Theseus," Pierre Herbart told him.

"When do you think the war will end?" asked Marie van Rysselberghe, as Malraux was emptying the few remaining drops of wine from the last bottle into her glass.

---

[2] In fact, ironically, Roland was to survive until a few days before VE-day, when a Swedish boat carrying a cargo of refugees for repatriation was torpedoed in the Baltic and sank with almost all hands. Roland was on board and was among the drowned.
[3] Present in the apartment were Gide's oldest and best friend, Madame Théo van Rysselberghe; her daughter, Elisabeth; the latter's husband, the novelist Pierre Herbart, Gide's spiritual son; and Pierre Herbart's brother. In her book *Galerie privée,* Marie van Rysselberghe has drawn a remarkable portrait of Malraux.
[4] Camus was still basking in the fame won him by his novel *L'Etranger,* published in 1942, one of the best sellers under the occupation. Luchino Visconti, the Italian motion picture director, later made it into a film.

"The Germans know they are beaten," said Malraux, "but they can't get used to the idea of defeat; or, rather, they don't accept it, they refuse to accept it. Hitler no longer counts his losses. What obsesses him is the idea of winning back what he has lost. The syndromes of schizophrenia are beginning to appear. The schizophrenic is cut off from the outside world. Confined with his ordnance survey maps, cut off from Europe, cut off from the world, Hitler launches imaginary armies, which he expects to perform a miracle. He draws plans, gets caught, bogs down, sets off again, stumbles, gets up once more. On the battlefront, the real one, his generals do their job, with the conviction of experienced technicians. But it's no longer a question of strategy; it's a matter of mathematics. The Nazis had both strength and numbers. They no longer have the numbers, but here and there they still represent a fanaticized moral force. Even destroyed, they will die indestructible. It is the battle of madness against sovereign reason. That is the danger—madness constantly appeals a decision. No judgment satisfies it."

"But, after all, there will be the irreversible verdict of the battlefield."

"Hitler denies it." Malraux was warming up to his subject. "He is less attached to his life than to his myth. He will commit suicide with exemplary firmness; it is the ultimate way of magnifying himself. But before that he will launch any number of counteroffensives. He won't let himself be taken prisoner; he is his own prisoner. I should not be at all surprised if Berlin were to become a new Stalingrad."

"What do you make of the objective wisdom of his marshals?"

"Since he came to power, Hitler has been the party chief, chief of state, and commander in chief. These triple functions required objectivity. But in his case the power of imagination has always prevailed over the desire to be objective. When a political leader is at the same time a conqueror, the phenomenon of the imagination is closely linked with the phenomenon of audacity. Hitler is a concrete example of this. When Mussolini governed, he did not imagine, he anticipated; this explains his boastful and finally timorous prudence. Hitler's rashness has no precedent in history. Even more than Napoleon, he has believed in his own irremovability, in the invincible constancy of his strength. Look how he assimilated Rommel's patriotic objectivity into an act of high treason. Today he commands alone, more feared than loved. His proconsuls tremble. Hitler today is a psychopathically subjective man— in contrast to whom Stalin is a craftily objective one."

"His people, who lauded him to the skies, no longer follow him."

"I am not so sure. The German people have had their nerves shattered by the Allies' wholesale bombings. And they are counting their dead. But they are not discouraged for all that. What is more, they are getting used to the slaughter. For them the apocalypse is an everyday occurrence. As for the morale of the German young people, it has been vanquished, but not broken."

"What about the secret weapons?"

"It's a race against time. Hitler will lose it. For having imagined too much and not anticipated enough."

"So when can we expect the capitulation?"

"In the spring. It will come with the thaw. But, as I said, Hitler will not capitulate. He will die without surrendering."

Once launched, Malraux could go on talking indefinitely. His index finger pointed at one face, then another, leaving nobody out. Malraux has always liked to play the oracle, to know everything before everybody else. Now, as the conversation took another turn, he spoke of his men in the brigade, with a certain tenderness, but a tenderness devoid of sentimentality. As he spoke, he could see in his mind's eye the forest of Saverne in the Rhine Valley, the double row of birch trees forming a hedge along the road he would travel at dawn. Strasbourg must be recaptured from the Germans. There was not a moment to be lost. The war was a succession of imperatives.

Before the entrance door on the rue Vaneau, the driver at the wheel of Malraux's car was getting impatient. Before leaving the apartment, his colonel had him prepare two substantial ham sandwiches. Malraux had talked, rather than eaten, his way through dinner, and the journey was a long one.

Before leaving Paris to rejoin the brigade, Malraux paid an unannounced visit to his friend Ernest Hemingway. They had not seen each other since one hot summer in Madrid. While the Nationalist troops were besieging the Spanish capital, writers from the whole world, including Hemingway, had met in a congress to discuss what position intellectuals ought to take toward the Civil War. Malraux had dominated those meetings.

In August of 1944, Hemingway, as a war correspondent, had been one of the first to enter liberated Paris.[5] Now Malraux found him in

[5] To General Leclerc, Hemingway was a busybody whom he could not restrain. For the irrepressible Hemingway, war was war, and he was as at home in it as a goldfish in an aquarium. Even Philippe Leclerc, the liberator of Paris, could not hold back such a troublemaker, who slipped into the capital in a jeep ahead of the advance guard.

his apartment at the Ritz, stark-naked, in the arms of two young women. The warrior's repose!

On November 23, 1944, Strasbourg was liberated. The Alsace-Lorraine Brigade was the first French army unit to enter the city; at Malraux's order, its ancient cathedral, which had been closed and transformed into a museum by the Nazis, was reopened for worship. On December 15, for the Te Deum celebrated by Monseigneur Ruch, Colonel Berger was seated in the first row of the faithful.

With the energy born of despair, Field Marshal von Rundstedt launched a last counterattack in the Ardennes. This last-ditch offensive threw the American front into confusion. The battle was a tough one. In the last two weeks of December the Alsace-Lorraine Brigade took heavy punishment. Malraux, constantly on his feet, would shout to his men to take cover.

He had established his command post in Strasbourg, in a formerly Jewish-owned building on the rue du General de Castelnau, a street that the Germans had christened *Roseneck,* or "nook of roses." His three battalions were stationed between Lingolsheim and Strasbourg, ready to intervene on the threatened southern sectors of the city.

On January 1, 1945, the darkest period in Strasbourg's history began. The American command was obliged to call up vital reinforcements to block the German counterattack, and in order to shorten their communication lines the Americans decided to plan a general retreat and abandon Strasbourg. It was a logical decision, which made sense from a military and strategic viewpoint, but it met with head-on French opposition.

Strasbourg could not and must not fall again into the enemy's hands. It would be disastrous for the French army, which had barely been reborn, and for the majority of the city's population, which had so enthusiastically welcomed the liberating Allied troops. Were the Nazis to return to Strasbourg, they would not hesitate to shoot everyone who had manifested delight at the Germans' forced departure. In their four years of occupation, the Nazis had found willing collaborators in Strasbourg as elsewhere.

During the night of January 2–3, the American troops retreated to the west of the Vosges Mountains. The American command, however, left at the disposition of the Alsace-Lorraine Brigade a contingent of artillery, 105 pieces, and a battery of antitank guns.

In the defense plan, the north of Strasbourg was to be held by the

Third African Division under General Augustin Guillaume, while the defense to the south was entrusted to the Alsace-Lorraine Brigade; its instructions were to keep a close watch on the Rhine between Plobsheim and Daubensand, to detect any attempt by the Germans to cross.

Because of the precarious situation on this front caused by the American withdrawal, the French carried on constant harassing operations. Colonel Berger's patrols were meant to give the enemy the impression that the French army was present in strength. German reconnoitering units were frequently engaged, but the men of the brigade were growing fatigued and beginning to lose their nerve.

On the night of January 2–3, General de Lattre de Tassigny, commander in chief of the French First Army, had received General de Gaulle's orders. They were categorical: the capital of Alsace was to be held at all costs.

Confronting the threat to Strasbourg, General Guillaume brought up his Third African Division to the north of the city on January 5. This made the French front extend along more than 135 miles.

That afternoon, the enemy made an advance toward Haguenau. The Third Division repulsed the attack.

On January 7, the Germans struck in the area held by Malraux's unit, to the south of Strasbourg, demonstrating their varied activity by sending strong patrols to attempt a Rhine crossing in boats and by infiltrating the French lines. Everywhere Malraux's men turned the enemy back.

On January 5, General von Maur, commander in chief of the German army of the upper Rhine, had given an explicit order to his troops: "I place all my confidence and hopes in you to enable me to announce to the Führer that the swastika flag again floats above Strasbourg!"

From his command post in *Roseneck,* Colonel Berger sent a communiqué to all the men of his brigade: "You will hold your positions at all costs. In case we have to fall back upon Strasbourg, you will fight, no matter what happens, to hold the city, street by street, house by house. We shall never surrender Strasbourg. . . ."

Barricades of overturned streetcars and automobiles, bolstered by paving stones, had been thrown up in the streets. Strasbourg was ready.

The daybook kept by Captain Landwerlin, Malraux's liaison officer, records the German attack of January 7 on the southern sector of the city:

At 6 A.M., thirty or so tanks of the Feldherrenhalle Brigade unleashed their attack from the Colmar pocket. This violent advance had as objective the Krafft bridge and, as final goal, Strasbourg. The offensive developed between the Ill and the Rhone Canal of the Rhine. At 11 A.M., the enemy attained the bridge over the canal, near Krafft, and cut our communications by establishing a barrage between the canal and the Rhine. On Monday, the 8th, a German plane passed, dropping leaflets inciting the men to surrender: ". . . in case of refusal, you will die under the fire of the German artillery and infantry. . . ."

The men were exhausted. They had spent more than a week on continual alert in foxholes filled with snow, and the total lack of sleep had considerably weakened them physically. In spite of heavy German artillery fire, they held on and fired off all their weapons until they ran out of ammunition. The temperature fell to about zero Fahrenheit.

Two commando units, encircled at Gerstheim, received orders to withdraw toward the French positions on the Ill. All night long they moved through German crossfire, their clothing frozen stiff, many of them with frostbitten feet. Every motion was agony, and they had run out of food.

The column kept on moving through the woods toward the upper Rhine, which they forded, and at last reached the left bank of the river. They were sustained by one resolve: not to surrender, not to yield to the enemy. . . .

By February 11, the Germans had not managed to throw back the French beyond the Rhone-Rhine Canal and the Ill, as they had been commanded to do. It was obvious that the attack had failed. Strasbourg was safe.

"The glory with which the Alsace-Lorraine Brigade covered itself," Father Pierre Bockel has written, "and the symbol that it carried would undoubtedly have justified its participating in some spectacular victory manifestation. But Berger preferred to leave the parading to other units, that were fresher, better dressed, and better trained to present arms."

At his Strasbourg headquarters, André Malraux could easily have broken free of Colonel Berger. The circumstances in liberated Alsace and the popularity of Colonel Berger were such that it would have been mere child's play for him to profit from the situation. However, he came neither as conqueror nor as partisan, but simply as liberator. "And now, it's up to you, gentlemen!" he said to the Alsatians, who were deeply grateful for the respect and tact he showed them. And when the last German had recrossed the Rhine, Malraux left as he had come.

A homage worthy of being quoted was given him by the father of five soldiers in the brigade, Jules Albert Jaeger. "One does not often encounter greatness on one's way; when one does run across it, hats off!" says Monsieur Jaeger, who tells the following moving story:

In the heat of battle during the French campaign, André Malraux was sorely afflicted in what was dearest to him. His young wife was victim of a fatal accident and this was a terrible drama for him. I had tried, in a few words, to write him my deepest sympathy. He had not answered me, which was quite natural. Shortly after the 23rd or 24th of November, 1944, I met him by chance in the main square of Altkirch, when he had just received the order to embark his brigade and lead them toward the tricky and dangerous operation involved in the capture of Dannemarie. He found time to stop.

"So, you are going to see your boys? You will find them a few steps from here in the village they have just occupied...."

A moment of silence.

"You wrote to me . . . thank you . . . I would have liked to answer you. Please do excuse me . . . one must not lay too much stress in public about hours of hardship but must rather keep them to oneself . . . but you are very kind."

Swiftly, his face twisted by the spasmodic tic that enlivens and sometimes distorts his expression, he set out again toward the duty he had laid down for himself.

The soldiers of the brigade had signed an engagement that was valid until the complete liberation of Lorraine and Alsace. When, by May of 1945, this was an accomplished fact, some of its elements signed up with the First Army and continued to fight as the campaign moved on into Germany. Colonel Berger decided that his role was finished, and the brigade was accordingly dissolved. Without flourishes of drums or trumpets.

12.

Enter de Gaulle . . .

It was in 1945 that André Malraux first met General de Gaulle. It was a meeting that would prove decisive in both their lives. The encounter was arranged by Captain Claude Guy, a friend of Malraux's, who was acting as aide-de-camp to de Gaulle in his capacity as head of the provisional French government. Guy brought the two men together at the War Ministry on the rue Saint Dominique in Paris for what was supposed to be a ten- or fifteen-minute interview. It lasted an hour and a half, and on the way home afterward de Gaulle suddenly turned to Guy, who was sitting beside him in the car, slapped him on the knee, and announced, "He's great, your Malraux!"

Thus began an association that would become deeper once de Gaulle went into his self-imposed exile after the war. Malraux was probably the most intimate friend the general—a man not given to close friendships—ever had. It was an association based on mutual admiration; their colloquy was that of two great minds united by their humanism. Ministers could come and go, but Malraux was immovable. He was and is the very soul of Gaullism.

To believe that Malraux underwent a fundamental change of ideas for this to be possible is not to know him. De Gaulle represented for Malraux an aspiration that fully explains his loyalty to the chief of Free France: to give to the French the consciousness of the greatness that they had in themselves and that they did not know they possessed.

Those who preserve a nostalgia for the Malraux who wrote *La Condition humaine* say: How could he have changed so? From the Communist that he was, here he is a Gaullist! Father Bockel has an answer to this:

Malraux is no more a Gaullist today, in the political sense of the term, than he was a Communist as a revolutionary in

175

Indochina or as an aviator in the Spanish Civil War. He has in fact never been attached to any party or persuasion. He has always been, in his various involvements, simply a militant for the liberation of man in the events and circumstances that history has offered. "It is a matter of profound indifference to any of us," he exclaimed at the Sorbonne just after the war was over, "whether a man is a Communist, an anti-Communist, a liberal, or anything else, because the only real problem is to know, above those structures, in what form we can re-create man!"

If the minister appears to have submerged the revolutionary and the adventurer—though being a minister is in itself a considerable adventure!—I think I can say that deep down Malraux has continued to be what he always was. But in the life of a man like him there is a time for nomadic adventure and a time for sedentary adventure, a time for the barricades and a time for the memoirs, a time for tearing down and a time for building, a time for bearing witness and a time for speaking.

There is also the fact that history offers itself in different ways to the men who make it. When the Rubicon has been crossed, one must come to a stop, but there is perhaps something better to do than to go fishing.

De Gaulle formed his second cabinet, to replace his provisional government, just after the legislative elections held in October, 1945. Those elections witnessed the triumph of tripartism—Socialists (SFIO), Communists, and the Christian Democrats (MRP)—and the collapse of the prewar political parties, including Edouard Herriot's and Edouard Daladier's Radical Socialist party. De Gaulle had held a national referendum, the first of many, to establish the pattern his government should take, and arranged that each of the parties should be represented in his twenty-one-member cabinet, including the Communists, who were allotted five seats. One of them was Maurice Thorez, the secretary-general of the French Communist party.[1] As minister of information, de Gaulle appointed André Malraux. The general had admired his prodigious intelligence from their very first meeting, and he recognized that in the person of Malraux he was associating himself with

---

[1] When a high-ranking official criticized de Gaulle for allowing Thorez to return to France from exile after the liberation, on the grounds that he was nothing but a deserter, and a nobody, the general replied acidly, "A deserter, *monsieur*, is not a nobody."

the most brilliant and generous features of the intellectual left wing in politics.

It was a short-lived government, however. Within two months, General de Gaulle, wearied and exhausted by the avid horse-trading of the three major parties, retired to Colombey-les-Deux-Eglises to draft his memoirs. His was an impressive departure.

On January 19, 1946, members of the government were peremptorily summoned to assemble in the Hall of Arms of the Ministry of National Defense at noon on the following day. Wearing his army uniform, the general entered the room punctually at the stroke of twelve and addressed his ministers in measured tones:

> The exclusive regime of the parties has reappeared. I disapprove of it. But short of establishing by force a dictatorship I do not want and which doubtless would turn out badly, I do not have the means to prevent this experience. It is therefore necessary for me to withdraw. . . . This decision is irrevocable and takes effect immediately. If you fail, I shall at least remain intact. I thank each of you for the collaboration you have given me in these historic times. I consider my mission ended.

He rose, shook hands with each of his ministers in turn, and strode out of the room.

In fact, de Gaulle could no longer govern, with the different political parties constantly bickering on every occasion about everything, both in the Council of Ministers and in the National Assembly. Disgusted by the electoral chicanery, by the backstage deals (which, in his opinion, had destroyed the Third Republic), he was saying good-bye to the Fourth Republic, which he had tried to put on its feet.

Later in 1946 the new constitution was approved and in the elections held that December, Vincent Auriol, a pillar of the SFIO, was named president of the Fourth Republic, while Léon Blum, the idealist of intellectual socialism, became premier. However, Blum's regime lasted barely a month. For the next twelve years, until de Gaulle's return to power in May, 1958, there was a veritable square dance of ministries— a succession of twenty-four in half as many years!

When de Gaulle resigned, Malraux left with him. Both men believed in the part the individual man plays in history, in what he can manage to create. For both, France's worth lay in what she could give to the world. To André Malraux's mind, during the twelve years that de Gaulle remained bereft of power (from January, 1946, to May, 1958), the general never ceased to be "of the greatest interest to France."

"Why?" someone asked Malraux.

"Because de Gaulle's format is grandiose!"

What did Malraux and de Gaulle have in common?

Chiefly, a sense of grandeur. Both were devotees of the rostrum, the monument. A kind of fatality, worthy of ancient drama, has always weighed upon the life of Malraux. He recognized the same quality in the general. For him, Charles de Gaulle was and will always be a man who set his mark on destiny.

Writer though he is, Malraux is first of all a man. He stands apart as a writer, belonging to no clan and fitting into no conventional category. As early as 1930, Drieu La Rochelle had called him "the New Man." His novels reflect his own life. His art books deal with his fundamental concern, to explain the work through the man who has created it. For Malraux the writer is the man.

Malraux has written less than his contemporaries, Aragon, Sartre, Giono, Montherlant. In compiling a list of the titles these men have published (some thirty to forty each), one finds that Malraux has barely ten books to set against them. "Why don't you write more?" Gide once asked him. "Because living doesn't leave me enough time," was Malraux's answer. If he does not live, he does not write. If he does not get himself involved in an expedition into the jungle or a revolutionary adventure, he does not bring back the material, the substance for a book. Malraux creates only on the base of something that he has lived; imagination and the technical "embroidery" come into play afterward. So it is with the museums he has visited. If, in the case of Goya, to mention only one example, he does not carry out a study in time that is a model of patience and of "anxious research" (the anxiety of curiosity being in his case the motor of knowledge), he cannot publish a work like *Saturne,* his essay on the creator of *The Horrors of War.*[2]

In a survey on writers, who were asked, "Why do you write?" Gide replied: "To be reread." The Norwegian, Knut Hamsun: "To pass the time." Hemingway: "To sell books." Giraudoux: "For my own fun." Malraux replied: "Out of inner necessity." Writing, in his case, is thus a fundamental vocation and a vocation that pays. This is

---

[2] *Saturne,* an essay on Goya, was serialized in the *NRF* prior to publication by Gallimard in 1950. Gallimard reissued it in April, 1970, as part of Malraux's *Le Triangle noir,* three essays on Saint-Just, Choderlos de Laclos, and Goya.

encouraging. For Malraux, from ten books, has earned more money than many others with forty.

How does Malraux write? Regularly, with the inveterate discipline of a Paul Valéry, but especially when the passion for writing becomes tyrannical. All his books, from *La Tentation de l'Occident* to *Anti-mémoires,* have been written in the heat of creative fever. What he strives for is perfection in the fury of creation. He spent more than a year working on *La Condition humaine.*

But the writings that have required Malraux's greatest mental concentration and the maximum of effacement before his subject have been introductions, the essays, the meditations on art. This titan's work has been interrupted by politics, but Malraux is bound to take it up again; someday it will be brought together and published in several volumes. "If I have preferred General de Gaulle to art," Malraux confesses, "it is because in following him I was convinced that I was serving men best."

In 1946 Jean-Paul Sartre, the high priest of existentialism, was at the peak of his fame. After a spectacular success in the theater with *Huis-clos,* he had published in succession the first three volumes of his great novel fresco, *Les Chemins de la liberté.*[3] In his stride he also had launched a monthly review, *Les Temps Modernes,* which catalyzed his philosophical thinking and on whose editorial board all his friends and disciples were to be found. He firmly hoped that it would take the place of the *Nouvelle Revue Française,* which, under the direction of the late Drieu La Rochelle, had dishonored itself during the occupation by collaborating with the Nazis and ceased publication at the end of the war.

Les Temps Modernes was being published by the house of Gallimard, of which Sartre, with his companion Simone de Beauvoir,[4] and Albert Camus were the leading writers at this time of postliberation.

In the winter of 1946-47, de Gaulle came out of his retreat in order to pronounce a violent condemnation of tripartism (the coalition of the three leading parties in France, the Communists, the Socialists, and the Christian Democrats) and the return to a past that had been believed gone for good. Encouraged by his chief henchmen, among them

---

[3] Published by Gallimard in four volumes. The most significant in setting forth his philosophy are *Le Sursis* and *La Mort dans l'âme.*
[4] She won the Prix Goncourt in 1955 with *Les Mandarins,* dedicated to Nelson Algren. Her first book, *L'Invitée,* was published in 1943 and was very favorably received. Her best-known works: *Les Deuxième Sexe, Mémoires d'une jeune fille rangée.*

Jacques Soustelle, Christian Fouchet, René Capitant, Louis Vallon, Edmond Michelet, Gaston Palewski, Pierre Clostermann, and Malraux himself, Charles de Gaulle was thinking of founding the *Rassemblement du Peuple Français* ("Assembly of the French People"), the RPF. It would have its headquarters on the rue de Solférino, and its membership would have as nucleus the old *Compagnons de la Libération,* de Gaulle's cohorts who had fought with him and assisted him during the war.

His condemnation of the parties, given at an RPF assembly in the Palais d'Orsay in February, 1947, was categorical and overwhelming: "*Françaises, Français,* General de Gaulle speaking. Thirsty for power and carried away by the intoxication that it produces, the politicians want to have France at their mercy. They should be serving France; instead they make France serve them. Against this menace— the degradation of *la patrie*—I solemnly take my stand. . . ." De Gaulle spoke of "politicians," but the specific menace he had in mind was communism, which was increasing its power in Europe with every month. The iron curtain had already descended over Eastern Europe. He, and Malraux too, deeply feared a possible Communist takeover in France.

The thunderous voice of Colombey was heard throughout the land. Against this dramatic, tempestuous, peremptory voice a handful of Paris intellectuals rose up. Existentialism[5] counterattacked over the radio.

Simone de Beauvoir went so far as to speak of the rebirth of fascist militarism and called de Gaulle a gravedigger of democracy, comparable to a Franco, to a Salazar. Jean-Paul Sartre followed her, expounding the theme of the Roman despot whose design it was to govern alone after having suppressed all social liberties.

"We know what the coming of a general to power would hold in store for us—the gag, the damper, the denial of the right to live for which so many heroes have not been afraid to die. . . ."

Yes, this was Sartre speaking, Sartre, who—vying with the Communist party—was trying to exert his influence over a certain element of youth that had come to the fore with the liberation. Going the gamut "to prevent the tiger from biting before it should be too late," Sartre was also preparing an explosive editorial for the next issue of *Les Temps Modernes.*

[5] The philosophical movement founded by Sartre, according to which "existence precedes essence"; "man is not what he says he *is* but what he *does.*"

This radio broadcast with Simone de Beauvoir caused a sensation and had wide repercussions in both literary and political circles, at which the government frankly rejoiced. Edouard Herriot, the cultivated republican leader of the Radical Socialist party, over which he still presided, as he presided over the National Assembly, also gave his blessings to the thunderous offensive of the revolutionary new humanists. Though Herriot was now an aging lion whose roars had grown a little hoarse, he had long nursed a deep hostility to de Gaulle, accusing him of wanting to juggle with the tricolor and make it assume only one color, that of Gaullism.

The fact that Sartre had the support of the government mattered little to Malraux, who was preparing a smashing counterattack. Abusive words had been spoken, unfair tactics had been used, a monument had been defaced: this was no way to treat a general who had saved France and but for whom *Les Chemins de la liberté* would never have appeared in the bookshops, except to be turned into pulp.

To call de Gaulle a fascist, a dictator, future liquidator of human rights, and betrayer of the heritage of Michelet and Gambetta, those preachers of freedom! For Malraux no insult could be worse.

There was no way of taking back what had been spoken over the radio. Malraux was not going to lower himself by begging Sartre to publish a retraction. But he would challenge him on another ground than that of the airwaves.

What he did was to deliver an ultimatum to Gallimard, his own publisher: If Jean-Paul Sartre, ex-professor of philosophy at the Lycée Henri IV, who had become a millionaire by having his plays *Les Mouches*[6] and *Huis-clos* performed with the approval of the Franco-German censorship, did not refrain from debunking General de Gaulle in *Les Temps Modernes,* Malraux would quit the publishing house of Gallimard, of which he was the chief asset.

The weight that he was throwing into the scale was enormous, for Malraux was much more than Malraux: Malraux also meant Gide, and the whole elite of the *NRF.*

The head of the Gallimard publishing firm, which, with Flammarion, was the leading Parisian house, was Gaston Gallimard, a sagacious and opportunistic Norman whose own behavior under the occupation had not been a model of unimpeachable patriotism. This crafty patriarch, head of his own dynastic firm, was faced with a de-

[6] *Les Mouches* was Sartre's first play. It was first produced in Paris in 1943.

cisive choice. Malraux's influence was sovereign. It was not the influence of age, but that of the war hero before whom Sartre, the man
of letters, would be fighting a losing battle. Sartre's war service had
been fought only with a pen, at a table at the Café de Flore in Saint-
Germain-des-Prés, before a stack of blank paper and coffee cups.

Malraux did not beat about the bush. He told Gaston Gallimard
that, if Sartre did not capitulate, he (Gallimard) should not only stop
publishing *Les Temps Modernes* but cease financing the review at all.
If Gallimard did not agree to this, Malraux would leave.

The matter was settled in twenty-four hours. Sartre would remain
a Gallimard author, but *Les Temps Modernes* and all its files would
move from Gallimard's offices on the rue Sebastien Bottin to the rue
de l'Université, where it would henceforth be edited by René Julliard,
an up-and-coming publisher who would make his name and fortune by
discovering Françoise Sagan.

The Malraux-Sartre quarrel marked a permanent break between
the two writers. They had nothing further to say to each other. In
reality, though, had they ever had anything to say to each other?

The radio broadcasts of the existentialist pair had lasted only a few
weeks. Malraux and Sartre would have other occasions to confront each
other, but here again they would be unevenly matched.

There is an interesting comment on Malraux in an article by
Sartre, published just before the controversy erupted, in *Valeurs* (issue
of October 1946–January 1947), entitled "Writing for One's Epoch."
It may well represent the last fair judgment of his great contemporary
that Sartre was able to make:

> It is highly improbable but theoretically possible that the
> twenty-first century will preserve the name of Drieu [La
> Rochelle] and will discard that of Malraux; in any case it will
> not espouse our quarrels, it will not mention what we call
> today the treason of certain writers; or if it does mention such
> a thing, it will be without anger or contempt. Why are we
> concerned with this? The thing that matters is what Malraux
> and Drieu mean to us. There you have the Absolute. For
> Drieu, in certain hearts, there is absolute contempt; for Malraux
> an absolute fraternity that a hundred posthumous judgments
> cannot breach. For Malraux, living, there is a strong pulse of
> warm blood in the heart of the epoch; Malraux, dead, will be a
> quarry for history. Why must the living man concern himself

with what his dead features will be? It is, of course, because a man lives beyond himself. He peers into the future, is preoccupied with happenings after his physical death. The measure of a man's presence and weight is neither his fifty or sixty years of organic life, nor the borrowed life he will live through the centuries in the minds of others; it is the choice he makes in the temporal cause that is larger than he. They say that the Marathon runner died an hour before arriving in Athens. He was dead and he kept on running; he ran, dead. He was dead when he announced the victory of Greece. It is a beautiful myth, for it shows how the dead still continue to act, for a time, as if they were living. For a time—a year, ten years, perhaps fifty years, a limited time, in any case; and then they are buried once more. This is the measure we propose for the writer: so long as his books arouse anger, embarrassment, shame, hate, love, even if he is no longer anything but a shade, he will continue to live. Afterward, the Deluge. We are for an ethics and an art that are bounded by time.

Not long afterward Sartre and the ex-deportee David Rousset[7] founded the *Rassemblement Démocratique Révolutionnaire*, the RDR, which would soon find itself opposing the mass, the dynamic force, and the electoral potential of that other *Rassemblement*, the Gaullist *Rassemblement du Peuple Français*.

Some twenty years later David Rousset was to realign himself and join the ranks of Gaullism.

[7] Author of *L'Univers concentrationnaire,* the first complete study of the Nazi concentration camps, and of *Les Jours de notre mort*, a novel about the deportation, written in 1947.

13.

"Monsieur Propagande"

The 1947 elections were the beginning of a Gaullist landslide. Four years later, the RPF presented 400 candidates. More than one-third were elected. Charles de Gaulle himself was positively stupefied. The day before, he had had a bare 14 elected supporters on the benches of the Assembly—just enough to form a group.[1] And here the French voters had sent 147 RPF (or allied) deputies to a Palais Bourbon that was abuzz with incredulity and amazement.[2]

Borne by the magic banner of de Gaulle, a tricolor hurricane had blown up. Before this new force, the political checkerboard suddenly took on a "new look." Many of de Gaulle's followers in this "coalition of hope"[3] had no political past at all.

The governmental combination of the three majority parties, the Communists, the SFIO, and the MRP, known as tripartism, had had its day. Only two great forces remained to confront each other, the Gaullists and those whom the general called the "separatists"—the Communists. Between these two blocs, these two antagonisms—neither of which could claim the majority necessary to assume the nation's leadership—a third force[4] was to assert itself, which numerically had

[1] A minimum of fourteen elected deputies is needed in the Palais Bourbon, the French parliament, to form an autonomous group that can be recognized as a party.

[2] It is worth remembering that though de Gaulle worked actively as head of the RPF movement from its inception until he disbanded it in 1953 because of its failure to gain ground with the French public, he himself remained in retirement at Colombey-les-Deux-Eglises. From 1953 until 1958 he was working on his *Mémoires de guerre,* the final volume of which was published in 1959, the year after his return as leader of the government.

[3] The formula is Malraux's.

[4] The term third force was first used by Léon Blum, the much-heeded leader of anti-Communist socialism. It designates the various democratic bodies in the spectrum between the two "giants," the Gaullists and the Communists, that would form an alliance to govern against the two enemies. The third force included the Socialists, the Christian Democrats who had not gone over to the RPF, the Radical Socialists, and the socialist democratic Union of the Resistance (at its head were to be found François Mitterrand

every opportunity and was going to make the most of it . . . a third force that for years would systematically exclude both Gaullists and Communists from the government.[5]

In the coalition of the victorious Gaullists one man had prepared the victory, having been given this assignment by de Gaulle himself—Malraux. From his headquarters on the rue de Solférino he had personally structured the general's speeches, launched a vast campaign of covering walls with posters and supporting them with slogans, and provided flocks of experienced speakers to back "somewhat timid" candidates.

This electoral springtime of Gaullism, through the *Rassemblement du Peuple Français,* was Malraux's basic responsibility. In a speech to the members of the steering committee, meeting at their rue de Solférino headquarters in the presence of General de Gaulle, he set out the lessons that the party should learn from triumph. This speech appeared in its entirety in *Le Rassemblement,* the RPF weekly, issued for the occasion in an edition of 500,000 copies. Some characteristic extracts follow:

> We did not expect that this victory, which constitutes a radical metamorphosis of the electoral body, would bring power into our hands. What has just taken place is not an election like any other. It is a vast phenomenon of confidence, of confidence not only renewed but increased. Until now, being a Gaullist was the result of a patriotic attitude and a courageous attitude in defending France. Until now, being a Gaullist meant a certain manner of being French, of thinking and acting as such. Until now, being a Gaullist was synonymous with pride, with dignity, with belief in a freedom to be won back, in a greatness to be renovated, and with hope in sacrifice. Gaullism was an act of faith in France. Today, Gaullism is still that, but with—in addition—something else.
>
> The act of faith in France incarnated in a man becomes a political reality still embodied in the same man—the one who has given back to men and who has given to women the right to express themselves freely in an election booth. General

and René Pleven). They formed what de Gaulle used to call *le bloc des remerciés*—"the bloc of those who had served their time."
[5] Pierre Mendès-France was the first premier of the Fourth Republic to ask Gaullists —Jacques Soustelle, for one—to join his government. This was in June, 1954.

de Gaulle has given back universal suffrage to the French. Today the French, through this universal suffrage and in the proportion of 23 percent (almost one out of four), have made known to de Gaulle that they are Gaullists first of all, that they prefer him, through the elected candidates who support his ideas.

Today this success has a political meaning because it represents a choice, a preference that amounts to a national upsurge, this upsurge being the emanation of a man who more than ever associates his destiny with that of a France which he has put back on her feet.

It is not our intention to politicize this success by transforming the affairs of France—as our predecessors have done—into an affair of politics managed by politicians. On the contrary, it is our duty to safeguard it, to defend it, and to extend it; for the French are never more fully, more perfectly French than when they are Gaullists. . . .

Compagnons, we have taken seats from the others, from the professional politicians. We do not intend to deprive them of their power, but so to act that the sovereign people will give it to us, consulting only their conscience, in the silent secrecy of our city halls on whose pediments the three sacred words— *Liberté, Egalité, Fraternité*—stand for the Republic!

And the Republic, once again, will never be as republican and French as in affirming its Gaullist faith.

Compagnons, time is in our favor. . . .

However, one cannot merely wait for time to do its work. The work of time must be provoked, precipitated. "A political movement is powerless in the immediate future, without the support that youth can give it—the new crop, the continuing force, the reality of tomorrow," as Malraux put it.

February, 1947: a mass meeting in the Vélodrome d'Hiver, and off he would go—the crusader in a gray flannel suit with fine stripes—to bring "those over fifteen and under thirty" to the RPF. Or, rather, those who did not already have their names on the tricolor card stamped with the cross of Lorraine. Among those hearts to be forged or won, many lived in the metropolis, many others in Algeria.

After a rapid tour of France, in his characteristic way Malraux went off to carry the message abroad. He returned to Marseilles on

"MONSIEUR PROPAGANDE"

June 28, 1948. Yves Salgues, the journalist and writer, has given me an account of what followed:

> We were there to welcome him at the Marignane Airport, Jean Joerriman[6] and I. . . . *"Compagnons, salut!"* Malraux greeted us as we went over to him, immediately adding, "What heavenly weather!" Then, suddenly coming down to political reality, "Is everything in order?"
>
> Everything was in order in the immense hall of the Hôtel Chateaubriand in Hyères. . . . The youth leaders of the RPF for the region of Provence and the Côte d'Azur had been invited for a militant informative meeting that evening.
>
> The hall, full but not overcrowded, had the well-organized look of meetings to which only the invited are admitted. Malraux drew a portrait of the chief and his *mystique*, Gaullism. He concluded, "We are not politicians—we are men of faith, of good faith."
>
> "And now," he said, "I want questions."
>
> There followed what stays with me as one of my most extraordinary recollections of Malraux.
>
> Department leaders, one and then another, raised their hands. Malraux asked for no information as to who they were. He identified them, having met them only once or twice. He recognized them by name, unfailingly. Tavernier, from Draguignan; Léandri, from Cannes; Andral, from Menton; Bonore, from Marseilles, et cetera. . . .
>
> "Political men are a special breed," Gambetta used to say. "They have no right to get tired."
>
> At three in the morning the meeting broke up. . . .
>
> The next day, which was Sunday, Malraux had got his breath back. We were at the Roches Blanches mansion, in Aiguebelle, the property of the Joerrimans in the Var. Three of us were lunching, Malraux, Jean Joerriman, and I. The menu: melon with port wine, roast pigeon with green peas, salad, pineapple cake; the wine, a Château-Lafite 1939, an excellent year for Bordeaux.
>
> Literature took precedence over politics. Oleanders, an emerald sea, summer sunshine. Malraux was calm, serene. He

[6] Son of the biggest hotel owner on the Côte des Maures and a close friend of Monsieur Clotis, Josette's father.

would deliver fearful blows and make carefully weighed eulogies, as he did whenever he was called upon to make judgments on people in his profession, colleagues.

I realized what an opportunity this was. Here I had Malraux, the elusive, "to myself" for three hours. I was interviewing him. He knew that I would not make journalistic use of his answers. But it could hardly be called an interview. Malraux took off and, once he was in midair, I was lucky if by a question slipped into the middle of a sentence I could bring him back to earth (or close to the landing field) once in a while.

I have culled from this monologue, from my lightning interruptions, which depended on the breathless pace that Malraux set, what have seemed to me—for the period—the most topical, the most captivating, and also the most timeless.

SALGUES: What do you think of Gide's *Thésée?*

MALRAUX: I draw from it a lesson that I hope would-be writers won't overlook. I mean the state of chronic dissatisfaction of the great writer whom people think of as taking his fame for granted and who—however great his mastery of language—feels the same anguish before a blank page that he felt when he first began to write, fumbling his way with Larousse or Littré within reach of his hand. Gide has never applied himself so diligently. After publishing more than thirty books, at well over seventy-five,[7] he, the most famous writer in Europe —more than famous, illustrious!—faces the challenge of writing in a state of piety much like that of a humble craftsman; as a Muslim entering a mosque goes and bows in obedience to the rites of the Koran. The moral of which is that a creator can take nothing for granted. He starts from zero every time. This is what makes creation so fascinating, whether it is in the field of painting, of music, or of sculpture.

SALGUES: What positive contribution does *Thésée* bring to Gide's work as a whole?

MALRAUX: It is undoubtedly the most accomplished of his works of art. And it is a young work, in line with his will to perfection. Put *Thésée* into the hands of a Japanese, an American, or a Greek student—why not?—who knows noth-

7 This was in 1947.

ing about Gide. The young fellow will never think this book is the product of an old man's laborious effort. Note, though, that there is nothing labored about *Thésée*. It represents hard work, yes, in spite of the fact that it exudes an atmosphere of facility. It's a false impression. Facility, no. Felicity, yes. The felicity is the fruit of a tremendous amount of work. How many hours of effort did it cost Gide to achieve this state of grace? How many times did he tear up his draft, start his manuscript over from the beginning?

SALGUES: To sum up, what is your opinion? Your critical judgment?

MALRAUX: Imagine that the Parthenon has a particularly beautiful metope. In Gide's work, *Thésée* would be that metope. In fact, it is a luxury. *Thésée* is neither a complement nor a supplement to the Gidian edifice as a whole. It is a gratuitous crowning. . . .

SALGUES: Koestler's *Darkness at Noon* continues to sell regularly. Three years ago the book shops could not keep up with the demand for it. Now people read it as a novel describing the tyranny of the Stalin regime, and no longer just to be in the swing, as in 1945–46.

MALRAUX: Koestler's best book is *A Spanish Testament*. It is the adventure of a man tied to the tragedy of a country. Every page of the *Testament* breathes sincerity. It is human and bare. Combining fiction with the Moscow trials, as in *Darkness at Noon,* is taking serious risks. The servitude of writing and the need to sell are increasingly being confused. It's the act of writing that corresponds to a necessity.

SALGUES: We all know your high regard for Hemingway.

MALRAUX: He is all the greater when he is true, as his language is the language of action, and sticks to the reality of beings, of events. *For Whom the Bell Tolls* is not a skillful novel, but a laborious fresco. It is his *Horrors of War,* his *Guernica.* Without making any kind of concession, except that he uses a love story as the basis for recounting the Spanish Revolution. Up to then Hemingway's novels had been relatively easy to read. *For Whom the Bell Tolls* is frankly hard to read. Yet he attracts readers. To date, Hemingway has earned two million dollars, without mentioning his motion picture rights. What is the secret of this unprecedented success? When the intrusion of fiction on reality does not displace its center of gravity, when the balance is maintained, when what is arbitrarily invented—the love story—does not distort the lived necessity—the war—it is possible to obtain, with a certain economy of means, an adequacy of expression and a density of substance that are the mark of outstanding works.

SALGUES: Do you consider *For Whom the Bell Tolls* a masterpiece?

MALRAUX: I consider it a powerful work, with a bravura piece, a central moment—the sabotaged attack, the launching of the offensive—which is a model of descriptive literature and which, keeping everything in proportion, can be compared to Tolstoi (the retreat in *War and Peace*) and to Stendhal (the Battle of Waterloo in *La Chartreuse de Parme*). As to the man Hemingway, I have reservations. I am afraid the personage may spoil the writer, that the legend in which he revels is prejudicial to the courageous, infantile, and boastful man he has always been. One runs a great danger when he tries to apply the "star system" to intellectuals. And that is what Hemingway does for himself, without a manager.

SALGUES: How do you explain the double fascination that the Spanish Revolution has exerted on both creators and readers?

MALRAUX: The Spanish war was the last romantic war. Hence its savagery, its horrors, its excesses, its violences. Hence also its anachronistic, sometimes old-fashioned aspects, verging at times on the comical; its fratricidal combats, the fury to win displayed by both sides, its mystical killings that Bernanos speaks of in *Les Grands Cimetières sous la lune,* its sanguinary crusaders, God who—for the first time—was "on the side of the wicked". . . . The anarchists went and picked oranges fifty feet from the enemy lines. There were more and more inquisition scenes. It was a war that each one waged for all, and that no one waged for himself. Never had heroism flourished in such disorder. . . .

SALGUES: Some readers have spoken of *L'Espoir* as a superior piece of reporting. Do you agree with this appraisal?

MALRAUX: A piece of reporting, yes—to the extent to which I limited myself to the truth of facts. Hence the abundance of anecdotes. But there is also the philosophic interpretation of the events. The war in Spain was the curtain raiser to the tragedy of Europe. A test war for the fascists, a war of cautious investigation for the Soviets, a war of lyrical illusion for the Republicans.

SALGUES: You like neither Sartre the man nor Sartre the writer?

MALRAUX: I don't like voices that have the insolence to make themselves heard without having deserved to be heard. What I do not tolerate in a work is a lack of nobility. I am allergic to Montherlant, but I am not untouched by the nobility of some of his attitudes, of his style, of his designs. On the other hand, I draw the line on a writer who uses his pen in the service of vulgarity. Giraudoux's literature of leisure has its good side; it is clean and healthy. Sartre's literature of engagement leaves a bad smell.

SALGUES: Doesn't his break with the Communist party seem dictated by an unquestionable honesty?

MALRAUX: The Stalinists covered the corpse of Nizan with filth and Sartre allowed him to be besmirched.[8] Nizan was his friend. Now he is trying to besmirch de Gaulle. There are statues on which one does not spit. As a philosopher, Sartre is confused. As a novelist, he has borrowed his technique from Dos Passos. As a dramatist, the structure of his plays is modeled after Bernstein and Bourdet. The theater depends on structure as much as on language. The existentialist theater learned to breathe on the boulevards.

SALGUES: Have you read *Les Mains sales?*

MALRAUX: No, but I know the plot. For anyone familiar with Communist methods, it is commonplace.

SALGUES: The Stalinists have labeled Sartre a counter-revolutionary. Do you consider him a revolutionary?

MALRAUX: He has no political experience. He does not know what a leftist party is. He has . . . never fought.

SALGUES: How do you see "his" RDR?[9]

MALRAUX: I don't see it, and it is hard for me to imagine it.

[8] Paul Nizan, professor of philosophy and author of a fine novel, *La Conspiration,* broke with the Communist party over the German-Soviet pact. He was killed during the German May-June offensive of 1940.
[9] *Rassemblement Démocratique Révolutionnaire.*

Salgues: Has it any chance of making an impact on youth?

Malraux: Neither on youth nor on the working masses.

Salgues: Do you consider that Sartre's success is based on an imposture?

Malraux: It is based on a misunderstanding; it has come at the point of convergence of two generations, in a postwar period that has not had time to effect a readjustment of values.

The *mistral* had begun to blow. The azure took on a metallic brilliancy. Malraux felt the need to stir, to walk along the seashore, to work out in his mind the speech he would be making that evening.

"I am anxious to know how many copies of the *Rassemblement* my kids have sold—in Toulon, Nice, Marseilles. . . . And if the young Communists who are hawking *L'Humanité-Dimanche* have been making trouble for them. It's a test. Youth has to be galvanized, prepared for future combats."

The revolutionary complaint from which André Malraux had often suffered had now taken the name of Gaullism, and had as its acronym the three letters RPF, *Rassemblement du Peuple Français.*

A third woman had appeared in Malraux's life. This was his sister-in-law, Madeleine, the widow of Roland, who had died en route to Sweden from his concentration camp just before the end of the war.

Since Josette's death Madeleine had looked after his two motherless boys, and on André's return from Alsace he had come to think of his small nephew, Alain, as his third son. A natural intimacy had grown between the dark, attractive young woman in mourning and "Colonel Berger."

But Malraux has the habit of never speaking of his love life. Unlike Hemingway, he has never written a line about any of the women he has loved.

In the spring of 1948, he finally divorced Clara, with whom he remained on easy, if not affectionate, terms, seeing their teen-age daughter, Florence, quite constantly. He had decided to marry Madeleine, and also that he wanted the marriage to be celebrated in Strasbourg, for understandable reasons. He so informed the mayor of the town,

Charles Frey, who was delighted, but distressed when Malraux revealed that he intended to get married in two weeks' time. Frey saw no reason for such speed. A residence of at least six weeks in Strasbourg and the publication of banns were necessary, "unless it is a case covered by article 169? . . ." Malraux reassured Charles Frey: No, there was no offspring in view, no urgent personal reason other than his own desire for haste.

He addressed himself instead to former members of his brigade. It was decided that the marriage would be celebrated in Riquewihr, the pearl of the Alsatian vineyard country, where René Dopff, one of his former battalion commanders, was assistant mayor. One day there appeared in the small grilled box fixed to the east gate of the small town a notice announcing the marriage of a certain Colonel Berger to a lady, Marie-Madeleine Lioux, "a resident of Riquewihr since January." But no one in Riquewihr knew her, either at the baker's or at the butcher's; her real residence, of course, was in Toulouse, rue Alsace-Lorraine. No matter. The notice was posted and residence established; the legality of the marriage was arranged for.

On March 13, 1948, at ten o'clock, four cars stopped before the picturesque city hall of Riquewihr. The local paper reported that four gentlemen, one of them one-legged, stepped down, accompanied by two ladies—"very beautiful," and carrying bouquets of roses and mimosas. Mayor Hugel officiated. Dopff, his assistant mayor, and Paul Diener-Ancel, another battalion commander, were witnesses. Bernard Metz, who had originally proposed Malraux as leader of the brigade, and the one-legged Bernard Collaine, who had been one of its most active recruiters and now worked for René Dopff in Riquewihr, constituted the "persons present" required by Article 165 of the French Civil Code. Octave Landwerlin, Malraux's old liaison officer, acted as master of ceremonies. It was a brigade wedding indeed.

The next day Father Pierre Bockel celebrated a Mass in the crypt of the Strasbourg cathedral "for the Alsace-Lorraine Brigade and its friends" in the presence of Monsieur and Madame André Malraux.

How does Malraux stand in the matter of religious belief? This is a question asked by many people because, agnostic that he is, he has so often come close to the religious universe, so often failed to conceal the attraction exerted on him by Christian mysticism, whose artistic expression seems to him to be the best that man has produced in the course of his history.

"I have always faced the spiritual problem," he says, "even in connection with the Hindu philosophers or the poets of the Koran."
Father Bockel answers the question as follows:

In the case of Malraux there is obviously a complicity between the Christian vision and the vision of man. Having a thirst for the absolute, he seeks it in man and perceives it in what he calls "the eternal part of man." In a letter that he wrote me on August 28, 1948, he defined it thus: "I call the eternal part of man his will to subordinate himself to what he feels is beyond him." He added, in connection with the future collaborations that he contemplated with men of the faith: "It appears to me essential that we should place the emphasis on our defense of the eternal part of man, whether or not we conceive it as linked to revelation."

However close he may be to the believing world, whatever may be his curiosity with regard to the mystery of grace—about which he never fails to interrogate his Christian interlocutor—Malraux remains an agnostic. At least, his fair-mindedness and his extreme diffidence do not authorize him to define himself otherwise with respect to religion. But there are times when, abandoning this defensive intellectual position, it is as though he were hearing Pascal's words: "Thou wouldst not be seeking me, hadst thou not already found me." I can still hear him telling me with a strange smile, "You know better than I that no one can escape God."

While he is, in the full strictness of the term, an agnostic, Malraux has an absolute aversion for atheism, which he considers a real imposture, an attack on man.

How far will he go? No one knows, and no one has the right to anticipate a future that belongs to him alone, that is a secret between him and God. I for my part would be averse to forcing this note, to saying more than has appeared to me, and to risk attributing as one of us a man whose destiny concerns him alone.

After the wedding in Riquewihr, the veterans of the brigade wanted to offer their colonel a souvenir of the day. When he was asked what he would like, Malraux, who somewhat mistrusted the good taste of his old *compagnons*, expressed the wish to receive a sculptured angle beam from an old Alsatian house. Despite the best efforts of the director of the Strasbourg museums, it was impossible to find such a rare piece of carving as that.

Instead, his friends of the brigade presented him with a superbly carved *dauphin de foudre*, a wooden batten that had once supported an eighteenth-century wine cask. The sculptured ornament on this piece represented two heraldic dolphins rampant. It was a gift of great value, particularly appropriate to a wedding in Riquewihr, one of the wine capitals of Alsace, his adopted province—most of all the gift enchanted Malraux because it was a reminder of his childhood and his grandfather, the master cooper.

The 1951 elections gave the National Assembly a right-center majority. Radicals (Edgar Faure, Pierre Mendès-France), the MRP (Georges Bidault, Robert Schuman), Independents with a conservative leaning (Antoine Pinay), and Gaullists (RPF) participated in the government in a succession of ephemeral cabinets.

The schism of the moderate parties, in the 1956 elections, finally gave the Communist party the advantage. In a precarious Republican Front coalition, the Socialists, led by Guy Mollet, and Radicals, whose chief was Mendès-France, ended up as the arbiters of the situation.

In 1955–56, the French government was finally obliged to recognize the sovereignty of Morocco and Tunisia. In Algeria, which had been in revolt since 1954, a bitter underhand struggle took the form of guerrilla attacks, armed attempts, and reprisals between the home forces and the Algerian *Front de Libération Nationale* (FLN).

The French people were deeply divided between those who wanted Algeria to remain French and those who were in favor of concessions, and the war—for so it was—provoked an at times violent opposition between the French colonists in Algeria and army officers, on the one hand, and the Paris government, on the other. France seemed to be as unable to make war as to make peace.

During the twelve years that the Gaullists call "the crossing of the desert," Malraux lived in Paris, in the villa he rented in the Bois de Boulogne for himself and his family. For the most part he was to be found in a vast room at the top of the house, a room more like a painter's studio, with bay windows opening upon the Bois. There the floor would usually be strewn with photographs that he was using to prepare the layouts of his volumes on art.

He did a great deal of writing on the subject during this period.

Between 1947 and 1949 he had published a work in three volumes, *La Psychologie de l'art*, then transformed it into a single volume, *Les Voix du silence*, brought out in 1951, the year André Gide died. *Saturne*, his essay on Goya, was published in 1950, another work in three volumes, *Le Musée imaginaire de la sculpture mondiale*, appeared between 1952 and 1954, *La Métamorphose des Dieux* in 1957, and *L'Univers des formes* in 1960. All were published by Gallimard.

But he was dreaming all the time of the great return of Gaullism. He knew that sooner or later de Gaulle would come back. "While France, defenseless, her spirit broken, slept through her dark night, this man, for four long years, held aloft her honor like an invincible dream."

By the beginning of May, 1958, France was in the midst of a political crisis on a national scale. The Algerian tragedy threatened to drag the country into a bloody revolution. Government succeeded government. Each found itself utterly unable either to put an end to the rebellion or to stand up against the intransigence of the French *ultras* (extremists) in Algeria.

Félix Gaillard, president of the Council (the premier), had been obliged to resign. "The preceding governments were nothing to envy," he said as he left office, "and the following government is to be pitied."

Pierre Pflimlin, deputy mayor of Strasbourg, was called upon to form a new government. Gaillard was a Radical Socialist, Pflimlin a Christian Democrat.

At the beginning of his attempt, Pflimlin, an energetic man of integrity, declared, "My program will be trenchant, like my character."

Meanwhile, in Algeria, revolutionary fever was rapidly mounting. It all began in Algiers on May 13, at four thirty in the afternoon, in front of the monument to the slain of the two world wars. Army units and civilian population alike had assembled to pay homage to three French soldiers who had been shot by the FLN. Eighty thousand demonstrators sang "La Marseillaise." Suddenly, about six in the evening, the young demonstrators began surging toward the Forum, the large open square in front of the Algerian government palace. The security guards were soon unable to control the crowd battering at the iron gates of the main government building, which yielded to the assault. The angry demonstrators managed to seize an army van. Some young fellows climbed the facade of the government building, and soon the first of them to reach the terrace waved a tricolor flag. By eight forty that evening, the palace was invaded.

A Committee of Public Safety was immediately formed in an

effort to quell the disturbance, and General Jacques Massu, commander of the regiment of parachutists, agreed to preside over it.

The capital was now cut off from the rest of Algeria. The inhabitants of the Casbah poured into the streets and fraternized with the Europeans. The Arab women burned their veils.

At 10:45 next morning, General Raoul Salan, charged by the government in Paris with maintaining order, appeared on the balcony of the government palace and addressed the crowd: "Friends, I am on your side, because my son is buried here!" Then, after a pause, he turned toward those nearby and shouted, *"Vive de Gaulle!"*

The Algerians did not want Pflimlin. Leaflets had been circulating in Algiers predicting that with Pflimlin heading the government, Algeria would be lost before October. The Algerians appealed to de Gaulle, who was at Colombey as he had been for the past twelve years. For twenty-four hours de Gaulle remained silent. Then, on May 15, at half past five, a declaration from the general was broadcast:

> The degradation of the state inevitably entails the estrangement of all the peoples associated with France, it disturbs the army in combat, and it brings about national dislocation and loss of independence.
>
> For twelve years, France, in the grip of problems too arduous to be solved by party regimes, has been engaged in a disastrous course.
>
> In former times the nation, in the depths of trouble, has trusted me to lead it en masse toward safety.
>
> Today, confronting the new difficulties that are arising, may the people know that I am ready to assume the powers of the Republic.

Pflimlin assumed office as premier at 1:20 A.M. on May 15. At 5:25 that morning he held his first conference of ministers and made his first appeal for discipline.

In Algiers, scenes of delirious excitement were renewed on the Forum every evening. "Ten million Frenchmen" was the slogan of the new Algeria, where two communities, Muslims and Europeans, fraternized, though they numbered only a little more than one million.

On May 16, the day after de Gaulle's broadcast, almost all the citizens of Algiers crowded to the government palace to shout their enthusiasm. On the previous night, local artists had painted effigies of de Gaulle—rejuvenated by close to twenty years, because the only models they had were antique photos of the de Gaulle who had led Free France!

At three o'clock on May 19, de Gaulle held a press conference, his first since 1955. It was broadcast live in America on three hundred radio and thirty-five television stations. A radio link with Pierre Pflimlin's office enabled the premier to hear the general's speech.

At the end of his broadcast, de Gaulle made this statement: "I have said what I had to say. Now I am going to return to my village where I shall remain at the disposition of my country."

Upon his arrival in Colombey-les-Deux-Eglises, a villager dared to ask him, "Do you think, general, that you will be called to power?" To which de Gaulle replied, "No, affairs are not yet in a bad enough way."

On May 27, Pflimlin, having refused the support of Communist votes to maintain himself in power, decided to abandon it and handed his resignation to René Coty, president of the Republic.

On May 29, at 8:45 in the evening, de Gaulle emerged from the Elysée Palace. He had just said yes to Coty, and accepted the task of forming a new government.

On June 4, General de Gaulle arrived in Algiers, where the excited population had been thronging the streets ever since May 13.

In the Forum, he simply told the ecstatic crowd: *"Me voilà!* Here I am! Long live the Republic! Long live France!"

Upon his return to Paris, de Gaulle at once established himself at the Hôtel Matignon, the seat of the premier, and began to put together his cabinet.

First as president of the Council of Ministers and then as president of the Republic, he deliberately set out to give France a regime possessed of stability and authority, yet without repudiating the democratic basis of the state. France now had its Fifth Republic.

When General de Gaulle called upon "the others"—the Debrés, the Couve de Murvilles, the Pompidous—to form his government, he remembered the one who was "not like the others": Malraux, the antimilitarist by birth, by training, by conviction, who had proved himself uniquely able to understand the imperatives of war and superlatively able to grasp the subtleties of politics. "I have been wounded several times in the service of liberty," he says. "If I support de Gaulle, it is because he does not attack it."

It was said that Malraux refused a $500,000 book contract with an

American publisher in order to serve as a minister in de Gaulle's government.

De Gaulle's first remark on foreign policy was to be, "We will tell other nations that they may count *on* France, but they must also count *with* France."

Malraux was to be his most faithful spokesman.

During his whole revolutionary period, Malraux had never ceased to combat the official—military—emanation of the governing power. Through de Gaulle he began and accomplished a conversion that is one of the most spectacular of this century. He saw Gaullism as "an antipolitical affair of rectitude and fidelity," which permitted no compromises.

De Gaulle never raised his voice against Malraux, although he had no compunction about giving others in the Council of Ministers a dressing down and calling them "ministers two republics late."

"What I ask of my men," de Gaulle once said, "is fidelity and adherence to my policy. It is a game that excludes trickeries as well as subtle intellectual reservations or silences that prepare triumphal barks. Malraux's strength and the esteem that I have for him have their source in that truth: he confesses, he cries aloud what he believes to be his truth, this being a truth that tries to be the truth of all, or at least the truth of the greatest number. He does not think for a few, he thinks for all, beyond social classes. He is a national who expresses himself in the context of the nation, that is to say an inspired nationalist connected to the orbit of international policy. This is why I entrust him with delicate, even perilous missions."

Journalist Gabriel d'Aubarède once asked Malraux if his political experiences before the general's return had nourished the writer in him as had his earlier combats. Malraux's reply deserves quoting at length:

> It is not politics that interests me, for I should then have become a member of parliament. What interests me is history. The resistance, prison, war—these remain. I was accustomed to fraternity in civilian life, and I commanded only volunteers. . . . In the resistance, what moved me most was the help that all of us had the experience of receiving in the worst days from people we did not know. France was the peasant woman who saw you pass surrounded by a German squad, which she thought was going to shoot you, and who stepped forward and

made the sign of the cross, in a region where people don't go to church. But I am not sure that the deepest experiences are fertile. Like many others, I have faced a false firing squad. Well, I have almost wholly forgotten what I experienced. Perhaps that is the only way life can continue. But how I should like to grasp the mysterious force that effaces and makes one forget everything. . . .

Well, the times of violence that have now and again filled or encumbered my life have left me with two obsessions, which I give you for what they are worth.

The first is fraternity. The mortal blemish of many European intellectual circles is masochism, the smug surrender of intelligence to stupidity mistaken for force. I recently gave an account of having seen Geneviève de Gaulle and Marie-Claude Vaillant-Couturier[10] return from the same Buchenwald prison and of being unable to forget their terrible resemblance. . . . Since it first formed a civilization there has been in humanity an invincible aspiration to a mysterious fraternal greatness. Let us render unto history what is history's and unto man what is man's.

My second obsession is that we are living . . . in a time in which men, instead of making the decisions that are necessary, choose to express their problems by tragedy in the best cases, by comedy in the others. But a civilization without transcendence like the one we claim to be erecting cannot be a civilization without wisdom. This is so true that a number of American intellectuals these last years have gone to find theirs from Gandhi. . . . What I call wisdom is not the disillusioned benevolence of Renan—even though he appears a genius compared to our recent masters—but the awareness of our real values and the determination to defend them. The wisdom of Europe will spring from Europeans, not from the Hindus nor the Tibetans. It may be that it will prove to be a tragic wisdom, but it must be a consciousness, not a spectacle. Otherwise the last actor can already be preparing the last funeral song for the last spectator.

But we have not come to that. It is not true that America is culturally foreign to Europe. It is a fragment of the Euro-

---

[10] Geneviève de Gaulle, a fervent Catholic and a leftist politically, was the general's niece. Marie-Claude Vaillant-Couturier was a Jewess and a Communist.

pean whole that includes it, just as England is a European fragment of a whole that includes England. We live as we can. . . . Whether we like it or not, we are between the atomic bomb and the birth of the first world humanism.

It is up to us to choose.

14.

A Gathering Storm

While women—love—have played a fundamental role in Malraux's life, men—friendship—have had an equally essential part in it. He has always been an exemplary friend.

There is no contradiction in this, for even though he recognizes that man suffers alone, that he dies alone, that solitude in the face of destiny is his lot, Malraux cannot imagine life without the constant support of "virile fraternity."[1]

Open as he is to friendship, he is wholly impervious to homosexuality.[2] In contrast to Hemingway, who displays a loud and impatient contempt for homosexuals (as witness his attacks on Jean Cocteau and Raymond Radiguet in *Death in the Afternoon*), Malraux leaves the question aside. For the good and sufficient reason that it is foreign to him, leaves him indifferent.

As a prominent member of the literary world, Malraux has always

---

[1] The theme is set forth in *L'Espoir* and is implicit throughout his work.

[2] In connection with T. E. Lawrence, Malraux has written: "The number of men in whose lives women have played no role should not be underestimated. A heterosexual presents no problem. In the case of a nonheterosexual it is obvious. Yet there are nonheterosexuals who are nevertheless not pederasts. I am not at all sure of the part played by 'inversion' in Lawrence's life. He went to Damascus at the age of thirty. From that time on he is not known to have had any masculine 'affairs.' I know of course that there is the dedication of the *Seven Pillars of Wisdom* to that dead lad. But Lawrence's life was not exactly a mysterious life, but an extraordinarily masked life. The fact that he was separated from women does not mean that he was a homosexual.

"Then came the time when Lawrence discovered his legend. There was nothing he could do about it. When the legend was born, that made him out to be a pederast in love with Arab boys, the *Seven Pillars* was not yet written. There is a close connection between the book and his life.

"The circumstances of his death are known. But few know the real reason for that fatal ride. Lawrence went to deliver a telegram to the post office on his motorcycle, racing at a hundred miles an hour. To avoid some children who were coming out of school, he crashed into a wall. In the text of the telegram, which was found on his body, Lawrence refused to meet Hitler, who had invited him to come to Germany."

had more friends than he knew what to do with, and very few enemies. Early on, and particularly after the publication of *La Condition humaine,* Malraux belonged to a sect, to a clan—the Gallimard "stable." This intellectual coterie, which was both united and closed, had a dominant influence in the literary world of the time, thanks in part to the Gallimard-published monthly review, the *Nouvelle Revue Française.* It was presided over by André Gide, France's leading literary figure, who had been painfully disillusioned by his trip to the USSR in 1936 and who felt for Malraux a close attachment that was never to weaken.

We have told how in this brilliant twosome Gide, often caught unawares in a spontaneous conversation, found himself "outdistanced" by Malraux with his encyclopedic range of knowledge—he knew everything, he understood everything, he had seen everything. It is difficult to realize how favored Malraux was without being aware that in the 1930s André Gide, Paul Valéry (who themselves were fast friends), and Paul Claudel (whom "the devil separated from Gide") were the *maîtres à penser,* the leading intellectual lights, of the century. Malraux, who dazzled them, was scarcely more than thirty. In the *NRF* establishment he stood out like a character in a novel. Drieu La Rochelle said of him at this time: "Malraux's best novel is his life. He will write it some day."

Of all his many friendships, two are particularly noteworthy. The first, with Drieu La Rochelle, lasted with intensity for years, for although the two men took diametrically opposed political paths, they had a great deal in common. Drieu, like Malraux, was on the warpath against *littérateurs* in carpet slippers. He was haunted by the legend of the warrior monks of the Middle Ages, and ready to go to war. The Spanish Civil War, however, was to find him on the side of the rebels, of the Francoists—in other words, on the other side of the barricades from Malraux. Only Drieu had fought in World War I,[3] and it is fascinating that, after an identical point of departure marked by the need to *"changer la vie"*[4] and a "moral" joining of the Communist party, the two could continue their friendship as their interests drew them apart.

In his book *Avec Doriot,* published in 1932, Pierre Drieu La Ro-

---

[3] His book *La Comédie de Charleroi* is a baroque and stirring account, told in flashbacks, of one of the deadliest battles in the conflict.

[4] "Change life"—an anguished plea uttered by the seventeen-year-old poet Arthur Rimbaud—became a rallying cry for successive generations of poets.

chelle drew (in a devil-may-care style, as was his habit) the pattern of his political evolution from international communism to communitarian nationalism. He was an influential member of the originally Communist, later extremely reactionary, *Parti Populaire Français,* founded by Jacques Doriot, which after the German occupation became an outright collaborationist group.

Malraux was to evolve from a militant Trotskyism to a fighting nationalism that espoused the ideal of General de Gaulle.

Despite their poles-apart political views, the two men never lost respect for each other. They met for the last time in 1941, when Malraux made a secret and risky visit to Paris on personal affairs. After the armistice in June, 1940, Drieu La Rochelle had assumed the directorship of the *Nouvelle Revue Française,* succeeding Jean Paulhan, who had resigned, and would have liked some pieces by Malraux. But nothing was forthcoming. Gide refused to contribute to the *NRF,* which became more and more markedly pro-German under Drieu's direction, claiming that it was more new than French.

Drieu La Rochelle also acted as editor-in-chief of *L'Emancipation Nationale,* a weekly of revolutionary rightist tendency.[5] After the liberation of Paris, he fled from his apartment on the avenue de Breteuil, because Emanuel d'Astier de La Vigerie, Malraux's friend in the resistance, who was later minister of the interior in de Gaulle's first government, had signed a warrant for his arrest.

Drieu tried and failed twice to commit suicide. The first time, it is said, he was so carried away by a detective novel he was reading that in order not to miss the end he did not take his second dose of barbiturate. The second time he cut his veins in the bathtub, which began to overflow. The concierge, seeing the bloodstained water leaking out under the door, called a doctor. Drieu La Rochelle was saved, much against his will. He finally killed himself by taking poison in November, 1944. In his will, deposited with his lawyer, he had dictated instructions as to his burial: seven women (his "seven widows")[6] and two men were to follow his hearse. The two men were Bernier, director of the Marxist review *Clartés,*[7] and Malraux. But Bernier was a prisoner somewhere in Silesia, and Malraux was busy retaking Strasbourg from the Germans.

Malraux has always kept enemies or adversaries at bay by his

[5] "I hate those lying words, left and right," Drieu La Rochelle repeatedly proclaimed in his editorials in *L'Emancipation Nationale.*
[6] He was actually married four times.
[7] The only professionally valid magazine published by the Communists prior to 1939.

dignity, and it can be said that his most momentous friendship—with Charles de Gaulle—was born of the same determination not to capitulate when one must lift one's head.

To the French journalist Michel Clerc, who asked him in an interview, "Why are you a minister of de Gaulle's?" Malraux answered:

"Because when I met de Gaulle I found myself for the first time before a man who exacted no less of others than he did of himself. There was in him no kind of comedy. He was neither a comedian nor a tragedian—he was a man.

"In the game that is beginning we give ourselves fifty years. If we die, we shall die, heads high. But we shall not die. We are at this juncture in a state of historic grace. We must make the most of it. A state that does not understand that it faces very deep transformations cuts off its arms and its legs."

Malraux believes that France is living through a new French Revolution. Nothing and no one will stop it.

"If it is not a revolution that we are living through, then it is our death agony that is beginning."

What interests him in this revolution is not the derailments, the sabotages, the ambushes typical of the ones he had lived through in the past; it is a return to a certain order, the plotting of a renaissance, a spectacular reconciliation of France with greatness.

On September 5, 1958, Malraux, on the place de la République, addressed the nation to ask it to vote for General de Gaulle:

> . . . What the Republic means to us we have never understood so well as during the years of the occupation. On the deserted pedestals the voice of the Republic said: "They may have removed my effigies but no one has been able to replace them. If it is in the power of no one to tear me from the hearts of the French, it is not because I am for them the memory of disastrous political wranglings, the justification of everything that has imposed on my illustrious face the mask of defeat: it is because, absent or present, I am an ineradicable part of your fraternal pride. . . ."

> In 1941, the chief of the Free French declared, "We say *liberté, égalité, fraternité* because our will is to remain faithful to the democratic principles that our ancestors derived from the genius of our race and that are the stake of this war for life or death. . . ."

Beyond the legal texts, however well drafted (and never-theless imperfect as are texts and men), you will vote for the will to national resurrection or for the effacement of our coun-try, in response to a man to whom history has given the right to call us to witness but whose undertaking can obtain its legitimacy only from you.

No one can rebuild France without the French. And the Republic cries out to all what the muffled voice of the exiled Republic said to them only yesterday: "I want to become France again."

Among you many still are those who heard night after night: *"Ici Londres. Les Français parlent aux Français. Hon-neur et Patrie. Vous allez entendre le général de Gaulle. . . ."*

Ici Paris. Le Paris de tous ses quartiers, depuis la Porte d'Italie jusqu'au Rond-Point de la Défense. Ecoute, pour la France République de bronze, la réponse de la vieille nef glorieuse: "Ici Paris. Honneur et Patrie. Honneur et Patrie. Une fois de plus au rendez-vous de la république et au rendez-vous de l'histoire, vous allez entendre le général de Gaulle."

On September 16, 1959, de Gaulle offered his plan for Algeria: free-dom of choice for the Algerian people, including independence if they voted for it, within four years of ending the current revolt. He rejected negotiations with any rebel Algerian government. The three choices he put before the Algerian people were secession, integration, or internal autonomy.

Despite the general's efforts, his personal standing and prestige, the Fifth Republic was faced with the same difficulties in Algeria as the Fourth, further aggravated: the tenacity and intransigence of the National Liberation Front, the obstinacy of the supporters of *l'Algérie française*, a chain reaction of acts of violence in Algeria and in the capital itself, a succession of plots.

The mother country, dramatically clinging to her colony in distress, was rent by factions and witnessed the insurrection of the French in Algeria, the underhand rebellion of the military, the terrorism of the OAS (*Organisation Armée Secrète*) that struck the very streets and homes of Paris with its dreaded *plastiques*.

Suddenly there came an end to the noisy demonstrations intended to prove that Algeria would remain French despite the determination of its "sellout," the traitor de Gaulle. Ended was the time of the delirious crowds tearing up the paving stones on the rue d'Isly, the main street of Algiers, as they shouted out their slogans: *"Fraternisation tri-co-lo-re . . . L'Algérie à la France . . . C'est l'Algérie qui le veu-eut."* The barricades of the hotheaded Lieutenant Lagaillarde[8] were still standing in the geographic and trembling heart of Algiers, but the rebellion had spread to greater numbers of its civilian and military leaders.

What had been the insurrection of a handful of colonels had become the cause for a considerable fraction of the army in Algeria. Whole regiments went over to the dissidents' side. What had been a revolt was now a revolution.

"In the whole history of clandestinity," Malraux was to say, "there is not one leader, not one movement, that has not faced financial difficulties. The OAS, on the contrary, is swimming in opulence."

The OAS had coordinated its tasks, taken stock of its forces, and then it had gone into action—or, rather, it had flung itself recklessly into action. Without the slightest political discernment. Without the slightest sense of the broader context outside Algiers itself. While minimizing the aura that (even more abroad than at home) surrounded the figure of the president of the French people. To such a point that it was no longer action, but activism, a frenzied craving for action at all costs.

On Saturday, April 23, 1961, came the putsch. The putsch of what de Gaulle called *un quarteron* ("a foursome") of generals: Maurice Challe, the former chief of the air force, who was the commander in chief, Edmond Jouhaud, André Zeller, and Raoul Salan,[9] who assumed the leadership of the subversion. General Massu,[10] the victor of the battle of Algiers (won against specialists in urban guerrilla fighting and the door-to-door terrorism to which the sordid alleys of the Casbah lent themselves), chose a wait-and-see policy. But the elite of the colonels (Gardes, Godard, Argoud—and others like Lacheroy[11]) were willing to face the risks of opprobrium and the penalties of prison for life or the firing squad if the putsch failed.

[8] The instigator of the erection of the first barricades, in January, 1960.
[9] The most spectacular figure of the OAS, of which he was the brains. Arrested on the eve of Easter, 1962, the former commander in chief in Indochina was sentenced to life imprisonment at the end of a sensational trial in June, 1962. He was pardoned by de Gaulle in July, 1968.
[10] Commander in chief of the French forces in Germany. Massu went into retirement in August, 1969.
[11] These took refuge in Spain. Argoud was captured in West Germany, where Hanover was for a long time the collecting point for the OAS exiles, before de Gaulle eventually arranged for them to be amnestied.

Overnight on Saturday, April 23, the First Foreign Regiment of Parachutists (*Premier REP*) assembled around Algiers and began to penetrate the city in small groups. The Forum was deserted, the city asleep.

General Fernand Gambiez, commander in chief of the troops in Algeria, was made prisoner in his car. The parachutists entered the General Delegation headquarters, where Jean Morin, delegate of the French government, announced by telephone to Paris: "I am no longer free."

There had been but one casualty, a noncommissioned officer of the guard at the television station. Everything had taken place in the silence of the night, and within a single hour.

That morning, at seven o'clock, the town woke up to the sound of the rebel radio. The *paras* were everywhere. The street corners were guarded, the avenues were enfiladed with machine guns. The Algerians who were partisans of the mutineers felt this was another May 13. The crowds chanted, *"Algérie française,"* as they made their way to the Forum.

On the balcony of the government palace, the four leaders of the complicity sang "La Marseillaise." They were Generals Challe, Jouhaud, Zeller, and Salan. Salan was the last to arrive at the rendezvous, having only just come from six months of voluntary exile in Madrid.

The conspirators had effectively seized power in Algiers, and, apart from certain sectors held by units whose loyalty to the president of the Republic was unimpeachable, they were now in control of a large part of Algerian territory.

For the enthusiastic and fraternal masses of May 13, 1958, there had been only one general. Now de Gaulle was stricken from the ranks. He was no longer wanted. His power, and the men who exercised it, was no longer recognized.

Michel Debré, in his capacity as premier, reported the news to the chief of the French that same Saturday. "Those people want my hide," de Gaulle growled. "They won't even get my shirt!" He thought for a moment. "I'm disappointed in Challe," he went on. "I thought he was loyal. He let himself be influenced. He's a weakling. Salan, on the other hand, likes intellectual adventures—and others, too. He may have to pay dearly for this one. Like many colonial chiefs, he is a gambler and a sybarite. After his execution, he'll have plenty of time to play cards. I wonder—is pinochle allowed in hell? I hardly imagine

Jouhaud knows how to play bridge. Zeller, yes. He is a *demi-mondain. . . ."*

De Gaulle did not seem to take the matter tragically. France had confronted him with other crises; and that malign tumor—Algeria— had already given him trouble. This time the trouble was serious, but ticklish rather than dramatic. De Gaulle had a trait special to certain great men; he faced facts squarely, while seeming to conceal their gravity beneath a verbal sally.

What could those rebel generals expect from the powers whose support they must necessarily solicit? For they could not cut Algeria off from its capital, isolate it from the rest of the world, and doom it to asphyxiation. No help was to be expected from the UN.[12] If they had seized power in Algiers, it was in order to seize it also in Paris. Did they have a sufficient air fleet? No. That being so, they would appeal—they would have appealed?—to the United States. But John F. Kennedy had his head on his shoulders. He would not lend a single plane. "No, the parachutists won't swim across the Mediterranean! . . ."

How did Paris react?

At dawn on Sunday, April 24, after a night of standby alert, the gendarmerie's tanks took up position in front of the Palais Bourbon and the Grand Palais, near the presidential palace of the Elysée. All the city buses were ranked in a file, ready to block the cross streets.

Determined to alert the people of France to their responsibilities, de Gaulle addressed the nation that day in a speech marked by firmness; the dramatization of the subject was deliberate. He felt the need to awaken in every citizen a sense of historic emergency and arouse the nation's patriotic conscience. *"Mon cher et vieux pays, nous voici une fois de plus dans l'épreuve.* ["My old, beloved country, here we are again in a time of trial."] This seizure of power has an appearance of power: a foursome of retired generals! . . . In the name of France, I demand that every possible means be employed to bar the way to these men. The future of usurpers should only be that which the strict enforcement of law assigns them."

At six o'clock that evening a sudden downpour plunged the capital into an autumnal cold.

"A good shower is worth ten thousand security police . . . when

[12] It was by a very narrow margin that France won a majority in the General Assembly. Her intervention in Algeria was morally condemned.

they are caught unawares. But rain doesn't bother parachutists—their outfits are waterproofed." With this pertinent comment, delivered in a waggish tone, Malraux entered into the arena.

De Gaulle's firm tone, heightened by the vibrant solemnity of the voice, and Malraux's insouciance were in marked contrast to the genuine call to arms sent out over the airwaves at 11:45 P.M. that Sunday. Michel Debré, the premier, went on television and made no effort to conceal an anxiety that verged on panic. The country was in danger. Every Frenchman, every Frenchwoman must put himself and herself in a state of legitimate defense. Paris would be the target of the criminal generals, to be sure, for there was the seat of power. "The parachutists are coming! Go to meet them, by car, by bicycle, or on foot!"

André Malraux, minister for cultural affairs, set up his headquarters in the Ministry of the Interior, on the place Beauveau. To be kept informed at first hand. And to fight. "The rebel army must be knocked out," he had said in the Council of Ministers. "And I shall climb into the first tank."

From the Elysée Palace, where de Gaulle had not left his study, it was impossible to make contact with Algiers. No telephone communication came through, either from the headquarters of the French administration, or from the airport of Algiers, nor from Bône or Constantine, Algeria's other chief towns.

Paris was suddenly on a war footing. Within three hours of Debré's appeal, the courtyard of the Ministry of the Interior was flooded with volunteers. Malraux and his aides saw to it that they were provided with equipment, while within the building Roger Frey, the minister, and his secretary-general, Alexandre Sanguinetti, consulted the file of the *Algérie française* fanatics who might be involved in case of a morning attack by the parachutists. In Corsica, in the provinces, no agitation was in evidence. With forced gaiety, Sanguinetti declared, "Here we are not worried. We have Malraux to defend us."

When General de Gaulle was told that Malraux had become "Colonel Berger" once more and was recruiting, recruiting . . . and that he had chosen the place Beauveau to quarter his troops, so as to keep an eye on the nearby Elysée Palace—"There's a man who never fails to surprise me," said the general, who was feeling the strain. And he added, "There's a man!"

The man in question had had arms delivered to him by the *Garde Républicaine,* the *Gendarmerie Mobile,* the security police. He assigned tasks and responsibilities, designated those who would maintain liaison between the various groups. He explained his street combat strategy. The airfields—Orly, Le Bourget, Villacoublay, Toussus-le-Noble—were bristling with stakes, making it impossible for planes to land.

If rebel soldiers were to manage to land outside the regular airfields, they would be intercepted by fast tanks and units of infantry posted round the gates of Paris. Still to be considered was the case of local infiltration, and of planes landing their human cargo at protected points, which would enable them to form groups, spreading out over the Invalides esplanade, the Champ de Mars, the racecourses, the stadia, the wooded approaches—Boulogne, Vincennes—the sloping lawns of the Butte Chaumont, those of the Monceau and Montsouris parks. Those points, which lent themselves to hide-and-seek, had to be watched.

Paris was organizing her resistance. The alert had brought about a civic night watch that was animated by Malraux. A well-ordered bustle prevailed in the Beauveau camp, a combination of feverish courage and controlled fear that had taken hold of the big court in which the motorcyclists of the protection brigades gaily made their motors roar. Volunteers arrived in ever greater numbers. Many of them brought their uniforms and guns with them, and soon two thousand men were equipped, all of them experienced army men, seasoned in street fighting. Said their war leader—the inexhaustible André Malraux, who, at the age of sixty, managed to combine the experience of maturity with a youthful fervor: "The parachutists will be here in three hours, or never! They shall not pass!"

When night fell, a rain squall shook the horse chestnut trees on the avenue Marigny.

"The weather is on our side," said Malraux.

Mad contradictory rumors circulated throughout the city: Salan had sent an emissary to President Kennedy to explain to him that an independent Algeria meant a Communist Algeria; 125 four-engine jet planes designed for troop transport had left Florida for Algiers; the regiments operating in the Aurès Mountains had gone over to the generals in the putsch; throughout France the OAS was getting ready for its big night.

The night would be a sleepless one on the place Beauveau. De Gaulle had called Malraux on Roger Frey's private line. Just to say two words to him: *"Malraux, merci."*

"Roll yourselves up in those blankets," Malraux ordered his *com-*

pagnons. "Only every other man must go to sleep. You can relay one another."

At five o'clock, when the gray, misty dawn rose over Paris, Malraux scanned the sky. "Now we can go and sleep like babies. It's over. There's no longer any danger of their coming."

Next day, Monday, the *"Non!"* of the contingent in Algeria made itself heard. Young enlisted men had heard de Gaulle's broadcast appeal and had sabotaged as best they could the orders of the insurgents, shouting "Long live de Gaulle!" in the barracks, while aviators painted the cross of Lorraine on the roofs of hangars.

There Challe, the aviator, suffered his first serious setback.

Then came a warning shot from the navy. Vice Admiral Jean-Marie Querville, a former Free French follower, who commanded the Algerian fleet, happened to be in Algiers. Summoned by the rebel generals to align himself with them, he refused and managed to escape on a fast launch and reach his base at Mers-el-Kebir. There he boarded the squadron's escort, the *Maillé-Brézé,* which made as if to move out to sea.

When the parachutists from Oran arrived in tanks and jeeps at the gates of the maritime base, the *Maillé-Brézé* turned back and leveled her guns on them. The parachutists retreated, in deadly fear of a naval blockade.

De Gaulle had given clear instructions to his armies: "Employ every means, including gunfire." But by the time this message was made public, Challe had already written the letter in which he gave himself up. Toward eight o'clock, however, Salan, who had not surrendered, had announced the mobilization of eight divisions in Algeria over the rebel radio of Algiers. The loyal military authorities promptly decided to blockade Algiers, and surrounded the city during the night. Recognizing that they had lost, the parachutists evacuated the government palace, departing in the direction of Zeralda, from which they had come. Once loaded aboard their trucks, they broke into song—movingly, in spite of everything—chorusing a well-known song of Edith Piaf: *"Non, je ne regrette rien, rien de rien, ni le mal, ni le bien . . ."*

Challe and Zeller had already surrendered.

Salan, Jouhaud, and the colonels disappeared into the maquis of the subversive underground. It was the end of a nightmare that had made republican France tremble.

De Gaulle had won. During an extraordinary meeting of the Council of Ministers he publicly thanked Malraux, who replied, "Paris was well worth a sleepless night, *mon général!*"

"De Gaulle has no friends," Malraux had once said. This he could no longer say. The night of April 24 had sealed a hoop of steel round the two men.

André Malraux has justly been called "the man whom death continued to haunt." One month later, on May 23, death, which had struck him through those near and dear to him—his two brothers, his beloved Josette—drove him implacably back into solitude by taking his two young sons.

Gauthier and Vincent had gone down to the island of Port Cros, close to Hyères, where the Clotis family lived, to spend five or six days and "work in the sun," as Gauthier put it. Gauthier, twenty-one, was very athletic, loved boxing, which he practiced, and had a room in which he lived alone in the Latin Quarter. He had just passed his end-of-the-year examinations preparatory to a political science course. He was very studious, and was preparing to take an examination in English on his return to Paris. His favorite writer in the language was Hemingway.

Vincent had four passions—underwater fishing, speeding on a motorcycle (he had a BSA 650 cm^3), French literature, and motion pictures.

Though only eighteen, Vincent was already engaged to Clara Saint, daughter of a South American businessman, and they planned to marry later that summer. She was a year older than he. For Clara's birthday, her father had given her an Alfa Romeo, a Giulietta model, which she lent to Vincent so that the brothers could use it on their vacation. They had left for Hyères on May 18. They stayed at the villa Anémones, the home of Madame Marcelle Henry, whom they called their "island godmother." This fine old lady was the owner of the island of Port Cros. She had been a close friend of Monsieur and Madame Clotis, the boys' grandparents, and, having known Gauthier and Vincent since they were small, felt for them all the affection of an authentic grandmother.

"On the Monday of Pentecost," Madame Henry told me, "Father Moulin came to say Mass in the chapel on the island. All three of us attended it, and then we had lunch with the father. On Tuesday the boat *Iles d'Or* brought us back to the mainland, to Le Lavandou. Gauthier and Vincent drove me in the Alfa Romeo to the Salins d'Hyères, where I had left my car. The two boys drove well, but very fast. At my age one is frightened of speed. When they left me, I can still see them leaning over the door of my car, telling me jokingly, 'Be very careful, godmother, don't drive too fast. Try to be good. . . .'

"Then they had added, 'We want to be in Paris this evening. . . .' "

Toward eight-thirty that night a motorist on Route Nationale 6 passed an Alfa Romeo Giulietta that was smashed against a tree, less than a mile and a half from the village of Lacanche, between Chagny and Arnay-le-Duc. He notified the proprietor of the garage in Lacanche, who went at once to the scene of the accident.

"It was frightful," he reported. "The car was wrapped around a tree. I glimpsed a human body smashed against the windshield. It was the driver. A few yards away on a grassy knoll lay another corpse. The two bodies were taken to the Hôtel Dieu hospital in Beaune."

The most reasonable hypothesis about the accident was that the car, driven at great speed on a slippery road, had gone into a skid and crashed with terrible force against the tree, on the opposite side of the road. Gauthier, who was at the wheel, was killed instantly, Vincent, who was thrown clear, a few moments later.

The following afternoon, André Malraux stepped from his black car in the court of the Beaune hospital. In a room of the clinic Father Bourgeon, the dean of Beaune cathedral, had prayed all night by the bodies. That night, it was Malraux, adventurer, minister, father, who sat all alone with his two dead sons.

Next day, the coffins were carried from Beaune to the church of Saint-Germain de Charonne, in Paris. Following a requiem mass celebrated by Father Bockel, they were buried in the small Charonne cemetery close beside a gray marble tomb that bears a simple inscription in gold letters: "Josette Malraux Clotis."

One day, long before, Josette had said, "I am frightened when I look at the lifelines in my children's hands. They stop short, like mine, in the middle of the palm."

214

15.

Ambassador to the World

It could be said of Malraux, as of Antigone, that "he has a certain experience of misfortune." Within a year of his sons' deaths an attempt was made on his life by OAS activists. On February 7, 1962, twenty-two-year-old Jean-Marie Vincent, an important member of the OAS in Paris, drove, with three accomplices, to the vicinity of Malraux's house in the avenue Victor Hugo, on the edge of the Bois de Boulogne. Vincent gave a plastic bomb to one of the young men with him, who placed it on the sill of a ground floor window.

Vincent and the others stood guard with machine guns and smoke bombs at the ready.

It was about one o'clock in the afternoon, a time when everything is quiet in that residential part of Paris, and most people are at lunch. In due course, the bomb went off, and the OAS terrorists made their getaway. What they did not know was that the ground floor was occupied by the owner of the house, a Monsieur Renard, who rented the upper floors to the Malraux family. The innocent victim of the explosion was Renard's four-year-old daughter, Delphine. She was playing in her bedroom after lunch, before going back to school, and was seriously wounded in the face. It was feared she would be totally blinded. The surgeon had to take more than a hundred stitches in her face to prevent her from being permanently disfigured, and Delphine was on the operating table for three hours. When she recovered consciousness, her father told her, "We had a car accident. The suitcases fell around you and one of them struck you. That's why it's so dark." The child would never again be able to see out of her right eye.

The perpetrators of the outrage were arrested a few day later.

On March 18, 1962, representatives of the French government and of the provisional government of the Algerian republic met at Evian, a spa on the shores of Lake Geneva, and signed a peace pact. The following day a cease-fire was ordered in Algeria, the country that was now to become an independent nation. The Algerian war was over at last.

To rebuild or to maintain French ties of friendship in what had once been called France's empire was now the task of General de Gaulle and his government.

As spokesman for his president, André Malraux served as the prestigious traveling salesman of Gaullist thinking. In the course of his ten-year service as minister of culture, he made the circuit of the globe, visiting all the countries he had once known well, with the exception of Spain, where he will never return as long as Franco, whom he despises, is in power. A sampling of his speeches, graceful, sonorous, profound, reveals much about the man behind the minister of France who was "the hero and the herald of French culture," according to Emanuel d'Astier de La Vigerie.

In December of 1958, in Tokyo, he said to the Japanese: ". . . the old civilizations must establish contact and learn to know one another, not in order to rediscover their past, but in order to build the future together, for it is not certain that the prodigious past which has been that of Iran, of India, of Japan, of France, will stand up in the face of the Marxist prediction.

"Either we believe that the world's destiny is wholly linked to political and economic evolution, or that its object is the maintenance and the creation of human values. It is not obvious that these two possibilities are contradictory. The decisive problem of the world can be summarized as follows: How will a new civilization that is now beginning be able to reconcile the desire for freedom and that of social justice?"

Visiting Athens in May, 1959, he proclaimed the greatness of Greece from the height of the Acropolis: "Of all the values of the spirit, the most fecund are those that spring from communion and from courage. . . . A secret Greece rests in the hearts of all men of the West."

That August and September he traveled to Latin America.

In Santiago de Chile, he was about to address two thousand students when a firecracker thrown from the balcony burst on the stage of the amphitheater, leaflets fell in handfuls from the ceiling, and some twenty voices rang out: "Algeria! Algeria!"

Malraux, unfazed, cried out: "When I was nineteen and I believed in a cause, I did not serve it with firecrackers and leaflets. I served it with my life, and I paid for my faith, as for my mistakes, with my blood. I have always served the world's oldest nobility, the dignity of men, and I don't authorize choirboys to teach me liturgy. . . ."

And he went on: "Arise, Lazarus! We cannot revive the dead, but France is beginning to know how to revive the dreams of nobility."

Two thousand students, on their feet, acclaimed him.

In Brazil he used these words: "In a country that is fifteen times the size of France, sixty million inhabitants—half of whom are less than twenty—have passed from walking on foot to the airplane without having known the stagecoach or the railroad. We are already in the twenty-first century. . . ."

Ten days after his return to France, Malraux discovered a rose petal forgotten in one of the pockets of his jacket. "It is the symbol of this journey," he said. "Latin America has entered into the world's destiny. Despite powerful obstacles, it is the continent of hope."

In Mexico, August of 1960:

"The envoy of an old country of liberty has come here to tell why and how each of its gestures, for nearly two years, has unswervingly served the same cause. It was well for me to have come to tell Mexico what were France's achievements in the Franco-African community, what its objectives were in the policy of self-determination in Algeria. In the course of all the conversations that I have had, there has emerged very gradually a strange realm of common truths. Mexico's passionate anticolonialism has found, I believe, in what I have come to tell it, both reasons for reflection and reasons for hope. It has understood, at the same time, our ordeal and our determination to find a remedy without renouncing our fundamental *raison d'être*."

In the month of May, 1962, France's minister for cultural affairs visited the United States. He had first met the Kennedys when they made their triumphant visit to France the previous year, a few brief days after his sons' deaths. Despite his grief, he had been most gracious, particularly to Jacqueline Kennedy, who now wished to return his hospitality. The morning of his arrival in Washington with Madame Malraux, Jackie took him to visit the National Gallery of Art. Its director, John Walker, was exhibiting for the first time a painting by John Copley representing the artist's family. To set it off effectively, the painting had been hung alone above a bed of green plants. The director was waiting for compliments.

Malraux looked at it briefly and, leaning toward Jacqueline Kennedy, said to her, "Certain paintings belong to the history of

217

humanity, others to the history of the United States. I am very happy to see this one for this *second* reason."

Nevertheless, Malraux left the National Gallery very much impressed to have seen again what he called its only masterpieces: a fifteenth-century *Madonna with Child* by Domenico Veneziano, the *Christ Chasing the Moneylenders from the Temple* by the young El Greco, and the *Girl with a Broom* by Rembrandt.

At one point, before a woman's portrait by the fifteenth-century Sienese painter Neroccio, Malraux leaned toward the director.

"Did you know," he said to him, "that Neroccio was Modigliani's favorite painter?" The director did not.

"He knows everything, he knows everything, it's incredible!" John Walker exclaimed afterward.

The visit lasted a good hour. In each room Malraux himself described the paintings and commented on them. "You're the guide today," said Jacqueline Kennedy. As they were leaving the museum, someone asked Jackie what her favorite paintings were.

"Oh, that's easy," she said. "My favorite paintings are those *he* likes best."

A student asked Malraux if in that year of 1962 he would still write *La Condition humaine*.

"Absolutely not," Malraux replied. "The circumstances are no longer the same. For me the end of the human condition is called Budapest."

That evening President and Mrs. Kennedy gave a banquet in the White House in honor of French Minister for Cultural Affairs and Madame Malraux. It was served in two separate dining rooms. In one, the State Dining Room, the President had Madame Malraux on his right. In the other, the Blue Room, the French minister was at Jacqueline Kennedy's right.

At the end of the dinner, the President of the United States rose and delivered the following speech:

Ladies and gentlemen:

I want to express a very warm welcome to all of you, and particularly to our distinguished guests, Monsieur and Madame Malraux.

This will be the first speech about relations between France and the United States that does not include a tribute to General Lafayette. It seems that almost every Frenchman who comes to the United States feels that Lafayette was a rather confused sort of ineffectual, elderly figure, hovering over French politics, and is astonished to find that we regard him as a golden, young, romantic figure, next to George Washington our most distinguished citizen. Therefore he will not be mentioned, but instead I will mention a predecessor of mine, John Adams, who was our first president to live in the White House and whose prayer on occupancy is written here. John Adams asked that on his gravestone be written, "He kept the peace with France."

I am very glad to welcome here some of our most distinguished artists. This is becoming a sort of eating place for artists. But they never ask *us* out!

I want to tell you how very pleased we are to have so many distinguished writers and artists and actresses and creative thinkers. You know, one of the great myths of American life is that nothing is pleasanter or easier than lying around all day and painting a picture or writing a book and leading a rather easy life. In my opinion, the ultimate in self-discipline is a creative work. Those of us who work in an office every day are actually the real gentle livers of American society.

We do not manage our cultural life in this country, nor does any free society, but it is an important part. It is one of the great purposes. And I would hope that this tremendous energy obtained in the intellectual life of America could be communicated not only to people in this country but all around the world.

There are so many more people playing musical instruments now, going to symphonies, going to the theater, to art galleries, painting, than anyone realizes. And it is our hope that Americans will begin to look about them and realize that here in these years we are building a life which, as I say, develops the maximum in each individual.

Now we have the best model that we could have this evening in welcoming Monsieur and Madame Malraux. I suppose all of us wish to participate in all the experiences of life, but he has left us all behind. We are the descendants of early founders who were themselves men of great variety and vitality. But he has led an archaeological expedition to Cambodia, been connected with Chiang Kai-shek, Mao Tse-tung, and has been active in the civil war, participated in the defense of his

219

country, been involved with General de Gaulle, and has been at the same time a great creative figure in his own right. He has left, I think, most of us way behind.

So we regard him as an honored guest in this country—as participants in the cultural stream and also as admirers of those who travel the far horizons of human destiny. So we are very proud to have him. And we are particularly proud to have him because of his association with a distinguished leader of the West.

A good deal has been written by some of our distinguished correspondents about the difficulties that have occasionally come up between the President of the United States and General de Gaulle. But I want to say that there is a tradition in that regard, with Franklin Roosevelt and Dwight D. Eisenhower. And General de Gaulle continues on his way, and has built for his country and his friends in Europe a strength which is the most valuable source of comfort to us all. I know that there are sometimes difficulties in life, but I hope that those who live in both our countries realize how fortunate we are in the last two decades to be associated in the great effort with him. And we are glad to have Monsieur and Madame Malraux here because we believe that they will go back to France and say a kind word for the United States—and its President.

So I hope you will drink to all of us, in the sense that you are leaders in our free society—and particularly to our distinguished leader whom we are very glad to have with us tonight —and most especially to the President of France, General de Gaulle.

In the Blue Room, André Malraux then rose to speak:

Mr. President, ladies and gentlemen:

I believe this is the first time it has happened to me, as a guest, to have to reply to a speech which I unfortunately have not heard.

I thank you for having welcomed me here by your masterpieces and, better yet, by your masterpieces as presented by Mrs. Kennedy. I can hardly tell you how deeply this welcome has moved me; but I say that I have been received here as I have never been. And I do not say it out of courtesy, but because this welcome has a meaning.

I visited long ago that other great country, Russia; amid its immense snows I then had the sense of a limitless hope. Here the feeling is different. Perhaps it expresses the very essence of the Western world—fraternal liberty.

One more word: the United States is today, outstandingly, the country that assumes the destiny of man. And it is the first time in history that a nation occupies such a place without having sought it. Through the millennia many countries have achieved first place by sustained efforts, at the price of innumerable human lives. There has been an Assyrian Empire, a Byzantine Empire, a Roman Empire. There is no American Empire. There is, however, the United States. For the first time a country has become the world's leader without achieving this through conquest. And it is strange to think that for thousands of years one single country has found power while seeking only justice....

Reversing the customary order, I therefore first raise my glass to thank you for your masterpieces and to thank the lady who showed them; I drink finally to the President of the United States, and to the people who have achieved first place among the peoples of the world, without having conquered it, without having sought it, and even without having wanted it.

Two days later the Kennedys invited Malraux to spend Sunday with them privately, at their country home in Virginia.

On that day Malraux spoke of France, of the future of the world, of de Gaulle. He expressed himself with verve, finding the most appropriate words, the most concise and telling expressions to convey his ideas, and more particularly those of the general.

President Kennedy listened eagerly, swinging rhythmically back and forth in his rocking chair.

Questioned about the French *force de frappe*, Malraux explained that France wanted atomic weapons not in order to fight alone against the Russians, which would be absurd, nor alone against her allies, which would be even more absurd, nor alone against anyone.

The general's idea was that France needed nuclear independence to reinforce her international position. A really independent state could not count on foreign force—American, in this case—to insure its security and affirm its will. Consequently France, in order to make herself heard and be no one's vassal, was building a nuclear arsenal.

The problem of NATO was linked to that of the *mystique* of the French army. An army must have an aim and a purpose. It can obey effectively within the context of European unification only if it fights for its own flag and not at all for a vague cause, under multiple command.

The Atlantic alliance was in no way at issue, insofar as it was an effort of the West to meet a common danger. On this level France and America had always had the same aims, and America, for the time being, was still the guarantor of European security.

What France wanted, Malraux told JFK, was to give its army a new luster again, to make it one of the bastions of European defense but not to subject it to a foreign command.

Malraux also said that to General de Gaulle's mind Algeria was only a transitional problem which, once settled, would enable him to take gigantic strides in the way of reforms toward the only objective he had ever had: to give back to France its voice as a great power by adapting it to the world of today and preparing it for the world of tomorrow.

In January of 1963, André Malraux returned to the United States, accompanying Leonardo da Vinci's masterpiece, the Mona Lisa, the loan of which he had arranged with the curators of the Louvre. The speech presenting the great portrait to President Kennedy deserves quoting:

> . . . Other illustrious portraits can be compared to this one. But every year a few poor madwomen take themselves for Mona Lisa, whereas no one takes herself for a figure of Titian, Raphael, or Rembrandt. When the ocean liner *France* left the port of Le Havre, to the bouquets of flowers brought for the living passengers was added a bouquet bearing an unsigned card on which was written, "For Mona Lisa". . . .
>
> The list of those who have been deeply affected by this painting is a long one and begins with its author. Leonardo, who spoke of his own painting with such moderation, once wrote: "I had the experience of painting a really divine work". . . .
>
> Many explanations for this can be given. I shall suggest only one.

The antiquity that the Italian resuscitated involved an idealization of forms, but the people of the antique statues, being a people without eyes, were also a people without souls. Eyes, the soul, spirituality—these were brought by Christian art, and Leonardo had found this same illustrious smile for the face of the Virgin. By transfiguring a profane face through it, Leonardo brought to woman's soul the idealization that Greece had given to her features. The mortal woman with a divine look in her eyes triumphs over the goddesses without eyes. It is the first expression of what Goethe was to call the eternal feminine.

The possession of masterpieces today imposes great obligations, as everyone knows. You have been good enough, Mr. President, to speak of a "historic loan," thinking perhaps of the sentiments to which it testifies. It is historic also in another sense, which does you great honor. If, upon my return, I am asked before the Assembly by some peevish deputy, "Why have we lent the Mona Lisa to the United States?" I shall answer, "Because no other nation would have received her as they have."

Through you, Mr. President—and through Mrs. Kennedy, ever present when it comes to uniting art, the United States, and my country—the most powerful nation in the world today pays the most splendid tribute that a work of art has ever received. Praise be to both of you—in the name of all the nameless artists who may perhaps be thanking you from the depths of the great funereal night.

One last word.

There has been talk of the risks taken in letting this painting leave the Louvre. They are real, even though exaggerated. But the risks taken by the boys who landed that day at Arromanches—without mentioning those who had preceded them twenty-three years before—were much more certain. To the humblest among them, who may be listening to me, I want to say, without lifting my voice, that the masterpiece to which, Mr. President, you are paying a historic tribute this evening is a painting he has saved.

In the course of a Canadian press conference in October, 1963, Malraux explained how he reconciled the Malraux of *La Condition humaine* and General de Gaulle's minister: "I formerly considered two things to be primordial, justice and the proletariat. General de Gaulle, whether you agree or not, is for me the embodiment of justice. Since *La Condition humaine*, there has been the war, and for me today there is first France and then the proletariat."

In December, 1964, the transfer of the ashes of Jean Moulin[1] to the Panthéon, burial place for the great men of France, moved Malraux to make one of his finest speeches, a funeral oration worthy of the seventeenth-century preacher Bossuet. It concludes with these words:

". . . Today's tribute summons only the song that will now be heard, the 'Song of the Partisans' that I heard murmured like a song of complicity, and then chanted in the fog of the Vosges and the woods of Alsace, mingled with the far cries of the sheep of the *tabors*, when the bazookas of Corrèze were advancing to meet von Rundstedt's tanks that were once again being hurled against Strasbourg. Listen today, youth of France, to what was for us the song of misfortune. It is the funereal march of the ashes that lie here. Next to those of Carnot[2] with the soldiers of the Year II, to those of Victor Hugo with *Les Misérables,* to those of Jaurès watched over by justice, may they rest with their long procession of disfigured shades. Today, O Youth, may you think of this man as you would have brought your hands to his poor shapeless face of the last day, to his lips which had not spoken; on that day it was the face of France."

The life of André Malraux completed full circle on the day that the minister for cultural affairs returned to China for the first time in thirty-five years. He had fallen ill, been advised to take a long sea trip for his health, and while in the Far East received de Gaulle's permission to make a formal visit to Red China and its dignitaries.

"We are hoping for a *rapprochement* between People's China and the West," Malraux said when he arrived in August, 1965. "But it is a problem and we don't know how to solve it."

("There is one Chinese fact that is extremely important," he told me recently. "It is the modernization of China. The transformation of China—I had not been back there since 1929—is startling, and far greater than that of the USSR, which I saw with the same time gap.")

[1] Jean Moulin (1899–1943) had been prefect of Chartres before June, 1940. He opposed the Germans, fled to London, and joined the Free French there. In 1942 he parachuted into the southern zone of France and became the chief organizer of the underground resistance. Traitorously denounced on June 21, 1943, he was terribly tortured by the Gestapo and died from the effects in the train that was deporting him to a concentration camp in Germany.

[2] Lazare Carnot (1753–1823) was one of the pivotal members of the Committee of Public Safety during the French Revolution, a great strategist and organizer.

Visiting India afterward, Malraux declared in New Delhi: "Between China and India there is no really serious problem. The real problems of China lie elsewhere. In the world's destiny there are real conflicts, which have real consequences. If there was a conflict between China and the United States, the consequences—and among them tens of millions of dead—would immediately make their effects felt on the world's destiny. Every one of us must hope that this conflict will not occur and make every effort to safeguard the peace."

That October, restored to health by his travels, the minister for cultural affairs mounted the rostrum before the members of the National Assembly to defend the culture budget:

> A special effort in behalf of youth is imperative, for it is during adolescence that a certain number of passions crystallize. It is rather rare for a person to acquire later what he has not acquired around the age of twenty. This is especially true of education. Everyone knows that any child can easily learn Chinese . . . for us it is more difficult.
>
> On the contrary, the body of psychological research that has been carried out in the past thirty years has shown that the age of culture is not youth, but the second part of life. The role of culture, if it operates in depth, corresponds to what the role of religion was formerly, having as it did an impact also on childhood and the second part of life. What was the life of Louis XIV? It was what you all know, up to the age of forty. His great virtues came to him between the ages of forty and forty-five. The idea that the king of France went to Mass with his mistress in order to find another one disturbed him not in the least.
>
> And Saint-Simon, who was not of a particularly religious turn, made a retreat at La Trappe every year for one month. . . .
>
> The truth of it is that we must not work for an "age category," as the ethnographers say, but try to understand why, in the realm of culture, the French should be considered to be dead by the age of thirty.

In April, 1966, Malraux was in Dakar, capital of Senegal, one of France's most successfully developing "associated nations."

"Cultural community is only possible for the sake of dialogue," he said, "the dialogue of the spirit, for France has nothing to sell, not even our values. Success? The future will tell. Africa is face to face with the world's destiny. . . . Africa has set out on the adventure of creation and adventure is its greatness."

The minister took advantage of his stay in Dakar to go to Casamance to make the round of the priest-kings who still exist, following old custom, in that province of Senegal. The mayor and the prefect have the material powers, but the kings and queens still serve as intermediaries between men, the spirits of the ancestors, and the gods.

After miles of a trail that wound between the enormous trunks of bombax trees, baobabs, and fig trees, Malraux reached the palace of Queen Sebeth, who governed the people of the Floups. The palace was a large round hut in the village of Sinagar. On the mud wall a heterogeneous assortment of aluminum pans and exquisitely shaped potteries. The queen, draped in a green muslin toga, had put on all her jewels—rings on all her fingers, a magnificent gold filigree necklace, an enormous brooch with false pearls. She at first took the minister for General de Gaulle.

Malraux offered her the customary gifts, a plug of chewing tobacco, a bottle of cognac. She presented him with the local fetish, a piece of raw wood decorated with three white moons, kept between the roots of a bombax tree, in an enclosure that only she had a right to enter every morning for a libation of palm wine. She invoked the spirit of the dead for the good continuation of the minister's voyage, pressing his hands for a long moment and taking him in her arms to bid him farewell.

"I like that queen," said Malraux. "She has a feeling for what is sacred, she has the gestures of a priestess."

Malraux, speaking at the Festival of Negro Arts in Dakar:

"What remains of a civilization if not its art? The most horrible, the most inhuman civilization of history was that of the Assyrians. What has it left us? The admirable 'wounded lion.' Africa must be present in the world. Africa is strong enough to make its 'imaginary museum' for itself. On the condition that it does not stop there. This is the message of France: 'May Africa conquer its freedom!'"

Malraux in Egypt, May, 1966:

"Your revolution has one prime objective, like all revolutions: to change the people's living standard. It is obvious that to change a people's standard of living without changing its spiritual standard is simply to lead it to disaster."

Malraux on Fidel Castro: "Today the revolutionaries who act are not often revolutionaries, they are thinkers, writers. Those who act because they have thought the revolution are, in this order, number one, Marx, and number two, Lenin, because Leninism is an ideology. Lenin was a man of genius in action, but he was also an ideologist. There are those who act by their prestige. There is no other word. In my opinion, Castro is infinitely more a revolutionary of the prestigious type than of the ideological type."

Malraux on the youth of yesterday and the youth of today:

> I am not a good judge to compare them. No one is a good judge. One is not obliged to accept the famous gap between generations, and, in fact, to accept it is madness. But neither must one pretend to understand too much. What was youth like when I was young? It was *les copains*. Today it is my sons. Or, rather, it *was* my sons. . . . To know youth is to be in it. It is not holding a dialogue with it. . . .

(It is interesting to note the curiously ambivalent attitude of the current student generation in France toward Malraux. His books are studied in schools and universities, his writings are constantly reissued, he is an honored guest at any educational institution he cares to address. For a large proportion of French youth, he is still a sure guide and a revered one.

(His relationship with the young generation of leftist intellectuals was sharply challenged, however, by the student uprisings of May, 1968. Quotations from his works appeared on the walls of schools and colleges, taunting him with sentiments from an earlier era. As the only government figure with a revolutionary past, he was the easiest to confront with his contradictions. To the student rioters, Malraux was the turncoat who had preferred power to carrying on the class struggle.

(Nevertheless, the son of David Rousset,[3] himself leader of a commando group who had to go into hiding after the May uprisings, probably spoke for the majority of his comrades when I interviewed him recently:

("Malraux was the front-rank leader of our dreams. . . . If, at the age of twenty, we had found him still the man whose works we had read when we were fourteen, a tremendous movement would have rallied us around him. But alas! he was no longer free—he had chosen

[3] Founder, with Jean-Paul Sartre, of the *Rassemblement Democratique Révolutionnaire*, who subsequently changed allegiance and became a Gaullist.

de Gaulle, chosen to side with the bourgeois state against the revolutionaries. . . .

("We had expected everything from Malraux and he disappointed us painfully. Hurt us, in fact. As de Gaulle's minister of culture, he accomplished some remarkable things. But his *maisons de la culture,* the superb exhibitions he arranged—what have they done to advance the revolution an inch? He was an incomparable patriotic minister, an irreproachable servant of France. But we are internationalists, and we expected more of him. We are disappointed in him, but that's a long way from regarding him with contempt. In our eyes, he is a great figure—above all for his concept of fidelity. When de Gaulle retired, Malraux left the government. Who else was capable of such an act of courage? A few others, maybe. But they don't *interest* us as he does.")

Malraux about women in action: "When, like Hemingway, you introduce a love story into a revolutionary combat, you are pulling the reader's leg, because if you are having a love affair you are not in a revolutionary combat. When Robespierre met Danton in the corridors of the Convention and the latter said to him, 'You're a traitor, Robespierre!' he replied, 'Idiot! No one is a traitor when he's making love'. . . .

"Men are in a good civilization for men because it is they who have made it. Women are in a bad civilization for women because it is they who have had to undergo it. There is no joint civilization. But I am convinced that we shall witness a penetration of masculine civilization by women."

On Europe: "[Though] building Europe is prodigiously difficult . . . [it] is the only really important thing that can be done in our time. But it does not consist in bringing people together who call themselves delegates or whatever in Strasbourg or elsewhere, because then we shall change nothing at all, we shall be doing what has already been done for a good while: an illusion of Europe, a false Europe."

Malraux on relations between China and Russia: "Everything that has arisen between capitalism and communism will arise henceforth between two realities, China and Russia, that is to say, two communisms. During that time one part of communism will become capitalist, while capitalism is fast becoming socialized."

On the responsibility of education: "In our machine civilization all the factories of the earth find a response in the factories of dreams. What comes through most powerfully in television and motion pictures is the organic power of sex and blood. Only the powers of the spirit can combat those demons."

In February and March, 1968, Malraux took his world travels full circle. He went to the Soviet Union, his first visit in thirty-four years. He began by visiting several large industrial cities in the south of Russia, then went to Moscow.

The Moscow visit began in Lenin's former office in the Kremlin. Malraux looked, asked questions. He remained for a long time near the windows of Lenin's apartment, gazing out over the Kremlin. He inquired through which gate Lenin used to enter the Kremlin. "The Troitsky gate," he was told, which was then the main gate. He examined in detail the military maps of the period of the Revolution that were hanging on the walls of the office. He looked at the statuette of a monkey given to Lenin by an American millionaire. Lenin had said at that time, "If humanity does not stop the armaments race, it will return to the state of this monkey reflecting on its past and holding a human skull in its hands."

Answering the toast of Ekaterina Furtseva on the traditional friendship between Russia and France, Malraux said: "I do not know what is the origin of this friendship—perhaps it was the fact that Catherine II considered herself a disciple of Diderot—but as concerns myself I salute this friendship between the Soviet Union and France. . . . I raise my glass to all those who have contributed to this friendship, the living and the dead."

At the Union of Soviet Writers, Malraux asked the question, "What is the present attitude toward Boris Pasternak, what position do Dostoevski and Tolstoi occupy?" "Dostoevski and Tolstoi are classics," was the reply, "and they are not a subject of controversy. Pasternak also is a poet who is almost canonized."

Constantin Fedin, having reminded Malraux of their meeting thirty-four years before, gave him a photograph of that period showing Malraux in the company of Pasternak and Meyerhold. (It is reproduced in this book.)

"We are looking forward to a closer *rapprochement* with France," said Fedin, "an essential *rapprochement*. On that depends the future of each. The time demands it. We all know the alternative to this *rapprochement*. We have experienced it and we have no wish to begin over again." Malraux replied: "Thirty-four years have passed, and here and now I again feel myself not a minister but a writer. In this half hour among you I have again experienced a sense of fraternity. There is an easy contact. This is why the French like Tolstoi, who wrote a novel against Napoleon. I raise my glass to fraternity, to the Soviet Union."

Malraux was received by Aleksei Kosygin. "Have you found any changes since you were here in 1934?" Kosygin asked. "Yes," said Malraux, "great changes. But the whole world is changing, and changing very fast. I also had a feeling of permanent change on my return from the Far East. I went to China three years ago. There has been enormous change."

"That is true," said the Russian, "but it is sometimes for the better and sometimes for the worse that the world changes. . . ."

The Palais-Royal, with its entrance at 3, rue de Valois: de Gaulle had given it to Malraux to serve as his ministry and his official headquarters.

When asked if he had any difficulty putting himself into the skin of a minister, Malraux used to reply with a story of Stéphane Mallarmé's. "One night the poet listens to the cats conversing on the tiles. A black cat asks his cat, 'And you, what do you do?' The poet's cat replies, 'I pretend that I'm Mallarmé's cat.'"

In February, 1969, André Malraux went to Nice. He went there in his role as minister of culture to lay the foundation stone—which had been detached from the Louvre—of the building that was to house the *Biblical Message* that Marc Chagall had offered to France.

He was stepping out of the official car with its tricolor insignia when a man stepped forward and splashed him with red paint, shouting, *"A bas Chagall!"*

The bystanders thought it was an armed attack, but Malraux, reacting promptly, "disarmed" his aggressor and in turn covered *him* with paint.

"It's simply an aesthetic disagreement," said Malraux calmly. "I don't want him arrested; there are screwballs everywhere. But I'm furious at him for having insulted one of our greatest living painters."

16.

The Lovers of Verrières

We come back to 1967, before Malraux's visit to Moscow. He had just returned to the world of literature after a ten-year absence with the publication of his *Antimémoires*. The book was a huge success; 340,000 copies were sold in three months after publication in France and the French-speaking countries. The American version he dedicated to Jacqueline Kennedy.

As the man nationally responsible for cultural affairs, he had a revolutionary idea. He proposed to Coco Chanel what he called "her little Louvre."

In fact, it was a double proposition. The right-hand gallery of the Louvre would be Chanel's to decorate, exactly as she liked, and as would best suit some forty masterworks to be chosen from the Louvre collections by Malraux. In the Grand Palais, meanwhile, on the Champs Elysées, Mademoiselle Chanel would exhibit her favorite models, in effect presenting a cavalcade of Parisian haute couture over the years.

The proposal was made in the course of a luncheon at Chanel's apartment at 31, rue Cambon, where the Coromandel screens are rated by experts as the finest in the world. Chanel asked the minister for time to think it over, and in fact the "little Louvre" did not in the end materialize. She had, however, had the good idea of inviting Louise de Vilmorin to the lunch.

The two had not met for thirty years. Malraux was now rich, a minister of state, an irreplaceable and much-relied-on adviser to the president of France. Louise had spent most of the war years in Hungary with her second husband, Count Pallfy. Since the war she had been living at her family château of Verrières-le-Buisson, writing mostly short stories and articles for *Marie-Claire* and other popular women's magazines. She had divorced Pallfy, who had since remarried; Malraux was living apart from his second wife, Madeleine.

There is no other way of putting it; for André and Louise it was a fated rediscovery. It was a chaste rediscovery, of brief duration, for Malraux had to preside at a council meeting at four o'clock at his ministry on the rue de Valois.

His chauffeur, at the wheel of the official black Citroën, delivered him to the meeting and then drove Louise out to Verrières, which is some forty minutes from Paris.

"Adieu, monsieur le ministre!" Louise cried, tapping on the window of the car.

"By no means *adieu!"* Malraux replied, blowing her a kiss. *"A très bientôt!"*

Which meant that the strokes of the bell in the baroque and charming *clocher* at Verrières were about to usher in a time of ardent dreams come true, after thirty-three years.

"We are Chateaubriand and Madame Récamier." (This is Louise speaking.)

"I wish I didn't have to leave you. I hate the work that tears me away from you."

"Don't try to lie! Work is more necessary to you than the air we both breathe."

"How agreeable to man is the woman who understands him!"

"How unlike you such language is!"

The setting was the eighteenth-century study—a former reception room—on the ground floor of the château of Verrières. Near the round table on which Malraux put his documents stood a tall chiseled glass decanter. Malraux had been a resident of Verrières only since May 1, 1969, four days after the departure from office of General de Gaulle.

The president had asked the country to vote on a referendum as to whether or not France should be divided up once more into its historic regions, instead of the departments that had existed since the French Revolution. If the yes votes won, de Gaulle had promised to deal at once with a labor problem that had for some time obsessed him: he wanted workers to participate in the running of the affairs in which they were employed. He visualized all workers, both intellectuals and manual laborers, sharing in the responsibilities and, of course, in the profits of the various enterprises.

However, the proposition had failed to arouse any real interest among the French people. Proprietors and managers were shy of it and noncommittal. Trade unions were skeptical. In his final appeal to the country before the referendum took place, the general had appeared on television and laid his own position in the balance, declaring that if the French people were to oppose the reform, he would no longer be honorably able to continue as their president.

"In provoking this vote," said Alain Poher, president of the Senate and as such de Gaulle's immediate second in the republican hierarchy, "Charles de Gaulle has given to this verdict the meaning of a vote of confidence and has declared that he will immediately submit to the will of the people."

"I have turned the last page of the chapter I opened in our history thirty years ago," was how de Gaulle himself put it.

The referendum vote, of course, was no. De Gaulle had no recourse but to resign. One presumes that he must have wanted to, for he had really engineered his own defeat.

Saturday, on the eve of the vote, André Malraux had been once again the spokesman for Gaullism. In a great lyrical flight, he exclaimed: "Napoleon wrote, 'I drew up my plans with the dreams of my sleeping soldiers.' General de Gaulle has often made his plans with the dreams of a sleeping France, because he had with him some French people who did not want to sleep!"

On Monday morning, when the referendum results were known, de Gaulle, at home at Colombey, issued orders to all his staff to leave the Elysée Palace at the hour when his functions would cease—that is to say, at noon.

"General de Gaulle regrets that he is unable to bid each one of you good-bye personally," the secretary-general of the Elysée told the two hundred employees who gathered around him, many with tears in their eyes. "We will all regard it as an honor to have served under his orders."

The archives had been emptied and the personal papers of the general were stacked in an official car that took the road toward Colombey. He would use them now only in compiling his memoirs.

"The spell is broken," was Malraux's epilogue to that day. He himself at once offered his resignation as minister to Alain Poher, who had become interim president until an election could be held in June.

Four months before, Malraux had rented for Louise and for himself a five-room duplex apartment, with a front view overlooking the rue Montpensier and the court side giving on the wonderful gardens of the Palais-Royal, from which could be heard the cooing of the pigeons in the horse chestnut trees.

Before finding this jewel, Louise had explored the Right Bank, the avenue Gabriel, and the avenue Matignon. Unlike most intellectuals, Malraux is not and has never been a man of the Left Bank.

André appointed Louise grand administrator of the premises. "Do something that is like you," he told her. She took on Pierre Franck to assist her with the decorating.

Malraux planned to live on the third floor, Louise on the second. The two entrances were independent of each other. "When he hears my voice on the ground floor he will come down," Louise said.

She took care of everything—of the craftsmen (she never used the word worker), the tiling, the painting, the china. "I want deeper sinks," she said, "and gray walls, a very tender gray." Malraux's clothes closets were of impressive size. "I need at least three dresses," said Louise. "I'll put some in his closets."

On May 1, Europe's Labor Day, André Malraux moved in at Verrières, and Louise, at dawn, presented her lover with sprigs of lily of the valley, her favorite flower, recalling the lilies of the valley in her first book, *Grâce de Sainte-Unefois,* written the year of their long-ago first meeting.

That afternoon they went, arm in arm, to visit their "little Palais-Royal," which was still in the hands of the painters.

"You have a sense of proportion. I congratulate you," said André to Louise, on seeing that she had had a partition removed to good effect.

"You have a sense of emotion, you know how to communicate it," Louise replied.

"Emotion is what traps you in love. Love is an anguish, a Moorish warrior's scimitar on your throat."

Always this colorful dialogue with overtones of the seventeenth century, which at times made one think of the maxim of Joubert, the author of a volume of *Pensées* and the confidant and friend of Chateaubriand: "Love is incomprehensible to those who do not share it."

Even for these two exceptional beings, love would be an almost commonplace phenomenon if we did not obscurely sense that their romance was beset by the hovering proximity of death.

Who—or what—brings death? As in the Greek tragedies, we can follow Malraux's footsteps through life by the perpetual trace of blood, of anguish, of loss.

Yet in meeting Louise for the second time he had found again what he had missed most since Josette died, what none of the women he had known since then had been able to give him—a cheerful presence, both active and restful.

"What kind of a woman is the woman of your dreams?" Louise pointedly asked Malraux.

"A woman with whom I am never bored. I imagine the ideal mate to be a bird of paradise who could be told to close her wings when I was intoxicated by colors."

"Do I intoxicate you with colors?" Louise asked anxiously.

"No, never. You make my head spin with colors, which is not the same thing. That is even the whole difference. Your plumage blends with your language."

This was Louise de Vilmorin's trump card. She distracted Malraux, who is very sensitive to boredom. She poked fun at him, made him roar with laughter. She was a brilliant talker, wonderfully adept at that forgotten art, conversation.

Malraux would scold her, "You're monologuing like a phonograph." But then he would correct himself. "After all, I love your worn and driveling disc."

"Are you being nasty?"

"No, I'm only severe. Especially with myself."

Plans were always a part of their conversation. They made them like a young couple. This pair, both close to seventy, each of whom looked twenty years younger, formed an authentic couple, a really young couple. Fastidious, like an academician who does not care a fig for the Académie Française (he has no ambition to join the "immortals" under the *coupole*), Malraux would buy his clothes at Lanvin's, on the faubourg St. Honoré. He would choose gray flannels, navy blue serges, coal black twist yarns. He wore an elegant wristwatch from Cartier. He had his hair dyed at his coiffeur's, a couple of doors from the Comédie-Française.

He had remained a gourmet, much attached to dishes he had learned to like as a child. But he was very careful and never ate a great deal. He quite liked salsify and potatoes and salad, detested all other vegetables—though if served a beef stew he would most politely eat up all the carrots on his plate—did not care much for fruit, always liked a dessert with his meals, either a *pithiviers*, his favorite cake, or a napoleon, or a pastry. He was eclectic; abroad he would eat the local food. In Paris his favorite restaurant was the exquisite Chez Lasserre, with its open-topped room that permits customers to dine alfresco. He usually chose grilled meats, loved good wine, especially champagne, and smoked quantities of French cigarettes.

He was finicky in the extreme. He would wash his hands, which he did at least a dozen times a day, only with liquid soap, reputedly better for the skin than the other kind.

A characteristic detail: a busy man, constantly on the move, a sought-after writer, retired minister—Malraux would tear up every morning and throw into the wastebasket the page of his calendar on which the previous day's appointments appeared. This caused Louise to say, "He destroys what he has experienced the day before. I on the contrary keep it like a relic. He has a horror of memory ticklers. I worship engagement books."

"A *bon vivant* but austere, tense, with a marked tendency to depression alternating with phases of exuberance." Thus he was defined by Louise, who added, "He is a man with permanent contradictions and one dominant trait—he has an uncommon faculty for forgetfulness. It's like a guillotine. Extraordinarily enough, this spontaneous desertion of memory is accompanied in his case neither by rancor nor by the slightest sense of guilt."

"When a thing is finished and classified," Malraux says, "I don't give it a further thought. Why go back? The torn page is no longer there."

"But," says Louise, "he is capable of an unflagging attention."

Malraux has no sense of money, which represents an abstract value for him, something one writes down in a checkbook that one hands to a third party or deposits in a bank. The apparently contradictory fact that he has an acute business sense and is uncompromising when it comes to a contract belongs in another category; Malraux in his daily life is completely indifferent to money. "Give me some sous," he would say to Louise, who would hand him a hundred-franc bill to go to his barber's. "I always slip ten francs into the right-hand pocket of his jacket for the *maître d'hôtel* at the restaurant and five francs in the left-hand pocket for the cloakroom."

One question haunts the mind. How could two beings so sorely tried have remained so youthful? For in her sentimental journey Louise de Vilmorin had carried just as heavy a burden as Malraux—with this difference, that Louise's life could be told like a fairy tale.

The family photograph in which the six Vilmorin children, four boys and two girls, seem to be posing for eternity in the Verrières dining room spells happiness and gracious living. The older sister, Marie-Pierre, who became Mapie de Toulouse-Lautrec (a cooking expert and an admiral's wife), spreads her radiance across the picture inside the frame that seems too small for those six tall bodies. To her left stands Louise, a black velvet ribbon in her hair, a braid over each shoulder, a dog of dubious ancestry, ears pointed, at the level of her dress hem. Behind, in sailor suits, standing in a row according to their heights, are the "four dear brothers," as Louise always called them— Henry, Olivier, Roger, and André.

Louise was never willing to part with this photograph of a family in which the children gave the orders. When she was away from her beloved home, she would see it every night "with its château of very humble riches," fragile and precious "as a morel in the dew of a spring morning."

Louise first left Verrières in 1924, when she was twenty-two, to marry a wealthy American. Her husband, Henry Leigh Hunt, was the son of good friends of her parents, and had known Louise for quite a while. He was an attractive man, with the physique of a *jeune premier*, who had served during World War I as an American liaison officer with the French army. His postwar days were spent on Wall Street, but he used to come home every evening with a white orchid, which Louise, dressing for dinner, would pin on as a corsage.

Hunt would have liked to interest his wife in business, in oil securities, for example. But in vain. She would not hear of it. "Oh, my love, how revolting," she said. "You think only in terms of dollars." And one fine day she packed up her trunks, said good-bye to the skyscrapers of Manhattan, and went back to Verrières.

It was at this time that she first met Malraux, a time of great personal uncertainty for her. In spite of the incompatibilities, however, the marriage lasted ten years, in the course of which Louise bore Henry Leigh Hunt three daughters, Jessie, Alexandra, and Elena. Louise made many back-and-forth trips between France and the United States. But in 1935, the year after Elena's birth, the break became final. They were divorced, quite amicably, and Louise came back to Verrières.

The "four dear brothers" were there to welcome the gay divorcée who would once again reign over the petunias of the French garden, just as she had done in the days before she left Verrières ten years earlier. Then she had queened it over a little society of bachelors, who she used to say were "in love with me with the tips of their hearts." Numbered in this were her cousin Honoré d'Estiennes d'Orves and the writer-pilot Antoine de Saint-Exupéry (both of whom died as heroes during World War II), and the mannered but elegant Bertrand de Saussine. Now these lovers were gone, but Louise still could give delightful parties. Well before twilight the champagne bottles would begin to pop. "Let us not depart from tradition!" the antitraditionalist Louise would recommend.

Malraux was never present on these occasions. Had they become estranged? Had they quarreled?

In 1936 the Spanish Civil War broke out and Henry de Vilmorin at once enlisted with the *Requetés*, fanatical supporters of Franco. We know, of course, on what side Malraux fought, and with what ardor. Louise backed her "dear brother." Malraux had met Josette Clotis, who had become his faithful companion. It was understandable that his relationship with Louise should have ceased, gently.

The Verrières home received all this world's notabilities. Louise's Grandfather de Vilmorin had been a close friend of Chateaubriand. Mélanie, Louise's mother, frequently entertained at her table the poet-diplomats Paul Claudel and Alexis Léger, better known as Nobel Prize winner Saint-John Perse.

"I was brought up amid the song of poets," Louise used to say. "One poet dominates them all: God. He is here everywhere present."

One wonders just how large a part affectation played in her language. "I was born to be carried away in golden coaches," she would toss out with a fantasy full of assurance.

In December, 1937, she *was* carried off in a coach. The destination was Pudmerice in Hungary and the coach was that of Count Pallfy, a Hungarian nobleman of an ancient family, who looked like Rudolf of Hapsburg and owned more than twelve thousand acres of forests full of deer. The tenderhearted Louise did not like the fact that he hunted, but Pallfy made it clear that, while his wife might rule the castle, it was he who was master of his ancestral acres, which he would use as he saw fit.

Louise made a flying visit to Paris in 1940, when her former husband took the three girls back to America for safety. She could not wish to keep them in France and expose them to the dangers of an occupation that seemed a foregone conclusion, but the result of enforced separation was that her three daughters grew up as Americans and married Americans after the war. She would often say that the real tragedy of her life was being separated from her children during World War II. She said good-bye to them in 1940 as little girls; she saw them again as young women, and strangers.

She returned to Paris for a longer stay in 1943, to supervise the making of a film from her novel *Le Lit à colonnes*.[1] Almost all the war years, however, she spent at Pudmerice with Pallfy, who would end up the conflict a ruined man, his estates confiscated by the Russian occupying troops. She divorced him, eventually, and he later remarried. As for Louise, she returned thankfully to Verrières and used every pretext to justify never leaving her childhood home again.

"O Verrières, I was dying of longing for you! My poor soul was withering." So she announced to her brothers as she crossed the threshold of that childhood home from which nothing could tear her away. Not even a possible third marriage. Not even her dearest love, André Malraux.

There is also a value of habit to be reckoned with. Louise de Vilmorin's entire work grew in the psychological climate of Verrières. That kind of mental atmosphere was what she needed in order to create. There was a touch of insincerity in Louise's personality, and when she confessed publicly that she considered literature "an immense bore," no one believed a word of it. For, after all, Louise de Vilmorin was doubly famous—for her life and her social dash, and for her work. One had to hear her exclaim—with what a frenzied appetite for society!—"Let's go to Maxim's and breathe the magic perfume of fame. I know of nothing more vexing for a woman than not to be recognized."

At Maxim's, Louise de Vilmorin played Madame de Sévigné. She reigned over the famous restaurant like a sultana of letters. The *maîtres d'hôtel* were at her feet. She was constantly being brought messages and *billets doux*. One almost had the impression that she was mobilizing the entire telephone switchboard just for her calls. Recognized she was, a hundred times rather than one. Even in her sixties she was fascinating; she looked years younger because of her infectious gaiety, air of distinction, and lively mind.

She deserved the admiration shown her by the patient, craftsman-like, meticulous quality of her work; her *oeuvre* forms a bloc like a

[1] Cocteau wrote the screenplay and Jean Marais was the leading man. It was the first of her books to be made into a film; the most famous was probably Max Ophuls's version of her *Madame de . . .* , made in 1953, which starred Danielle Darrieux and Vittorio de Sica.

magnificently set piece of jewelry. Never had Cocteau spoken more truly than when he said, "She writes with a diamond."

Never had Malraux spoken more equitably than when he said, "She does not write for the moment that follows, but for the future. She writes for the years to come. She writes for all time."

And then there was her poetry.[2] Louise de Vilmorin's expression was essentially poetic. Her complete works, in verse or in prose, mark the triumph of a scintillating femininity. For all Louise's heroines—*Julietta, Le Retour d'Erika, Les Belles amours*[3]—are women indeed.

After the stroke of luck of her first book, *Sainte-Unefois*, her second, *La Fin des Villavide*, caused the critics unanimously to agree that Jean Cocteau had not been mistaken. Talent was not a matter of chance with Louise de Vilmorin, but a virtue sustained with a constancy and a felicity that did her honor. But were it not for this constancy, could one speak of felicity, of a state of grace?

However this may be, she still disdained literature, or, rather, pretended to disdain it. "I don't like to write," she would say, "but it's still the easiest thing I have found to earn my crust of bread." With the poetry thrown in, Louise's writing gives an appearance of flagrant facility; but this is a false impression, a kind of optical illusion before the jugglings of vocabulary. The truth of the matter is that Louise always chose difficulty, that the blank page excited and discouraged her, and that every line, she said (but again she exaggerated), "cost me more than it cost a general to draw up a plan of battle."

Contact with André Malraux reduced her playacting attitude. "I already felt so small before Balzac," she told him. "Before you I am a dwarf."

"Don't make me higher than I am," Malraux retorted jokingly. And he added something he liked to say: "What books are worth writing, other than memoirs?"—even if, in a spirit of contradiction, one calls them "antimemoirs."

Malraux was in fact working on Volume II of his *Antimémoires*. It was Friday, December 12, 1969, at Verrières. The day before, Malraux had lunched with de Gaulle at Colombey. He would be spending four days going over the notes of an interview with the general that had lasted six hours. . . .

[2] *Fiançailles pour rire, Le Sable du sablier, L'Alphabet des aveux.*
[3] Other titles: *La Fin des Villavide, Histoire d'aimer, Une Fabuleuse Entreprise, La Lettre dans un taxi, Migraine, Le Violon, L'Heure maliciôse.* All her books were published by Gallimard.

THE LOVERS OF VERRIERES

As minister, Malraux used to rise at eight thirty, to be at the Cultural Affairs Ministry at ten. Now he got up at ten.

Louise would wake up at eight thirty and play three games of solitaire. This was a ritual with her. Afterward, she would dress and make up, and then go into Malraux's room to join him as he ate breakfast: tea with lemon and a croissant. From his bed he would look at Louise. His first glance was for her.

"How do you find me this morning?" she asked.

"Hirsute," Malraux replied (a laconic and *farfelu*[4] language imitated from Baron Clappique, a tragicomic character in *La Condition humaine*).

Half an hour later, Louise presented herself again in a different outfit. "And now?"

"Quite proper."

A third attempt, a third judgment.

"It will do," said Malraux. Then, "What am I saying? Great beauty!"

Louise would read the mail aloud. She would open *Le Figaro*, of which he glanced only at the headlines.

"*Cocottes*," he used to say. ("You might just as well make *cocottes* —paper roosters—with all this newsprint.")

At one o'clock André and Louise would drink a whisky in the Blue Salon, then have lunch, *tête-à-tête*. A lunch of "explorations," of "investigations." He speaks of civilizations, of his future writings.

At two fifteen they leave each other, each going his own way for the afternoon. Then, from five fifteen to six fifteen, another whisky in the Blue Salon, where the wood fire crackles in the big chimney.

Preceded by their two cats—Lustré, two agate eyes in a uniformly black coat, and Fourrure, a proud and highbred animal—Louise de Vilmorin makes a feline entrance into the Blue Salon.

"Ravishing," says Malraux, "but your hair is not sufficiently bouffant." For Malraux has a sure eye, he sees everything, notices everything, especially in women.

"My darling," says Louise to André, "in two weeks exactly we shall be flying off to Marrakesh. I just can't wait!"

"We shall stay at the Hotel Mamounia," he tells her.

---

4 An untranslatable word, perhaps invented by Rabelais, of which Malraux is excessively fond, and which he greatly contributed to putting back into circulation; farfetched, whimsical, zany, haywire, cockeyed, fanciful, either alone or in combination, are only approximations.

Louise does not yet know Morocco.

"I imagine iridescent sunsets."

"There are such."

"I see old English ladies taking tea around the swimming pool and munching cookies with silent melancholy and dignity. I'll talk to them. I'll amuse them. I'll put electric current in their bodies. Then they will eat like diabolical dolls."

"You're mistaken, my dear. You will see snake charmers, and peddlers selling sewing machines at a discount, but you won't meet Queen Victoria and her lady companions dipping their toes in the swimming pool."

"Well, *tant pis,* I'll look at you. That will be my finest recompense."

"A man, an intellectual, finds it difficult to be looked at when he works."

"Then I shall watch you dream . . ."

"I stopped dreaming so long ago, demanding child!"

"All the better reason for dreaming once more. For dreaming together."

"You are an incorrigible woman."

Followed by Lustré and Fourrure, Louise leaves.

Malraux, jealous, says to her, "They follow you. All right, you can keep them."

"I'll send one of them back to you!" says Louise.

Malraux had put off their departure forty-eight hours, setting it for Sunday, December 28, 1969.

"I feel a kind of difficulty of being, as Monsieur de Fontenelle might have said. A slight difficulty of being, for near you I have a mad desire to live."

Louise was expressing her sensation of having the flu. She used the words *sentiment de la grippe.* Everything, even illness, was a pretext for her insatiable need of poetic freedom. Poetry, which she considers "the essential anarchy."

"No mischief," Malraux retorted. "Influenza, this year, whether it comes from Hong Kong or the North Pole, is a serious illness—malign, perverse. You're going to take care of yourself strenuously. I warn you, I'm going to be uncompromising."

"I'm going to get well right away. Oh, my God! I should never forgive myself if I missed Marrakesh."

"A trip can always be put off. No one can be more delighted than

242

I that seeing Morocco is a little girl's dream come true for you. But reality comes before dreams. And reality, in your particular case, is called the flu."

"Who tells you that it won't be benign?"

Malraux looked at her sternly, then smiled, disarmed by Louise's pouting expression. "How do you feel?"

"I'll summarize at a gallop the way I feel," she said. "A stubborn headache, short circuits in the brain, lumbar shudders—my vertebrae are irritated—tingling heaviness in the legs; for the first time I have the sensation of having the legs of a very old woman, legs one hundred thousand years old—"

Malraux could not help smiling.

"My heart, which is ordinarily so calm, starts racing unaccountably."

"Ah!" Malraux exclaimed.

"And, finally, my eyelids are made of marble, eyelids that think only of shutting. Let's pull the shutters, let's pull the shutters!"

"My love, please, no more joking! Give me your hand and let me take your pulse."

A silence, punctuated by a burst of laughter from Louise.

"Reckless girl! You have a raging fever. All the symptoms of a classical influenza, but a violent one. Go back to bed. I'm going to telephone my doctor; he'll rush out from Paris."

"Let's not dramatize. Our family doctor will do. He knows us like a marionette master knows his dolls, and he lives no distance from here."

Malraux let himself be persuaded. Louise, in a dressing gown, was seated on her bed, her face pale and drawn, as though she were just recovering from a case of jaundice. Even the fever did not give a touch of color to her cheeks.

"You are an eternal little girl who deserves to be cordially spanked," said André tenderly, putting her back to bed.

This was Monday, December 15. It was a little after ten in the morning.

Three days in bed, with a trying fever that yielded only reluctantly to antibiotics. A painful and courageous convalescence, agitated by the fear of not being able to leave for Morocco. On Tuesday, December 23, Louise was up again.

"An illness is of no interest once you get the better of it," she said. "It's a trial of strength between the body and the microbes, which the medicines help you to kill. . . ."

On Christmas Day she seemed much better. Louise did not tell André that she was still dizzy and unsteady on her feet, however. Instead, in a burst of energy, but without letting anything untoward show, Louise actually went to Paris—to visit her sister, Mapie de Toulouse-Lautrec, who had also come down with "that tedious epidemic that must have come to us from Java or Timbuctu."

"This is madness," Malraux reprimanded her on her return. "You stay right here where it's warm. Verrières can at least serve to protect you, even if it has to be against yourself."

On Friday, December 26, at six in the afternoon, Louise was taken with fits of dizziness. Her heart pounding furiously, she went up to her room to lie down. But an intestinal artery had ruptured and there was nothing to be done.

At 7:22 P.M., she who has been called "the twentieth-century Princesse de Clèves" drew her last breath.

On December 27 the press announced the decease of Louise de Vilmorin. André Malraux, whose name was listed last in the notification, officially associated himself with the affliction of the family. By his height, his personality, his world stature, he dominated this bereavement that overwhelmed him. Would he who all his life had carried on a dialogue with death, he whose daily life had never ceased to lead a procession of dead that he could not forget, recover from this last blow of fate, which had cut short a love that was rejuvenating his life?

"I do not doubt the existence of God. I doubt his sense of justice toward a humanity that has its right to love."

Yesterday a butterfly intoxicated by the sunny prospect of an African vacation, yesterday a superbly garrulous and unreservedly happy spirit, Louise today was extinguished forever. Happiness had made her look twenty years younger.

"The dead are ageless," said Malraux.

From all sides expressions of sympathy came pouring in. General de Gaulle wrote a long letter to his *compagnon*. The relay of virile fraternity was functioning. Malraux, who had known such great love, perhaps did not realize that he was so much loved on the level of friendship.

Friendship took the form of physical presence. All the Vilmorin family, the young and the not so young, rallied round Malraux. Then a friend from Gaullist days appeared on the scene to help Malraux in this difficult moment; he did not leave him alone for an instant. For Malraux, in his despair, was in danger. Gaston Palewski, one of the first Free French to join de Gaulle in London, now president of the Constitutional Council, had long ago become a legend of exquisite politeness. It was not reserved for diplomatic occasions; his was the politeness that comes from the heart.

Palewski arrived at Verrières shortly after dawn. He arranged to take in hand one of Louise's dying wishes. For—who would have imagined it?—Louise had made a will. This gay actress who made so many people laugh had anticipated her death.

"I want a coffin of oak wood, with very thin sides, almost transparent, if possible, so that my body may as soon as possible come into contact with the firm, fresh earth. Dust thou wert, to dust thou shalt return. But living and flying dust."

André de Vilmorin, her dear brother, visited the cabinetmaker in Verrières-le-Buisson to bespeak the special coffin.

"A dear craftsman," Louise seemed to be saying, "who understands very well what I want as a last envelope."

Louise had decided that she wanted to be buried in the park at Verrières, but "I think a tomb would make a sad impression. So I have had the idea of a stone bench, with perhaps a bronze table on which children can come and have their tea parties." As far back as 1961 she had planned the bronze table—"light, light, weighing no more than a bubble on the grass of the meadow in which my soul will breathe inside the oak. On the bench beside it shall be inscribed my motto, *Au Secours!* in characters traced from my handwriting, and then my special symbol, the four-leaf clover."

Louise had also visualized the manner of her death, had wanted to be warned of it in advance by her doctor, told that she had only two days to live. Then she would have prepared for her departure, lying on an elegant bed, surrounded by her family and her dearest friends, so she could bid them good-bye with a smile, in a fashion that would suit both them and herself.

Alas! she was cheated of this gracious leave-taking; her "dear brothers" and Malraux were determined she should not be cheated of her desires about her final resting-place.

Louise had asked that she be buried beneath a cherry tree in the park, one similar to that whose leaves had sheltered her first games. The request was categorical. It had its roots in a dream she had had since she was a child, and that concerned childhood. She asked that her seventeen grandchildren and grandnephews be allowed to come and pick cherries, jumping from the bronze platform, on which they would also be able to play hopscotch.

"The cherries will rain down on my tomb. The children will feast on them."

Such was her wish—to rest under the fruit tree of a private park and transform this most unusual cemetery into a small playground with its songs and shouts. One can well imagine that there was a problem to be solved at a government level.

Gaston Palewski made it his business to persuade the minister of the interior, and soon afterward the prefect of the department of Essonne formally gave permission for Louise to be buried in her own garden—in conditions he courteously described as "so unusual, so poetic."

Would the religious service be another problem? After all, Louise had been twice divorced and, in the eyes of the church, she was currently living in sin. The church had become modernized, it was true. "God has put water in his wine," Louise used to say.

("Ask the priests," she would answer, when asked at what date her marriage with Malraux would take place. "They are the only ones to get panicky about getting married.")

Edith de Vilmorin, the wife of Roger, another of the "dear brothers" (Henry and Olivier were no longer living), went to see the parish priest of Verrières-le-Buisson. There was no real reason why he should make difficulties—and in the end, he did not.

The headstrong Louise once again had her way. She had the last word. Not a mock funeral, but a happy one, without a taste of ashes, with, even inside the church, an anticipatory fragrance of cherry blossoms, and beautiful singing by the celebrated choir of Saint-Eustache.

The cherry tree was planted in June, 1970, by Louise's daughter Jessie. Louise's body lies somewhere beneath the soft turf.

"We don't know exactly where she is buried," says her brother André. "But her spirit is everywhere at Verrières! . . . All three proprietors of the château and the garden live here now—my brother Roger, my nephew Sosthène de Vilmorin, and I, with our respective wives and children. And so does André Malraux, who is doing us the kindness of staying—I hope for a very long time—in one of the guest apartments in this big house."

With the affectionate help of her family and friends, Louise de Vilmorin had won the most difficult wager of her gay but far from frivolous existence. "The wager of the clover leaf against the sepulcher," Irish Catholics would say in similar circumstances.

Louise's clover-leaf emblem will be cut into the bench beside her tomb, in the shadow of those big, sweet cherries called *coeurs de pigeon*.

As for André Malraux, he had lost *his* wager: love, the last love, did not take him to the end of the road.

17.

A Man Alone

"Mon ami, you are wearing your heart in a sling!" said Madame Récamier one day to Chateaubriand, who was suffering from a broken heart.

Malraux was wearing his heart in a sling. He continued to live at Verrières as one of the family, welcomed by all. Back and forth he would go in the big park, one walk before noon and one after five o'clock, stopping for a long time beside the cherished grave.

Malraux nevertheless remained Malraux. Overwhelmed by fatality, he defied it, head held high. His brain was too luminous to allow the least darkness to creep in.

"Every man is linked to the world." This sentence summarizes the whole philosophy of his work. Despairing, but on his feet, Malraux has remained linked to the world. Twenty-six years of understanding friendship united Charles de Gaulle and André Malraux. Now de Gaulle too is gone, and his faithful minister is most truly a man alone.

Bracing himself against destiny—France first, private grief second —Malraux presents that long period of service thus, summarizing an era, drawing a balance sheet, opening vistas.

"I want to be frank with you," he told me. "You are doing your best and I hope I can help you. I detest complicity in a biography. I appear. I don't stay in the wings, but in no sense do I want to be the man in the Chinese shadow theater who pulls the strings."

My interviews with him were conducted before de Gaulle's death, in the Blue Salon at Verrières, and, as I have mentioned, I had to take all my notes by hand because Malraux cannot work with a tape recorder. It was an exhausting but exhilarating labor. Malraux had recently come back from a visit to de Gaulle, and his vision of this long relationship was uppermost in his mind.

"In the beginning, I was an adviser of the general's. But I don't much believe in *éminences grises*. We are no longer in the time of the cardinals.

"When I met the general for the first time, I had a mythical idea of him. To me he was the contrary of a politician. A Frenchman, since Charlemagne and Jeanne d'Arc, has always loved to identify himself with a myth, which commands him and which he venerates.

"My entry into de Gaulle's cabinet immediately followed our first meeting, after Strasbourg's final battle. While I handled cultural affairs, Louis Vallon was in charge of economic questions and Michel Debré of the Justice Department. Georges Pompidou became a part of the team in the fall. Gaston Palewski had presented him to the general. Pompidou was connected with the general's private affairs and with the Anne de Gaulle Foundation, which was close to Madame de Gaulle's heart.[1] A marginal role, in short, but an essential detail. The fact that Pompidou dealt with good works, thus finding himself in frequent contact with Madame de Gaulle, played an important part in his future."

"What are the striking things about de Gaulle that attracted you to him, for initially nothing deep seemed to bring you together apart from the fight against the Nazi occupation?" I asked.

"The general wanted the unconditional submission of capitalism to the state. This was the governmental act that appeared to him the most urgent. I myself found the idea attractive and necessary."

"You are obviously attracted to the general. Is this attraction mutual?"

"While I feel an affection for him, I do not know what his feelings for me are, except for the desire to help me."

"Your contempt for 'politicians' is well known, as is your admiration for historic figures who are above politics. One single historic figure: de Gaulle. Why?"

"His fundamental disinterestedness impressed me. He acted less for the present which he assumed than for the future that he bore within himself. General de Gaulle's extraordinary effort consisted in wanting to create a world policy with France, in making our country a force that would be heard in the concert of the most listened-to nations. He was not a reticent president, at least not as reticent as

---

[1] Anne de Gaulle was born retarded and died at the age of twenty. In her memory the de Gaulles founded a small institution for retarded children, which was supported almost entirely out of the royalties the general received from the various volumes of his *Mémoires*.

people have said. If he did not get along with Eisenhower, he came to an understanding with Kennedy. Between Kennedy and de Gaulle, in fact, there was a joint bond. They belonged to the same 'family.' Going to Dallas for Kennedy, passing by the Petit-Clamart for de Gaulle[2] meant the same thing, the same sort of attitude. There was no major reason to go to Dallas, but one can see very well why Kennedy— who had been warned of what might await him there—still decided to make the journey.

"It is the knowledge 'I must go' that de Gaulle shared with Kennedy —the idea that if life must end there, *eh bien!* so much the worse, or maybe so much the better. . . .

"What makes me say they belong to the same family is their similar attitude toward their own historical role, the way in which they always place themselves in relation to a history that is more important and much bigger than mere stories. Very few people know what really lay behind the assassination in Dallas. Bobby Kennedy knew it all. The last time he came to Paris, he told me, 'Now it is my turn. . . .' "

Malraux's face was somber, brooding. There was a pause before I asked my next question.

"Were you, as legend has it, the first person to read the general's *Mémoires de guerre?*"

"I did not read the entire manuscript. I read only the portraits. The *Mémoires* are really two books—first, a great book by a great historian, the book of the man of destiny. The other book is an honors list. . . ."

"When did the general read your *Antimémoires?*"

"He was getting ready to leave for Canada to raise that big hare, Quebec, when I handed him the pages concerning him. He answered me with a telegram: 'Admirable in all three dimensions.' I never found out what the three dimensions were."

"Why did you leave when de Gaulle retired?"

"It would have been indecent for me to stay."

"Would you go back into the service of de Gaulle?"

"Yes. He remains France's best chance, whether in power or not."

We spoke of youth, which he regards as a very serious problem, but a worldwide one that does not only concern France. For Malraux there is a crisis of civilization, a crisis of youth—rather than a youth

[2] The most nearly successful attempt on de Gaulle's life was made at Petit-Clamart, a Paris suburb, as de Gaulle was driving to Colombey with his wife, Yvonne, in August, 1962. Twelve shots hit the president's unarmored car, but miraculously no one was hurt.

crisis. At the time of the student rioting in May and June, 1968, he was the first in the Pompidou cabinet to define and isolate the real problem. I asked him how, if he had full powers, he would have solved it.

"By patience," he replied. "That is in fact what happened."

"In connection with that 'red and black spring,' you spoke of an absence of hatred among the commandos of certain factions. There is one haunting question. If Malraux had not been a minister, would we have seen him at the Charléty Stadium?"[3]

"No. Its lack of seriousness would have kept me away. The crisis itself was serious only by its bringing together of the university explosion with the proletarian revolt. The irrational element in those May events was a *jacquerie*. Afterward, France felt like getting back into its slippers."

As early as 1946 Malraux no longer believed that there might be another revolution in France. Revolution is made by the proletariat or it is not made at all. According to Malraux, the Communists are using eroding tactics, at which they are most adept, and are not contemplating seizure of power.

"What do you think of America?" I asked him.

"The role of the United States in history can be conceived only on the scale of a world policy. The United States would do well to be conscious of this. Kennedy understood the real problem. Johnson never really took an interest in the *destiny* of the U.S.A. He was interested in problems of domestic policy in a narrow electoral sense. Nixon seems to want a personal and original foreign policy. He has learned a great deal, to begin with, in Vietnam. To carry out a great policy one must have the will. After the will to conceive it, one must have the will to make it a reality. They are not the same.

"That is the real question. Does America want to have the policy of her power or does she not? The chief problem is that of the third world. Nixon seems to be aware of it. At least, he says he is. Does America want to be number one everywhere and always, or does she not? Any failure would bring her back to her original point of departure."

"What about Russia?"

"The Russian 'wall' is already tottering. It budged in Budapest, it budged in Prague, it can budge elsewhere. European communism

---

[3] Scene of a huge political rally on May 27, 1968, at which the leaders of the student revolt addressed a crowd of some thirty thousand. The majority were students and young workers; former Premier Pierre Mendès-France was among those present.

has lead in its wings because of the birth or the rebirth of nations. That is the most absolute fact. In the twentieth century Nietzsche has won out over Marx. In the Soviet Union the obsession with Germany is an unbelievable phenomenon. No matter how often it is repeated that the threat of a reunification of the two Germanys is not serious, no one believes it.

"I had a meeting of one hour and twenty minutes with Kosygin. When I came into his office, there on his worktable was the passage of the *Antimémoires* that deals with Mao, translated into Russian. For twenty minutes he spoke to me about West Germany. The German presence in the Soviet Union is more marked than the Chinese presence. From East Germany a nationalism may develop in a new form, and this worries the Russians, even though they control East Germany. In West Germany there are the Americans—and this exasperates them."

Malraux reflected a moment. "What is appealing in Kosygin is a deep humanity. For years he would leave his office every evening saying to himself, 'Perhaps it will be tomorrow.' Two of his colleagues were shot under Stalin and Beria.

"The impression he gave me is that the Communist party is stronger than ever. The party does everything, it controls everything, everything stems from it. Its presence is crushing. It is so powerful that as from today the Soviets would be quite able to get along without all their satellites."

Remembering that Malraux had first met Stalin as long ago as 1932, I asked him for his recollections of the dictator.

"Stalin would be silent, letting his interlocutor speak and waiting five minutes before saying a word. Five minutes of utter silence is a very long time! Stalin gave the impression of being seated at the bottom of his inferno and seeming to want to say, 'Go ahead! Just come and try to get me, let them come and try to make a second Germany in Russia! They'll get a welcome, all right.' With his black Ivan the Terrible moustache, and the artificial epaulets of his uniform made to fill him out and give him more of the appearance of the terrifying warrior—Stalin never explained anything, never gave himself away, and never ceased to look you in the eye with his stony gaze, so that after a while you ended up by being really scared."

"And China?" I asked.

"China's object is China. The third world, which is not world communism, looks to China, and China is ready to open its arms to that world, whose leader it expects to become. A part of Mao Tse-tung's policy is based on this. He is delighted, but he knows quite well that Zanzibar will not save Peking, and he never believed that it could.

"The last time I saw Mao he said to me, 'What is terribly frustrating in building a Chinese ideology is that the word *liberty* does not exist in our language.'"

He shifted a little in his seat. "Most of the statesmen I have met have seemed to be bound by alienating elements or forces that have prevented them from playing the role that they should have played. Ben-Gurion and Nasser, for instance, wanted to make peace and ought to have made peace, but they were held back from doing so by their extremist followers. But Mao is not bound in this way. His problem is that he is obsessed by the difficulty of deciding who should succeed him. Chou En-lai does not want it. Lin Piao does not have the capacity. That is what torments Mao, causes him real distress."

The case of Israel is brought up. In his *Antimémoires* Malraux dwells more on the Nazi concentration camps than on the Jewish people who were their chief victims. He does not talk much about Israel. Yet no one could suspect him of indifference, having defended the Jews as he did before anyone believed that they would suffer the fate of martyrs. At the time he published *Le Temps du mépris* in 1935, Malraux was serving as president of the International League Against Anti-Semitism. Yet in his most recent work he passes over the drama of Israel in silence. I ask him how he sees it.

"The English, when they were masters of the Middle East, decided to take a piece of the former Turkish empire and make Israel out of it. Then the Arab world came into being and spread. But it was not the English who made this world; it was a direct consequence of decolonization. The creation of Israel was pushed, as it were, by the destiny of the Arab world that was born of this decolonization. We thus come to the heart of the contradiction. The Algerian affair, too, was closely linked with the destiny of the Arab world. Obviously, it cannot finish in the same way for Israel."

"The Balkans came out of the 1912 war badly," Malraux continued, "and in 1914 it was already evident that the Balkan crisis, by killing the peace, would sweep away the whole previous universe, would carry away the old world. We should be careful not to put the problem in terms that are no longer valid, for, once again, Israel was essentially born from the unexpected upsurge of the Arab world.

"But the Israeli question will not be settled either by demanding the departure of its subjects nor by extermination, as the Germans attempted to do in 1940–45. For the time being, the problem is insoluble. . . . There are historic constants: problems of this kind are always solved by great men."

"What about the conquest of the moon?"

"The Soviet Union is in a phase of thinking things through, of research, of tests. The Americans are making the most of the momentum they have acquired, of their considerable advance, and, with the wind in their sails, they are launching a succession of ventures and piling up successes. They are in a phase of audacity and full of confidence. But the situations are reversible."

I asked what he meant by that, exactly.

"That the one who leads the dance today may be outdistanced tomorrow by his adversary. The Russians are greatly attached to the religion of the state secret. They hang out the flag once their success is confirmed. It's an advantage. The Americans practice an astronautical policy of self-confident giantism. They almost go so far as to give detailed press conferences on the exploits of their Apollos before they are even launched. 'We are the stronger. Nothing and no one can prevent our getting to the moon.' This does not prevent tens of millions of Americans, from the Klondike to Hawaii, from praying for Glenn and his comrades. It's a carnival, but a mystical carnival. It is impossible to exaggerate the extent to which spatial supremacy has awakened national feeling in the U.S.A."

"Spatial supremacy, with the moon as its objective! But surely you're not expecting a revenge of Atomgrad and the Luniks over Cape Kennedy and NASA?"

"I am expecting a spectacular venture on the part of the Soviet scientists. Of this the Red cosmonauts are convinced—time works in their favor. Their surest ally is patience. It is not only a question of reaching the moon, but of thoroughly exploring it, of ensuring its conquest. . . . The real question is: Will the moon be a sterile conquest? A spectacular odyssey without profit either for the spectators or for the actors?

"When Christopher Columbus and his famished sailors, on the verge of physical exhaustion, close to delirium, landed in Havana, a world rich with enormous possibilities opened before them: Florida, America and its vastness, as Chateaubriand poetically described it in *Atala* and in *René*. The moon, on the other hand, offers us no prospect of a lyrical and human future—no Far West, no Mississippi, no gold diggers—this is the folklore aspect. For history, no immigrants from

all the countries of Europe drawn to a new world of which the fascination made itself felt beyond the seas. No northerners and southerners
already at odds in a racial conflict. No romanticism and no realism. No
New York on the horizon! If a few mineralogical specimens are to
conclude the most gigantic, the most costly undertaking in all history,
admit that the spoils of the voyages to the moon will be meager."

Malraux was categorical: "The conquest of the moon is the first
great discovery that brings no profit. Perhaps it is the first great
healthy discovery. But the greatest power of the human mind has
produced something that is sterile—to such a point that one wonders
if thé role of the collective unconscious has not been prejudicial to this
adventure of scientific enthusiasm."

I asked what he thought about using the moon for strategic or
scientific purposes.

"I don't believe in the setting up of secret bases on the moon,"
Malraux says shortly.

Reminded of Henri Bergson's remark that "science without conscience is the ruin of the soul," I ask him if he thinks that conscience
is threatened by science.

"Science does not depend on metaphysics," he replies.

I was reminded of the meeting of Malraux and J. Robert Oppenheimer, which Haakon Chevalier had finally engineered in 1953, when
the atomic scientist was on a visit to Paris, just before the Oppenheimer
affair came into the open. The two met in Malraux's Bois de Boulogne
house and talked for an hour, with Chevalier occasionally interpreting
but mostly acting as a dazzled listener to the extraordinary dialogue
between two men, so different in mind and temperament but each
supreme in his field:

> The discussion, after an exploratory phase, became centered
> on Einstein's unified field theory, which Malraux considered an
> extraordinarily fruitful contribution, not only for science but
> for art, and which Oppenheimer systematically tore apart. . . .
> As we left the house, Malraux accompanying us to the gate,
> his two sons, Gauthier and Vincent, thirteen and ten respec-
> tively, timidly appeared in the background. Malraux called
> them and introduced them to Oppenheimer. When they were
> out of earshot, Malraux told 'Opje' that Gauthier, who was
> studying physics, had asked him in a whisper, "Is that really
> Oppenheimer himself?" . . .

Commenting on this discussion as we drove away, Oppen-heimer said, "Malraux has some understanding as to what science *isn't*. But he has no conception of what science *is*."[4]

I asked Malraux, "Do you feel there is a threat to the arts?"

"No," he replied. "Painting is inexhaustible; invention is not. Literature has recourse to permanent quotations of which people some-times understand nothing. Painting belongs to a much vaster past; it needs no translator."

A few last questions:

"Do you feel you have carried out your contract as a revolutionary —that is, as an internationalist socialist?"

"No. But what Frenchman has carried it out?"

"Your contract as a soldier? As a fighter on all fronts?"

"Yes."

"Your contract as a minister?"

"Partially."

Malraux's judgment of his ten-year term in office is a fair one. There were some important achievements: the putting through of a law to protect the ancient quarters of cities, such as the Marais in Paris, the Balance at Avignon, Uzès, Metz, and others; the rehabilita-tion of such important monuments as Les Invalides, where Napoleon is entombed, the Grand Trianon at Versailles, the châteaus of Cham-bord, Vincennes, Fontainebleau, and the cathedral at Reims. He also created the Orchestre de Paris, under the direction of Charles Munch. He had the Louvre renovated, and had many important buildings and monuments cleaned—probably one of his most noticeable achievements as far as the visitor is concerned. The filled-up moats of the Louvre and the Invalides were dug out anew; the Grand Palais, on the Champs Elysées, was completely transformed and made into a center for big international art exhibitions. A really significant contribution

---

[4] In his book *Oppenheimer: The Story of a Friendship* (Braziller, 1965), from which this extract is taken, Haakon Chevalier goes on to tell of Malraux's reaction to the downfall of Oppenheimer and his penetrating analysis of the scientist's motivations:

"When I described to him and read passages from the transcript to illustrate it, the impotence that Oppenheimer had displayed when confronted with certain accusations, his hesitancy, his contradictions, his inarticulateness, Malraux said, 'The trouble was, he accepted his accusers' terms from the beginning. He should not have allowed them to shift the battle to their ground, where they were sure to destroy him. He should categorically have refused to answer questions about the political opinions or associ-ations or affiliations of his friends and associates. He should have told them, at the very outset, "*Je suis la bombe atomique!*" He should have stood on the ground that he was the builder of the atom bomb—that he was a scientist and not an informer.'"

was the launching of a project to inventory all the French national monuments; it is a compilation that will take years to complete, but it is an important beginning.

Malraux is proudest of the establishment of *maisons de la culture* in several cities, though he had hoped for more popular enthusiasm to back up these projects.

But there was much left unaccomplished, dreams that were realizable but not realized, either through lack of time or because of insufficient funds.[5]

Among them was the bringing to life, by setting up luxury shops, of what has been called *le Quai du Néant,* the fragment of the Seine between the place de la Concorde and the Pavillon de Flore, which is in the process of becoming a secondary freeway. He has left to his successor, Edmond Michelet, such costly projects as the redesigning of the Jardin des Tuileries, the development of the Invalides esplanade, the transformation into historic sites of various artists' houses—those of Rouault, Braque, Modigliani, Pascin, Juan Gris. . . .

"He is a man who travels a great deal, even in the Council of Ministers," de Gaulle once jokingly said of Malraux. He is also a man who was surrounded by adversaries but is not known to have enemies.

Malraux will live beyond his death: that is the destiny of great men. But perhaps the greatest testimony to his fame will come from five words that everyone who has known him can utter in pointing to his place, in some Spanish inn, in some hovel in Corrèze, a corner of Alsace, or else in the Elysée, in the château of Verrières:

"Here a man has passed."

[5] "Monsieur Malraux is an expensive minister," said Georges Pompidou, who was then prime minister.

EPILOGUE

In his Mémoires d'espoir, *Charles de Gaulle wrote of Malraux:*

> ... *The Council of Ministers met once a week, rarely more frequently. I always presided and on my right I had, and would always have, André Malraux. With this brilliant friend at my side, I somehow believed that I would be shielded from the commonplace. The image of me that this incomparable witness reflected continuously fortified me. In a debate, I always knew that his lightning judgment would help me to dispel the shadows.*

On Monday, November 9, 1970, at seven thirty in the evening, Charles de Gaulle took possession of a new and second destiny. Three days later, he was buried, as he had wanted, in his village, with the young men of the countryside to carry him to rest in the earth, "that good earth of Champagne, coveted by every invasion force."

His friend André Malraux did not hear the news until the morning of November 10, when his chauffeur told him. His first reaction was disbelief. He had seen de Gaulle quite recently, at Colombey, in excellent physical and mental health. In addition, there had been so many false rumors about the general's health, so many "greatly exaggerated" reports of his decline. But this time it was true.

Among the other Compagnons de la Libération,[1] André Malraux, his face drawn with grief, wearing as his only decoration the cross of the order, attended the funeral at Colombey while the great figures of the world, as de Gaulle had wished, were present only at the memorial services held later that day at Notre Dame in Paris.

[1] Created by General de Gaulle in 1940 to honor his most valiant companions in the fight to free France.

EPILOGUE

"I knew," Malraux explained to me, "that the general wished to be buried in the style of the orders of chivalry, in the presence of his family, the members of his order, and the people of the parish. But such a funeral would imply that the body of the deceased knight should be visible, rather than in a closed coffin covered with a flag. The presence of the bishop, too, added to the religious ceremony an air of pomp and state that would have been absent had the old curé of Colombey, the Abbé Eugène Drouot, of whom de Gaulle was so fond, presided. He had died only a few months before.

"In the church there were a couple of moments of intense emotion: the arrival of Madame de Gaulle, her face ravaged, and that of Philippe, her son, who bears such a resemblance to the general that he might almost be the phantom of June 18."[2]

Outside the church, thousands of people lined the streets of the tiny village, standing patiently in the cold beneath the gray November skies. In his instructions for his funeral, prepared as far back as 1952, de Gaulle had set down his wishes for the exact conduct of the burial: "The men and women of France and of other countries of the world may, if they wish, do my memory the honor of accompanying my body to its last resting-place."

"The most moving moment for me personally," Malraux told me, "was on the road leading to the cemetery, when an old peasant woman began to cry out, 'He said everyone could be here! He said everyone!'

"I stopped and took her by the arm and said to one of the soldiers lining the road, 'Let her through, she speaks for France.'

"And the soldier stood aside."

[2] The date of de Gaulle's call to the French people to join him and Free France in resisting the Germans.

259

BOOKS BY ANDRE MALRAUX

Lunes de papier. Galérie Simon, 1921.

La Tentation de l'Occident. Grasset, 1926.

Les Conquérants. Grasset, 1928.

Royaume farfelu. Gallimard, 1928.

La Voie royale. Grasset, 1930.

Vie de Napoléon. Gallimard, 1930.

Oeuvres Gothico-Bouddhiques du Pamir. Gallimard, 1930.

La Condition humaine. Gallimard, 1933.

Le Temps du mépris. Gallimard, 1935.

L'Espoir. Gallimard, 1937.

La Lutte avec l'Ange. Geneva: Skira, 1945. (Later published as *Les Noyers de l'Altenburg.* Gallimard, 1949.)

Oeuvres complètes. Geneva: Skira, 1945.

Scènes choisies. Gallimard, 1946.

Esquisse d'une psychologie du cinéma. Gallimard, 1946.

Goya: Dessins du musée de Prado. Geneva: Skira, 1946.

Le Musée imaginaire. (La Psychologie de l'art, Vol. I.) Geneva: Skira, 1947.

La Création artistique. (La Psychologie de l'art, Vol. II.) Geneva: Skira, 1949.

La Monnaie de l'absolu. (La Psychologie de l'art, Vol. III.) Geneva: Skira, 1950.

Saturne. Gallimard, 1950.

Les Voix du silence. Gallimard, 1951.

Vermeer de Delft. Galerie de la Pléiade, 1952.

La Métamorphose des Dieux. Gallimard, 1957.

Le Musée imaginaire de la sculpture mondiale. 3 vols. Vol. I, *La Statuaire.* Vol. II, *Des Bas-reliefs aux grottes sacrées.* Vol. III, *Le Monde Chrétien.* Gallimard, 1952–1954.

Antimémoires. Gallimard, 1967.

Le Triangle noir (Saint-Just, Goya, Choderlos de Laclos). Gallimard, 1970.

EDITIONS IN ENGLISH, IN ORDER OF PUBLICATION

The Conquerors. Translated by Winifred Stephens Whale. New York: Harcourt, Brace & World, 1929. (Subsequently published by Random House.)

Man's Fate. Translated by Haakon M. Chevalier. New York: Random House, 1934.

The Royal Way. Translated by Stuart Gilbert. New York: Random House, 1935.

Days of Wrath. Translated by Haakon M. Chevalier. New York: Random House, 1936.

Man's Hope. Translated by Stuart Gilbert and Alistair Macdonald. New York: Random House, 1938.

The Psychology of Art. Translated by Stuart Gilbert. Three volumes. New York: Pantheon, 1949–1950.

The Voices of Silence. Translated by Stuart Gilbert. New York: Doubleday, 1953.

The Metamorphosis of the Gods. Translated by Stuart Gilbert. New York: Doubleday, 1960.

MALRAUX

The Temptation of the West. Translated by Robert Hollander. New York: Random House, 1961.

The Museum Without Walls. Translated by Stuart Gilbert and Francis Price. New York: Doubleday, 1968.

Anti-Memoirs. Translated by Terence Kilmartin. New York: Holt, Rinehart and Winston, 1968.

INDEX

INDEX

Cassou, Jean, 10, 150
Castro, Fidel, 227
Causeries (Baudelaire), 8
Cendrars, Blaise, 10
Chagall, Marc, 230
Challe, Maurice, 71, 72, 207-209, 212
Chamfort, Nicolas de, 61
Chamson, André, 148, 161, 163
Oliand, Coco, 61, 231
Chantiers de la Jeunesse, 148
Chaplin, Charles, 11, 120
Charcot, Jean, 70
Chartreuse de Parme, La (Stendhal), 190
Chateaubriand, François René de, 238
Chaussade, M., 156
Chavigny de Lachevrotière, Henri, 36, 37, 41, 44
Chemins de la liberté, Les (Jean-Paul Sartre), 179, 181
Chevalier, Haakon, 116, 117, 255
Chevance-Bertin, General, 158
Chevasson, Louis, 5, 6, 19, 20-29, 55, 133
Chez Lasserre (restaurant), 235
Chiang Kai-shek, 33, 35, 49-54, 219
Chile, 216, 217
China, 33-36, 48-54, 252
Cholon, Saigon, 32, 34, 35, 44
Chou En-lai, 253
Christ Chasing the Moneylenders from the Temple (El Greco), 218
Churchill, Winston, 131
Cinémathèque, 126
Clair, René, 120
Clairon, Le (Paul Déroulède), 4
Clartés (review), 204
Claudel, Paul, 7, 11, 25, 58, 122, 203, 238
Clemenceau, Georges, 1
Clerc, Michel, 205
Clostermann, Pierre, 180
Clotis, Josette, 105-107, 116, 119, 127-130, 133, 134, 138, 151, 165, 166-168, 214, 234, 238
CNR. See *Conseil National de la Résistance*
Cocteau, Jean, 10, 55, 63, 64, 202, 239, 240
Cognacq, Maurice, 36, 38, 39, 43
Collaine, Bernard, 193
Combat (newspaper), 168
Comédie de Charleroi, La (Drieu La Rochelle), 203
Compagnons de la Libération, 180, 258
Connaissance, La (review), 7

Conseil National de la Résistance (CNR), 147
Copley, John, 217, 218
Cordier, Stany, 127-130
Corniglion-Molinier, Edouard, 70-102, 109, 132
Correyer, Sergeant Major, 97, 98
Cot, Pierre, 109
Coty, René, 198
Courrier, Le (newspaper), 39
Couve de Murville, Maurice, 198
Croix de bois, Les (Roland Dorgelès), 2

Daladier, Edouard, 176
Darkness at Noon (Arthur Koestler), 189
Darrieux, Danielle, 239
Daudet, Léon, 56
Death in the Afternoon (Hemingway), 202
Debré, Michel, 198, 208, 210, 249
Défense de l'Occident (Henri Massis), 53, 54
de Gaulle. See Gaulle
Delong, Camille, 39, 40
Derain, André, 10, 11, 14
Deuxième Sexe, Le (Simone de Beauvoir), 179
Diary of a Young Girl (Clara Malraux translation), 46
Diener-Ancel, Major Paul, 158, 193
Dietrich, Marlene, 116
Dieudé, Lieutenant, 140
Djibouti, French Somaliland, 19, 72-74, 94
Dopff, René, 193
Dordogne Valley, 138, 139
Doriot, Jacques, 204
Dos Passos, John, 191
Dostoevski, Feodor, 6, 11, 65, 229
"Double-Mètre," 141, 142
Doyon, René-Louis, 7, 8, 14, 25
Drieu La Rochelle, Pierre, 2, 56, 103, 167, 168, 178, 179, 182, 203, 204
Drouot, Abbé Eugène, 259
Du Yueh-sheng, 49, 50
Dufy, Raoul, 10
"D'une jeunesse européenne" (article), 54
Du Perron, Edgar, 46, 49, 55

Echo Annamite, L' (newspaper), 44
Echo de Paris, L' (newspaper), 104
Ecole Française d'Extrême-Orient, 17, 19

264

INDEX

INDEX

INDEX

INDEX

INDEX

T.0.